DATE DUE

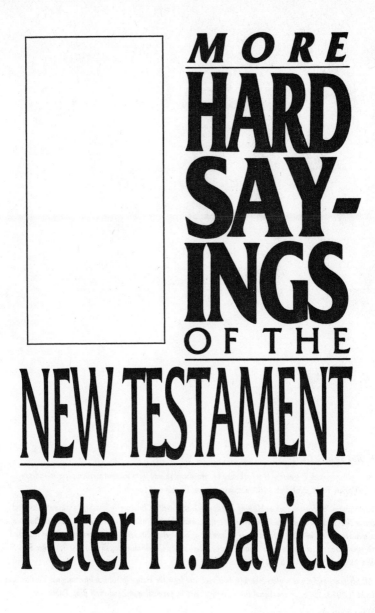

MORE HARD SAYINGS OF THE NEW TESTAMENT

Peter H. Davids

INTERVARSITY PRESS
DOWNERS GROVE, ILLINOIS 60515

InterVarsity Press is the book-publishing division of InterVarsity Christian Fellowship, a student movement active on campus at hundreds of universities, colleges and schools of nursing in the United States of America, and a member movement of the International Fellowship of Evangelical Students. For information about local and regional activities, write Public Relations Dept., InterVarsity Christian Fellowship, 6400 Schroeder Rd., P.O. Box 7895, Madison, WI 53707-7895.

All Scripture quotations, unless otherwise indicated, are from the Holy Bible, New International Version. Copyright © 1973, 1978, International Bible Society. Used by permission of Zondervan Bible Publishers.

Cover illustration: Dian Ameen-Newbern

ISBN 0-8308-1747-6

Printed in the United States of America ∞

15	14	13	12	11	10	9	8	7	6	5	4	3	2	1
03	02	01	00	99	98	97	96	95	94	93	92	91		

To Hugh H. and Doris M. Davids,
my parents.
I learned Scripture
virtually with my mother's milk
and from them both absorbed
a devotion to the God who speaks
in the Holy Scripture.
All of my work in biblical studies
has been built on this foundation.

Preface

In December 1989 I wrote a letter to one of the elders of Austin Avenue Chapel in Coquitlam, B.C. (where I had been teaching elder until that summer), stating that as I examined my life, one of my calls was to writing. In particular, I felt that God had called me to take the best of biblical scholarship and interpret it so that nonscholars can understand it and make some practical use of it. I am concerned especially with the bridge into the practical. Four hours after posting that letter, my telephone rang and James Hoover of InterVarsity Press was on the line, suggesting that I write this book. I did not say yes immediately, but it was almost as if his voice were the voice of God stating, "You have understood my call correctly." That is how this book got started.

My parents gave me a love for the Scripture. Although my father never studied Scripture formally, he used a good library of commentaries and exegetical tools for his own preaching in Plymouth Brethren churches. I grew up with Scripture read to me (and later read it myself) daily. In my teens, when I began to preach, commentaries and concordances were always at hand when I had a question. I built on this foundation while at Wheaton

College and Trinity Evangelical Divinity School. A paper I wrote at the latter institution set the stage for my doctoral work on James at the University of Manchester, where the late F. F. Bruce was Rylands Professor and head of our department. He was a good model to those who studied there, so I feel a special joy writing a book in a series for which he wrote the first volume.

Since my doctoral work the catholic, or general, Epistles have fascinated me. I have been interested in Acts since my youth, partly because of its importance to the Brethren. It has been a special pleasure to combine these two interests in one book. I took on the section in Revelation with more caution. John Calvin wisely did not write a commentary on Revelation. It is a work in which whatever you say is bound to offend someone. Yet at the same time it is Scripture, and its rich imagery made working with the various passages exciting.

While I have written this work as a call from God, I do not claim any divine inspiration for it. I have stood partly on the shoulders of some who, like my parents and Prof. Bruce and my thesis mentor the Reverend Canon Dr. S. S. Smalley, prepared me for this work. Others, including several of my thesis students at Regent College in Vancouver, especially Robert L. Webb and Mui-Lan Tay, have given me a basis for parts of this work through their own research. Still others have been cited in the notes. This work also has plenty of my own observations on the text. But in the end its inspiration is not measured by the cleverness of my own insights, but by the extent to which it faithfully explains the text of Scripture and makes it easier for the reader to understand the message being communicated. To the extent that it achieves these goals and gives its readers an idea about how to apply it in their daily lives, I have succeeded. I will have been a servant to God's Word and assisted in transferring that Word to obedience in the church. For that I will give thanks to God, who has provided the text and graced me with whatever gifts and energy are evident in this book.

Introduction

In one sense the title of this book is incorrect. Very little of what is included in this work is a "saying" of anyone. The title, in fact, is taken from the Gospels, where Jesus' ministry was recorded as a series of sayings. In John 6:60, responding to one such saying, his disciples observe, "This is a hard teaching ["hard saying" KJV]. Who can accept it?" From this verse came the title of the original work in this series, F. F. Bruce's *The Hard Sayings of Jesus*. Even though the literature under consideration in this volume is mostly history or letters, the title is still applicable.

The sayings are hard for three different reasons. Some of them are hard because we do not understand them. In many cases they can be clarified simply by adding some background information. In other cases (such as some of the material in Revelation), scholars are unsure of the author's real meaning, so we can only make the best informed guess possible. In such situations dogmatism is ruled out. But any way we look at it both of these categories are the easiest of the hard sayings. Either they can be figured out or they cannot. When they are explained, no problem remains. Those that remain unexplained should serve to increase our humility about interpreting Scripture. We do not yet know all that those writers did. If we accept this proposition, we can set aside these problems.

Another group of hard sayings is doctrinally hard. That is, the saying appears to contradict some other teaching of Scripture or clashes with doctrine that Christians have held for years. The disciples' comment in John 6:60 was made about a saying such as this. Since we as Christians hold our beliefs about the teaching of Scripture deeply and sincerely, we struggle with anything that appears to threaten them. At times it is possible to explain such Scriptures and leave the doctrines intact. Perhaps we are just misunderstanding the scriptural author, and when we understand what he really meant, we can see that there is no conflict. I suspect that the explanation of James 2:24 fits this category. But at other times a real conflict exists between what the author meant and our own doctrinal understanding. This is the real test. Will Scripture be allowed to correct our doctrine, or is our doctrine the grid through which we will insist on understanding Scripture? Either Scripture or our doctrinal understanding is the Word of God. When they conflict, we find out which one we have actually accepted as our final authority.

The hard sayings in the third category are not actually hard to understand. Rather, they are hard because we do not like what they say. They are hard to obey, and we would rather they meant something else than they do. James 4:4 and 1 John 2:15 may be in this category for some people. This book will be of relatively little help with this type, except to assure each reader that the scriptural author does mean exactly what was feared. The issue remains as to whether or not the reader will obey the Scripture. When it comes to obedience, a book cannot help. Each individual reader must decide. Thus, such sayings are in one sense the hardest of all, for we struggle with them most on the personal level.

What, then, is the goal of this book? It is to understand Scripture, especially some of the more obscure passages. By this we mean understanding what the original author intended to communicate when he wrote the words. That is, the author of each book of Scripture had something in mind when he selected the words to use in writing. Our assumption is that these words, when understood within his cultural context, accurately represent what he wanted to communicate. In fact, it is a good working assumption that what an average Christian reader in the first-century context in which that book of Scripture was written would have understood by the words fairly represents what the author intended to communicate. And this is what the church has accepted as the Word of God.[1]

The problem is that we are not first-century readers. None of us speaks Koine Greek (the language of the New Testament) fluently. Unlike most of the authors we are discussing, few of us are Jews. None of us are first-century Jews from the eastern Mediterranean world. We have not read the same books or had the same cultural experiences as the authors of Scripture had. We speak a different language.

Even our experience of the church is different. We know a world in which most churches are buildings with rows of pews and a platform of some type in the front upon which ministers of some description stand to lead worship. The authors of Scripture knew a church that met in groups of no more than sixty or so in private homes, usually at night. They sat around a table for a common meal something like a potluck supper, although for them it was the Lord's Supper. There was no such thing as ordination in our modern sense nor a difference between clergy and people. Leadership was quite fluid. Those who could lead were leaders. Furthermore, we know a church that is split into many different denominations and traditions. In the early period there was only one church, although it contained a lot of variety, even among the house churches in a given city.

We carry our Bibles into church, or take them out of the pews. The Scriptures in the early church (the Old Testament, if they could afford it, and perhaps late in the New Testament period some copies of a Gospel or two or some letters of Paul) were stored in a chest in someone's house and read aloud during meetings by one of the few members who could read. Finally, we know a church that looks back on 2000 years of history and stresses the fact that God has spoken in the Scriptures. They knew a church whose only history was the Old Testament and stories (even eyewitness accounts) about Jesus. What animated them was a common experience of the Holy Spirit and through him the living presence of Jesus in their midst. There was a dynamism (and often a risk) that even the liveliest of our groups has probably not fully captured.

With all of these differences, interpreting Scripture becomes the job of getting back into that ancient world and then understanding how it correlates with our world. To do so we will have to listen to the Old Testament and the sayings of Jesus that the authors we are dealing with certainly knew. We will also have to consult some of the works written by Jews in the period between 400 B.C. and A.D. 100, the intertestamental literature (much of it strange to our ears), which will show what first-century Jews, including the authors of Scripture, thought about various topics. In fact, one of our hard sayings, that in Jude, comes up precisely because Jude quotes some of this literature. Finally we will have to attempt to understand the culture and historical situation, for that, too, will be part of the author's understanding and something that he shares with his readers. This will enable us to translate not just the words but also the ideas of Scripture into our language.

The last stage of interpretation, however, is that of moving from the world of the New Testament into our modern world. Here we will have to be cautious. Some of the discussions and arguments Christians have had over the centuries were not issues in the first century. Our authors will have nothing to say about such concerns. They may refuse to answer our questions. In other cases we may have to discover the principle that informs the author's reasoning and apply it to our modern situation. But in most of the cases the real danger is in jumping too quickly into the modern situation. If we have not taken the time to grasp fully what the author of Scripture was trying to say, we will distort his message when we move into our modern period. But if we fully grasp it, we will be able to see where it applies, although it may apply in a different place than we thought at first.

The study of Scripture is an adventure, for the God who spoke still speaks. One of his ways of speaking to us is through Scripture as we take the time and trouble to study, understand and meditate on it. It is my hope that as we explore these passages each reader will discover the power of the Scripture again as the Holy Spirit makes it alive within him or her.

Introduction to the Books Being Studied

Unlike the previous New Testament works in this series, this book is not concerned with a single person, but with several authors. It would be nice to be able to write an introduction to each of the works being discussed, but that would take another book the length of this one. Instead, I have included a brief list of books that will give the reader the type of background information assumed in the chapters of this book. This is for simple reference, and not meant to be a complete bibliography.

Acts:
F. F. Bruce. *The Book of the Acts.* New International Commentary on the New Testament. Grand Rapids, Mich.: Eerdmans, 1954.

Hebrews:
F. F. Bruce. *The Epistle to the Hebrews.* New International Commentary on the New Testament. Grand Rapids, Mich.: Eerdmans, 1990.

James:
Peter H. Davids. *James.* New International Bible Commentary. Peabody, Mass.: Hendrickson, 1990.

1 Peter:
Peter H. Davids. *The First Epistle of Peter.* Grand Rapids, Mich.: Eerdmans, 1990.

2 Peter—Jude:
R. J. Bauckham. *Jude, 2 Peter.* Word Biblical Commentary. Waco, Tex.: Word, 1983.
Michael Green. *The Second Epistle General of Peter and the Epistle of Jude.* Tyndale New Testament Commentaries. Grand Rapids, Mich.: Eerdmans, 1968.

1-3 John:
S. S. Smalley. *1, 2, 3 John*. Word Biblical Commentary. Waco, Tex.: Word, 1984.

Revelation:
Robert H. Mounce. *The Book of Revelation*. New International Commentary on the New Testament. Grand Rapids, Mich.: Eerdmans, 1977.

Notes
[1]For further discussion of this evangelical hermeneutic, see Gordon Fee, "Issues in Evangelical Hermeneutics: Hermeneutics and the Nature of Scripture," *Crux* 26.2 (June 1990): 21-26, and "Issues in Evangelical Hermeneutics, Part II: The Crucial Issue—Authorial Intentionality: A Proposal Regarding New Testament Imperatives," *Crux* 26.3 (Sept. 1990): 35-42.

· C H A P T E R 1 ·

Send Us
into the Herd
of Pigs

The demons begged Jesus, . . .
"Send us into the herd of pigs."
He said to them, "Go!"
MATTHEW 8:31-32

In the age of Greenpeace and animal rights the idea that Jesus of Nazareth sentenced no less than 2000 pigs, one of the more intelligent mammals, to death by drowning by allowing demons to invade and terrorize them raises problems for most readers. Some just shrug them off because it is biblical history, but others rightly ask, Doesn't Jesus care about animals? In the Old Testament God does (for example, Prov 12:10). And even if Jesus did not care about pigs, shouldn't he have cared about the livelihood of the swineherds and the owners? He certainly did not ask anyone's permission. These problems are more important today than ever before.

The story in Matthew 8:28-34 and Luke 8:26-39 is drawn from Mark 5:1-20. In these accounts Jesus, confronted by a severely demonized man, does not immediately drive the demons out, but instead ends up in a short discussion with them. The demons request that Jesus send them into a large herd of pigs feeding nearby. When he consents, the demons do enter the pigs. The herd stampedes, rushes into the Sea of Galilee, and is drowned. This leads to the questions noted above.

Before we turn to the main issues, however, we need to deal with two less important ones. First, the name of the place where this story occurs differs among the Gospels and their translations, which points to a very difficult textual situation. In the best Greek text Matthew has Gadarenes, Mark has Gerasenes, and Luke agrees with Mark. Most modern versions translate the terms accordingly, but the King James has Gergasenes in Matthew and Gadarenes in the two other Gospels, for it is following a later, probably corrupt, Greek text. But to what town do these names refer?

One possibility is Gerasa, modern Jerash, about thirty miles southeast of the Sea of Galilee. Although it was a very prosperous town in the first two centuries A.D., it is unlikely that its lands reached the lake. The second possibility is Gadara, a site now called Um Qeia, five miles southeast of the sea. Its lands certainly reached the lake, for Josephus mentions the fact and its coins show a ship. The final possibility is that the reference is to a lakeside town. The site of modern Khersa has been suggested, but it probably gave rise to the corrupt reading Gergasenes after Origen's suggestion in the third century. Whatever the actual town (we will never know the names of all of the towns and villages on the east coast of the Sea of Galilee), Mark uses "Gerasene" to refer to its people and Luke follows him. Matthew (who likely wrote his Gospel in Syria, thereby closer to the site) prefers to refer to the town he knows, in the region he believed the place was located. Later scribes, not knowing any of the places, confused the matter. One thing is certain: all of the places named are in the Decapolis, gentile territory of the ten independent cities to the east of the Sea of Galilee.

The second preliminary issue is that Matthew mentions two demonized men, while Mark and Luke mention only one. This is a common problem in Matthew. For example, in 9:27 and 20:30 he mentions two blind men where the other Gospels mention only one, and in 21:2, 6 he says that two donkeys were brought to Jesus while the other Gospels mention only one. In each case it is not at all unlikely that two (or more) were present. Blind beggars (and other types as well) would group at city gates, a donkey young enough not to have been used for work would likely be with its mother, and more than one demonized person might find refuge in the same groups of tombs. But even if there is no necessity of seeing a historical problem, we may wonder why Matthew would mention two when one seems to do for the others. While other answers also may suffice, one reason is that Matthew's interest in the miracles is due to his Christology. That is, the miracles show the power of Christ. By mentioning two he heightens that power. The healing of one may have been a coincidence, but not the healing of two. Similarly, if two donkeys are brought to Jesus, the significance of his fulfillment of the Scriptures is underlined.

Concerning the major issues in this passage, it becomes clear that the Gospel writers were interested in quite different issues than those with which modern readers have struggled. We tend to romanticize the role of animals, while in the first century animals were raised for food or for other useful purposes. Everyone was familiar with animal sacrifice, whether for a secular marketplace or in the temple. We also see the economics of the story, while the Gospel writers were far more concerned with God's present provision (Mk 6:7-13) and future treasure in heaven than in preserving economic security now. Furthermore, we see the violence done to animals, while the Gospel writers were concerned with the violent destructive behavior of demons and their effects upon human beings (which they knew from firsthand observation). Therefore, the Gospel writers saw the whole story from another perspective.

In Mark, for example, Jesus comes into the land of the Gerasenes. Mark later notes that this is part of the Decapolis, underlining the fact that it is gentile country, even if it once belonged to Israel. In other words, Jesus is in an unclean land. The demonized man even uses a title for God ("God Most High") normally used by Gentiles. He lives in the tombs, an unclean place, the place of the dead. He is controlled by "an unclean spirit" (Matthew and Luke simply say he is "demonized"). The pigs, of course, are unclean animals (Lev 11:7; Deut 14:8), which Jews were not even to raise for others (so runs the rabbinic rule in Mishnah, *Baba Kamma* 7:7). So the unclean spirits go into the unclean pigs and drive them to their deaths, while the man who was in the place of the dead (and surely would soon enough die) is delivered and re-enters life (returns to his own house). From this perspective the pigs are not the issue—they are unclean—and the townsfolk miss the point when they see only their loss of pigs and fail to see the delivered man. Indeed, the pigs plunging into the sea may suggest that the unclean land had been freed of the unclean spirits with the removal of the unclean animals; but the people do not want salvation, preferring pigs.

Another set of issues is also present in this passage. This is the only exorcism in the Gospels in which the demons answer back to Jesus. In fact, they do so after Jesus commands them to leave the man (a detail not mentioned in Matthew). Their concern is that they not be tormented, that is, sent to hell (Matthew specifically adds, "before the time," meaning before the final judgment). Why would they say this? First, Jewish teaching was that demons were free to torment people until the last judgment (see Jubilees 10:5-9 and 1 Enoch 15—16). Second, Jesus' appearance and power to expel them looked to them as if he were beginning the final judgment too early. Therefore, the permission to enter the pigs is an admission that the last judgment is not yet taking place. The demons are still free to do their destructive work. Nevertheless, wherever the King is present he brings the kingdom and frees people from the power of evil.

There is no suggestion in this story that Jesus was not in control or that he was tricked. He had just stilled a destructive (perhaps even demonically inspired) storm (Mt 8:23-27; Mk 4:35-41; Lk 8:22-25). He remains the sovereign "Son of God" in the deliverance of the demonized man. But the account gives the Gospel writers a chance to point out that while the kingdom of God does come in Jesus, it is not yet the time of final judgment when evil will finally and totally be put down. Demons remain and act like demons, tormenting and killing what they inhabit, but they are limited in that Jesus could and still can free people by his power.

We moderns may not like the idea that demons do have this destructive nature, that of their master (see Jn 10:10, where the "thief" is an image for Satan). Jesus, of course, did not tell them to kill the pigs; the demons just did to them what they wished to do to the man in the long run. Nor do we like the idea that God is limited in his options here, choosing in his mercy to delay the final judgment, which would have been brought about had he removed the evil forces totally. But both of these facts underline the most important issue, the value of a person. So precious is human life that, when necessary, a whole herd of animals may be sacrificed for one—or two—people.

He Would
Not Let
Them Speak

*He also drove out many demons,
but he would not let the demons speak
because they knew who he was.*
MARK 1:34

E ach of the Gospels is designed to proclaim *who Jesus is,* to present him
to the world. The idea behind such Gospel proclamation is that once
people know who Jesus is they will commit themselves to him and
become disciples. But within the Gospels, especially in Mark, is the
curious phenomena of Jesus' commanding people *not* to tell others
who he is. If he wishes people to believe, why does he not allow the
open confessions of those who really know him? In the case of
demonized people, is this not one time that demons were telling the
truth? Could this mean that Jesus had doubts about who he was?
This is the problem of the so-called messianic secret in Mark.

In responding to such an issue we must look at the evidence. Jesus
commands silence on three types of occasions. The first involves
demons, who "knew who he was." The second involves people who

have been healed, who may not understand who he is, but who do have a story to tell about what he has done. "See that you don't tell this to anyone," Jesus says to a leper he heals (Mk 1:44; compare 5:43). The third occasion involves the disciples after they confess him as "the Christ" (8:30; 9:9). What is the purpose for all this secrecy? Each of these situations has a somewhat different explanation. We will discuss them in reverse order.

The disciples, whose confession Peter boldly states in Mark 8:29, had come to recognize Jesus over a period of time. They had followed him around, heard his teaching, observed his miracles and gone out at his command to do the same. Their faith had grown during that time. More important, Jesus had been able to define for them how he saw his own mission. Even though their understanding was far from perfect (the predictions of the cross still mystified them), their obedience made it relatively safe for them to think of him as "the Christ," or "the Messiah" ("Christ" is Greek for "Messiah"; both terms mean simply "the anointed one").

Unfortunately, Judaism did not have the same clarity about the Messiah and his mission. Some groups among the Jews were not looking for any Messiah. The golden age had come with the Maccabean victories in 164 B.C. As long as the temple functioned, deliverance was not needed. Others (for example, the people who wrote the Dead Sea Scrolls) believed in two Messiahs. One would be a descendant of David who would rule as king, while the other would be a descendant of Aaron who would purify temple worship as high priest. For both groups Scripture and the experience of Hasmonean priest-kings from 164—63 B.C. had proved that the roles of ruler and priest could not be combined. Still others were looking for a warrior-king who would deliver them from the Romans. In fact, several people presented themselves as candidates for the office (Acts 5:36-37 has only a partial listing), and one, Simeon Ben Kosiba, would lead the Jews to a final defeat in A.D. 135.

Therefore the title "Christ," or "Messiah," was a dangerous one. It would immediately excite people's preconceived imaginations about what that figure was supposed to do. It would mark him out to the Romans as a rebel leader. And it would close people off to

Jesus' own self-definition of his role. Because of this Jesus always referred to himself as the "Son of man." In Ezekiel this phrase means "human being." In Palestinian Aramaic it could simply be a modest way of saying "I" (similar to Paul's modesty in 2 Cor 12:2-3). But it also appears in Daniel 7:13 for a being who receives power and authority from God. Therefore the phrase had three possible meanings, and only context could determine which was intended. Because of this ambiguity, people had to listen to Jesus to see how he used the term rather than attach to it their own preconceived meanings. This is precisely what Jesus wanted and needed until he had accomplished all he had to do. So he told his disciples not to say anything until he had "risen from the dead"; he did not need their semi-understanding assistance in explaining who he is.

The people Jesus heals are another matter. Here the issue is in part modesty, for Jesus is not looking for a following as a wonder-worker nor does he wish to "blow his own horn." This must be the case in Mark 5:43, for many individuals knew that the child had died and they would recognize the miracle as soon as they saw her up and around the house. But Jesus was not looking for a string of requests to come to funerals! So he "gave strict orders not to let anyone know about this." This same motif can be seen in the "non-secrecy" of the previous incident. Jesus tells the delivered Gerasene man to "tell [your family] how much the Lord has done for you" (Mk 5:19). While the man then tells "how much Jesus had done for him," Jesus had drawn the attention to God rather than to himself.

A second concern in keeping the healed quiet is the problem of publicity. In the case of the Gerasenes Jesus was leaving the area, so publicity would be no problem. But the healed leper he tells to keep quiet (Mk 1:44) caused real problems when "he went out and began to talk freely, spreading the news. As a result, Jesus could no longer enter a town openly but stayed outside in lonely places" (v. 45).[1] This popularity was bad in two ways. As we see in Mark 6:31, it made life difficult. The situation appeared so crazy to his relatives that they wanted to take him into protective custody (3:20-21)! In fact, it even made ministry difficult, for frequently crowds became a hindrance in people's attempts to get to Jesus (2:2-4). Furthermore the popularity attracted the attention of the authorities, which could be dangerous (6:14). So this problem reinforced Jesus' own humble modesty about his healing activities.

Finally, we turn to the demonized. The demons did indeed know who Jesus was. In fact, they knew who Jesus was far better than even his disciples did, for only they use the title "Son of God" until the very end of the Gospel (15:39). We are never told what their motives are for crying out; it could simply be a spontaneous astonished wail upon meeting their match, or it may have had a more sinister purpose. Jesus always silenced them, whatever their motives. While he also never says why he did so, we can see from the text that he would have had several reasons for wishing to keep them silent. First, "the teachers of the law" associated him with Beelzebub, "the prince of demons" (3:22). Any tendency to show that he accepted the demonic would have given extra evidence to these opponents.

Second, to accept the testimony of demons about himself would give a precedent to his followers to accept (or even seek) testimony of demons about other things. This would threaten to make Jesus' movement an occult movement. Here is also a parallel to the temptation narratives in Matthew and Luke: Jesus will not receive the kingdoms of this world from the devil (4:9-10), and neither will he receive help in his mission from the devil's agents.

Third, and most important, Jesus' whole mission was a call to faith based on evidence, not on authoritative testimony. Jesus proclaims the kingdom of God and acts according to kingdom values. Those who take the risk of faith and commit themselves become disciples and learn more, but others receive teaching only in obscure parables (4:11-12, 33-34). When John the Baptist requests more information, Jesus simply tells the messengers to report the events that they saw (Mt 11:4-6; Lk 7:21-23). Only in the account of his trial before the Sanhedrin does Jesus make a direct statement about himself. Therefore the demons were short-circuiting Jesus' whole methodology. His command to them was a sharp "Shut up!" His invitation to the crowd at their expulsion was, "See and believe that the Kingdom of God has come."

Notes

[1]B. Malina, *The New Testament World* (Atlanta: John Knox, 1981), p. 122, argues that this was because the healed man's report included the fact that Jesus had touched him and thereby had himself become unclean. Jesus is thus forced to stay outside villages, where unclean people were to stay. While this is a possible interpretation, the fact that the text of Mark 1:46 stresses that many gathered to him and implies that he went back to Capernaum as soon as the crowd dissipated makes this a less likely interpretation.

No One
Has Ever
Seen God

No one has ever seen God,
but the only Son,[1] who is at the
Father's side, has made him known.
JOHN 1:18

John states quite clearly that no one has ever seen God. But is this the case? Isn't it true that Moses saw God (Ex 34:5-6)? What about Isaiah and Ezekiel? Isaiah says, "I saw the Lord seated on a throne" (Is 6:1; compare Ezek 1). And didn't the disciples see Jesus? If one replies, "But they saw Jesus, not God," then Jesus says, "Anyone who has seen me has seen the Father" (Jn 14:9). How, then, can the same Gospel author record this statement?

To understand Moses' situation we must not look in Exodus 34, but in the preceding chapter, in which God explains what is about to happen. Moses asks to see God's "glory." God consents, but adds, "you cannot see my face, for no one may see me and live" (33:20). The solution to the problem is for Moses to be hidden in a crack in the rock from where he could hear God's voice and experience God's presence, but not see anything until God had passed by. Then he could come out and see God's "back" or "afterglow." In other words, the text makes it clear that Moses never had a direct vision of God.

Ezekiel's and Isaiah's experiences are probably visionary. Ezekiel clearly states that he saw "visions of God" (1:1). Isaiah never states in chapter 6 that his experience was a vision, but in 1:1 he does call the whole book a "vision." It is this and the setting of the experience in the temple that leads commentators to believe that Isaiah is reporting a vision he had while worshiping in the temple. In other words, none of these experiences, nor that of John in Revelation 4, were direct experiences of God. They were spiritual events that were experienced as visual. Moses' experience was more direct in that God was in some sense physically present. That is not to say that the prophetic experiences were not real or did not have an effect on the recipient. In both Isaiah's and Ezekiel's cases they launched the prophet on his prophetic career. The visions permanently affected them, in some cases physically and mentally as well as spiritually. Yet they were not a direct viewing of God.

Jesus is another way of experiencing God. John's Gospel makes a consistent distinction between "the Father" and "the Son." It is clear right from the beginning that John places the Son (or Word) on a level with deity ("the Word was God" or "what God was the Word was," 1:1), even if the more difficult reading ("the only begotten God") in 1:18 is not accepted. But Jesus is also "the Word [become] flesh" (1:14) and thus present to human beings in such a way that he could be seen, experienced and touched (1 Jn 1:1). As a result our verse states quite clearly that in this form the Son, "who is at the Father's side, has made him known." So the answer to the question as to whether the disciples had seen God is Yes, but they did not see the Father directly. They saw Jesus, whose character and behavior are those of the Father. They saw the person who always spoke the Father's words (for example, Jn 7:16-17) and always did the Father's deeds (5:19-20).

There are, then, three ways in which living human beings have come close to a direct experience of God. Moses had the unique experience of God's coming as close to him as possible and his still remaining alive. The prophets in both the Old and New Testaments have had visions of God. And Jesus presents to us God in human form, apparently emptied of some of his preincarnate glory (Jn 17:5), but still a full representation of the character, will and deeds of the Father. Yet no living person has had a direct, unmediated experience of the Father. That, the prophet John tells us, is what will happen only after death, in heaven (Rev 7:9-10; 14:3; 21:3).

Notes
[1]We are following a reading in the NIV margin that has strong Greek manuscript support, but may well not be original. The NIV text, "God the only Son," is unlikely and is found in virtually no Greek text. More likely is "the only begotten God."

How Did Judas Die?

> With the reward he got for his wickedness,
> Judas bought a field; there he fell
> headlong, his body burst open and all his
> intestines spilled out.
> ACTS 1:18

While Luke's description of Judas's death is rather gory, Acts 1:18 would not be a problem were it not that Matthew seemingly has a different story. In Matthew's account, "Judas threw the money into the temple and left. Then he went away and hanged himself" (27:5). Matthew reports that the chief priests used the money "to buy the potter's field as a burial place for foreigners." Aren't these two contradictory statements about the death of Judas?

It is clear that Matthew and Luke have different concerns in mentioning the incident. Matthew is more interested in the purchase of the field, which he sees as a fulfillment of Scripture. He combines Zechariah 11:12-13 (the thirty pieces of silver and the potter) and Jeremiah 32:6-12 (buying a field), perhaps with overtones of Jeremiah 18:1-4 (going to the potter's house), and links them all under the better-known prophet's name. While it may seem strange to the modern reader to link passages on the basis of a common word or even of the ending of a word ("treasury" and "potter" sound similar in Hebrew), this was good Jewish exegetical practice. Thus Matthew wants to point out the silver-temple-field link far more than to explain how Judas died.

Acts has another concern, which is that Judas got what he deserved, a horrible death. (A similar situation is reported in Acts 12:21-24, where the author narrates the story of Herod Agrippa I's death.) The focus is not on the purchase of the field (which would have appeared a reward, especially to Jews for whom landowning in Palestine was important), but on his death in the field (which was ghastly).

Both authors want to point out that the field was called "The Field of Blood," thus memorializing the deed. Acts appears to connect the title to Judas's blood in his death, while Matthew ties it to the fact that the blood money paid for the field. It is hardly surprising that the same name might mean different things to different people.

A closer look at the two stories highlights gaps in the narrative that raise questions about the events. But the accounts are not necessarily contradictory. Acts is concerned that Judas's money and name were connected to a field. Whether or not the chief priests actually purchased it, perhaps some time after Judas's death, would not be a detail of concern to the author. His point was the general knowledge that Judas's money went to the purchase, which resulted in the title "Field of Blood" being attached to the field. Another possible reason for the name, also a concern of Acts, was that Judas split open and his intestines poured out. Such a defacing of the body, probably with the concomitant result of the corpse being at least partially eaten by vultures and dogs, was horrible in the view of the Jews, for whom proper burial was important. In fact, they even valued forms of execution that did not deface the outside of the body (such as strangulation) over forms that defaced the body (such as stoning, the worst form in their eyes).

Matthew points out that it was a guilt-motivated suicide, accomplished by the most common means, hanging. Suicide in Jewish literature is most often connected to shame or failure. (So 2 Sam 17:23; compare the other accounts of suicide in Old Testament history, which were normally to avoid a more shameful death.) However, since suicide by hanging was usually accomplished (at least by poorer people) by jumping out of a tree with a rope around one's neck, it was not unusual (nor is it uncommon in India today) for the body to be ripped open in the process.[1] I hesitate to say that this was exactly what happened, but it is certainly a plausible explanation.

Therefore, we will never be fully certain about what happened at the death of Judas. What I have shown is that there are certainly credible explanations as to how the two accounts fit together. I have shown how it may well have happened, not how it must have happened. In doing so we see that there is no necessary contradiction. Yet what is important in reading these narratives is to focus on the points they are making, not on the horrible death. With Matthew we see that Scripture is fulfilled even while those fulfilling it are driven by guilt and shame to their own self-destruction. And with Acts we see that sin does have consequences: Judas not only lost his office through his treachery but he came to a shameful end as well, an end memorialized in the place near Jerusalem named "Field of Blood."

Notes

[1]I owe this information to an Indian pastor well acquainted with such tragic events. There is, however, another translation of the passage: "Swelling up, he burst open, pouring out his intestines." While "falling headlong" is a more likely translation than "swelling up," which is first encountered in Papias's reported comments on the event, there is still no conflict, for a corpse left hanging would swell up and often eventually break open, resulting in the same defaced body to which Acts wishes to point us.

They
Cast
Lots

Then they cast lots,
and the lot fell to Matthias;
so he was added to the eleven apostles.
ACTS 1:26

The eleven apostles together with the women and Jesus' family were gathered in the upper room. Other unnamed disciples were also present. At Simon Peter's suggestion the decision was made to replace Judas, who had forfeited his office by his betrayal of Jesus. Unfortunately, the group of disciples contained not one but two qualified candidates, Matthias and Joseph Barsabbas. A decision has to be made. They pray. Someone brings out some dice. The dice are thrown and Matthias wins. He is from then on counted as an apostle, one chosen and sent by the Lord. This scenario is difficult for two reasons. First, if this procedure was of God, why isn't church business conducted in this way now? Second, if this method is not to be used now, how could it have been legitimate then? Did Matthias really become the twelfth apostle, or was this the first major postascension failure of the church, turning to worldly methods rather than waiting upon God?

The eleven certainly had a legitimate concern. Jesus had promised that the Twelve would "sit on thrones, judging the twelve tribes of Israel" (Lk 22:30). The situation that confronts them in Acts 1:26 is that now, as they await the inauguration of the mission to the world (Luke explains Pentecost more as empowering for mission than as the beginning of the church), there is a vacant spot. The issue was not that Judas had died. James son of Zebedee would also die, but he would not be replaced (Acts 12:2). The apostles believed in the resurrection of the dead, so in their eyes James was still available to take his place on his throne. Instead, the issue with Judas was that by betraying Jesus he had forfeited his place. A replacement needed to be found.

Some have suggested that Paul was God's choice as a replacement and that the decision in response to the perceived need here was a premature action. That can hardly be the case. First, one qualification they were looking for was that the person had been with Jesus during his whole earthly ministry (Acts 1:21-22). While many disciples other than the Twelve often followed Jesus, Paul was certainly not one of them. Second, the Twelve were oriented toward the "twelve tribes of Israel"; that is, their focus was and remained upon the Jewish-Christian mission. Paul was the great apostle to the Gentiles. Third, in his letters Paul never groups himself with the Twelve, but rather maintains the uniqueness of his own apostleship, in contrast to rather than in continuity with the Twelve and Jerusalem (for example, 1 Cor 15:8-9; Gal 1:12, 15). Finally, Paul knows several other apostles, such as James (Gal 1:19) and Andronicus and Junia (Rom 16:7). Thus, while all of the Twelve were apostles, not all apostles belonged to the Twelve. They had a unique role, and the eleven correctly realized that unique qualifications were needed to fill that twelfth spot.

The infant church's solution of casting lots or throwing dice was not unique to them. Throughout the Old Testament the lot was the normal means of discerning the divine will when a prophet was not available. It was the means of decision on the Day of Atonement (Lev 16:8) and was how the land had been divided (Josh 18:10). Centuries later, when the returning exiles wanted to know God's mind, they still used it (Neh 10:34; 11:1). More important than the historical examples are the instructions of Proverbs, which were understood as divine teaching. How could harmony be preserved when there were two contenders? "Casting the lot settles disputes and keeps strong opponents apart" (18:18). Could the dice really give *God's* answer? "The lot is cast into the lap, but its every decision is from the Lord" (16:33). In other words, since the decision in Acts was not automatic (two men were fully qualified), those gathered in the upper room had every reason in terms of both biblical precedent and biblical teaching to believe that God would make his will known through the lot. There was nothing incorrect in their procedure.

Why, then, is this the last time that we read about the early church using dice? In the next chapter, with the gathering fully organized (all twelve apostles in place), the Holy Spirit falls. The Spirit was also the Spirit of prophecy, whose departure from Israel had left them with only dice as a means through which God might communicate his will. But now in the wake of the coming of Jesus the Messiah the Spirit is back, not resting only on a few prophets, but on the whole people of God. Many of them received the gift of prophecy. From this point on Acts records prophetic words that explain decisions (for example, "the Spirit told me," 11:12), indicate people chosen for special roles (13:2) and apparently lead to consensus (15:28). In the church empowered by the Spirit, God speaks through that Spirit. It is therefore no wonder that in such a context the lot and similar indirect means of discerning the divine will (such as seeking omens from God like Gideon's fleece) were relegated to history. We who live in a church still filled with that Spirit can continue to be thankful that due to our direct connection with God we no longer have to copy the means that were necessary for the first ten days of the church after Jesus left.

• C H A P T E R   6 •

Salvation
Is Found
in No One Else

Salvation is found in no one else,
for there is no other name under heaven
given to men by which we must be saved.
ACTS 4:12

Today is a day of tolerance, of respect for the rights of others. When we read a statement like this one in Acts 4:12 we ask, In what way is it true that there is salvation in no one else? What does that imply about adherents of Islam, Judaism and other great faiths, not to mention the followers of the major gurus offering salvation and enlightenment?[1] And how is one saved by a name? Doesn't it take a person rather than just a name to deliver one?

The verse in question is the climax of Peter's defense to the Sanhedrin in Jerusalem. The author of Acts explicitly states that Peter was "filled with the Holy Spirit" when he made this statement (4:8, fulfilling the promise of Lk 12:11-12). It is, then, part of the core theology of the author, and not disapproved of in the New

Testament. Peter is referring to "Jesus Christ of Nazareth," the one raised from the dead and powerful enough to have healed a lame beggar. It is he who Peter claims is the sole bringer of salvation to Israel. The first issue to address, then, is the meaning of salvation.

Salvation itself is a special interest of the author of Luke-Acts. A broad term, it can mean deliverance from everything from sickness to sin, from political oppression to divine judgment. The lame man in Acts 3—4 had been saved by being healed, while Zechariah speaks of salvation in terms of deliverance from the political enemies of Israel (Lk 1:71). Acts 27:31 refers to rescue from a storm at sea as salvation. But a further issue is one of escaping divine judgment (Acts 2:21, 40). This escape is not only a rescue, but also has a positive side, namely, "that times of refreshment may come from the Lord" (3:19). This last meaning dominates the speeches in Acts, of which our passage is a part. Thus while our author certainly knows many meanings for salvation (for example, that Jesus is the one through whom physical healing comes), the stress in this passage is on what he believes is the most significant meaning, salvation in its fullest sense: deliverance from divine judgment and the release of the blessings of God. This type of salvation, he states, comes only through Jesus Christ.

It is significant that Peter makes this statement in front of Jewish leaders. Their Judaism, the closest one could come to Christian belief without actually being a Christian, could not save them. They needed the one "name," the name of Jesus. This theme of the exclusiveness of salvation through Christ is repeated a number of times in Acts, but perhaps Paul puts it most starkly over against Athenian Greek religion and philosophy when he states, "In the past God overlooked such ignorance, but now he commands all people everywhere to repent. For he has set a day when he will judge the world with justice by the man [Jesus] he has appointed" (17:30-31). In other words, the teaching throughout Acts (and the rest of the New Testament, for that matter) is that there is only one way to escape God's judgment and receive his favor, and that is through Jesus. This exclusivity is a consistent claim of the early church.

Obviously, this teaching goes against the grain of our age. We would like to think that salvation might also be found in Krishna or Buddha or Mohammed or simply in belief in God without specific Christian faith. This position, however popular it may be and tolerant it may seem, both contradicts the teaching of our passage (and many others in the New Testament, such as Jn 14:6) and is logically problematic. If the scriptural claim that God sent Christ to die for us is in any way true, and provided God himself were not confused, then none of the other existing ways is possible. Furthermore, if God sent his son to death when other ways of salvation already existed (such as through Buddha or Judaism) or would come into existence but not involve death (such as Islam), then God (assuming he understood) is either a masochist (due to the pain it caused him) or a sadist. In other words, the exclusivity of Christianity is rooted in the logic of the faith, as well as in the teaching of Scripture. It may be offensive to the modern mind but, like the offensiveness of being carried in a fireman's dirty, smelly arms from a burning building, it may be necessary. The cross has always been a scandal.

Given salvation's exclusive nature, what does Peter mean by stating that salvation is in a "name"? Again, we return to Peter's first sermon, where he states, "Everyone who calls on the name of the Lord will be saved" (Acts 2:21). Peter is quoting Joel 2:32, which in its Old Testament context meant calling on Yahweh ("the Lord" is the Greek term substituted for "Yahweh" to avoid saying the divine name emptily) for deliverance (rather than calling on Baal or some other god). The "name" stands for the person, for it is the "handle" by which one addresses the deity. It is just as if one were to say, "Anyone who appeals to the name of the Sovereign will be let loose from prison." Knowing that the present sovereign of Canada is Queen Elizabeth II, one would address an appeal to "Her Majesty Queen Elizabeth." But Peter in Acts 2 does not intend that one call on Yahweh. Instead he argues in the next few verses that Jesus of Nazareth is precisely the one God has made "both Lord and Christ" (v. 36) and therefore is the one to whom any appeal for salvation should be addressed.[2] This is also the meaning in our present verse. We appeal to Jesus, doing so by name. No other name is appropriate, not in the sense that another of the names for Jesus of Nazareth would be inappropriate, but in the sense that calling upon any other person, religious leader or deity will not work. It will take us to the wrong address, to someone or something which cannot save.

Therefore there is no mystical meaning in the name "Jesus." Nor is simply knowing or using that name what is intended. Rather, Peter is calling for a commitment to a person, which is what believing, or faith, means in the New Testament sense. We must cry out to him in repentance (which means turning from living one's life independent of the authority of Christ) and turn to him in obedience as Lord. The statement "Jesus is Lord" (and therefore the lord or "boss" of the person making the statement) was the basic confession of the early church (see, for example, Acts 17:7; Rom 10:9-10). This commitment to that person, the one named Jesus Christ, is what will bring salvation, whether in its broader or narrower sense. No other appeal, no other name, will do.

Notes

[1]Since I am Canadian, I note that in the Canadian context, with its multicultural ideal of cultural preservation and toleration (versus the United States' melting-pot ideal of cultural assimilation), this Bible verse appears positively racist. The Native American, the Jew, the Sikh and others all have their own forms of salvation. Isn't it racist to suggest that they will not find salvation in the way that their own culture dictates?

[2]Peter can make the shift from Yahweh to Jesus easily because in reading the Hebrew scriptures, 'adonay, "lord," was traditionally substituted for every place the consonants for "Yahweh" appeared. In the Greek version of the Old Testament the consonants for "Yahweh" were therefore translated by kyrios, "lord." This Greek term is used every time Jesus is called "Lord." So the term used in the Old Testament is the same as that the church was commonly using to refer to Jesus, making the identification of the two easy, especially since, according to the Gospel stories, God designated Jesus as his anointed one or Christ (Lk 2:11; 4:18; 9:20; Acts 4:27; 10:38). Furthermore, Psalm 110:1, a favorite text of the New Testament church, used "lord" in two senses in one verse, giving Old Testament precedent to the New Testament usage.

• CHAPTER 7 •

They Shared Everything They Had

All the believers were one in heart and mind.
No one claimed that any of his possessions
was his own, but they shared everything they had.
ACTS 4:32

Christians have enjoyed reading the summary of the church's behavior in Acts 2:42, but the author of Acts does not stop there. He goes on to describe what has been called "primitive communism" (vv. 44-45). Then he underlines it by describing it in more detail (4:32-35). Several questions arise from these passages, particularly for North American Christians who have tended to identify Christianity with capitalism. Surely, we ask anxiously, there is no expectation that all Christians would literally share their possessions? Don't these verses describe an idealized behavior of the church, later abandoned? Wasn't this the reason that the Jerusalem church became poor? If that is true, what, if any, is the relevance of these passages for today?

To understand these two passages we need to understand the methodology of Acts, the context of the passages and their meaning. First, we note Acts' methodology. The author is writing in an environment in which writing space is limited. Both Luke (the first volume in the two-part work) and Acts fill what would be the longest scrolls available in that day. Thus, the author must compress the text in his effort to fit a massive history within a limited scroll. Any word of Jesus that appears in Luke does not appear in Acts. Conversely, the saying that appears in Acts 20:35 does not appear in the Gospel. Another way the author shortens the text is by describing a topic once and then abbreviating it in succeeding references. The gospel messages in Acts are given in their fullest form the first time they appear and after that only in abbreviated form. New material, however, is given in full. Pentecost is the fullest description of filling with the Spirit; only variations are mentioned later. Acts 2 and 4—5 describe what the experience of the early church is supposed to be like. New details are added later, but the basic description of the church is not repeated. We expect, then, that these passages show how the author believed church life should be lived.

Second, both Acts 2 and Acts 4 fall within a context of the filling of the Spirit. Acts 2 includes Pentecost and the initial evangelistic thrust of the church. In the general description of life in the Spirit-filled church (vv. 42-47) we discover three elements: (1) signs and wonders, (2) evangelistic outreach and (3) sharing (teaching, food, possessions, prayer). In Acts 4 the believers respond to persecution with prayer for boldness (vv. 29-30). Again the church is filled with the Spirit. Again the three elements appear: (1) signs and wonders (5:12-16), (2) evangelistic outreach (4:33; 5:14) and (3) sharing (4:32—5:11). In this last passage the author chooses to expand upon the sharing aspect, first describing it and then giving two examples. For the author of Acts, sharing (often translated "fellowship") is a key mark of the Spirit-filled church. It is not a historical curiosity.

Third, what does the author intend by these passages? We can immediately lay to rest the idea of a "primitive communism" in which everyone turned all of their goods over to the community upon conversion. That has been a viable way of life for some Christian communities, but it is not what was happening in Acts. The description of selling one's goods in Acts 2:45 is expanded in Acts 4:34. In both cases the verb tense indicates an on-going process.[1] Whenever a need came to light, those having goods sold them and brought the money to provide for the need. As if these descriptions were not clear enough, in Acts 5:3-4 the author makes it plain that such generosity was not a legal requirement; it was the lie, not the failure to give, for which Ananias and Sapphira are condemned.

What was happening in the Jerusalem church, then, was simply that "they shared everything they had" (Acts 4:32). What had been an ideal to some of the Greek philosophers has been realized by the power of the Spirit in the church. Because they were "one in heart and mind" all thought of possessiveness vanished. They shared freely with one another. This resulted in powerful evangelism and an experience of grace, perhaps indicated by the signs and wonders (v. 33). Consequently, they realized the goal of Deuteronomy 15:4 ("There should be no poor among you"): "There were no needy persons among them" (Acts 4:34). Why was that? To hear of a need was to search one's heart to see if one could meet the need. As soon as a need was announced those with possessions would want to share (since the Spirit had removed their possessiveness and joined them in heart to their poorer fellow-Christians). They shared by bringing the money to the apostles, probably because (1) the apostles would know if the need had been met already and (2) the apostles would guard the anonymity of the donor. Later Jewish charity rules valued the anonymity of both donor and recipient. Joseph Barnabas is viewed as a good example of this practice. Ananias and Sapphira appear as negative examples, trying to fake the impulse of the Spirit and by deceit get the apostles to think of them as more Spirit-filled than they are. But, as someone observed, "in the church in which the lame walk liars die." The same Spirit that is present for signs and wonders is also present for judgment.

We should not imagine, however, that this practice is what impoverished the Jerusalem church. On the one hand, there were plenty of reasons for that church to become poor. Jerusalem was not in a good economic position, being off trade routes and not in the best agricultural area. Its main business was government and the temple, but the Christians were probably given only limited access to the revenues from either of these sources. Also, evidence in James indicates that the church experienced economic persecution, both in terms of legal oppression and in terms of "last hired—first fired" discrimination. The church had a large group of apostles to support (unlike the tentmaker Paul, a fisherman like Peter could not support himself on a mountain), many visiting Christians to feed and care for, and probably a large proportion of older believers, since many older Jews moved to Palestine to die and be buried in its soil (such pious dislocated people would be especially open to the gospel). To add to its problems Jerusalem experienced more than one severe famine during the 40s. We can read reports of Queen Helena of Adiabene sending relief to Judea, as well as rabbinic references to famine and poverty in Jerusalem. All of these would conspire to make it difficult to maintain the church in Jerusalem. But for the early Christians it was important for symbolic reasons that a large Christian presence remain in that city. It is no wonder that Paul took up a collection to support this church (Rom 15:26; 1 Cor 16:1; 2 Cor 8—9).

Acts, of course, is giving us historical precedents, not a pattern to be slavishly imitated. It shows what happened when the Spirit was present in power, not necessarily how the church must live today. However, we have already noticed that there is no other pattern for church life in Acts. The frequency of meetings may have dropped to once a week as the church moved into the gentile world (because the church was no longer located in one small city where meeting was easy and because the large group of slaves in the church made frequent meetings more difficult), but our author mentions nothing about a change in the charitable spirit. In fact Paul in 2 Thessalonians 3:6-15 deals with an abuse of church charity that assumes some system of sharing was in place. He tells the abusers to "shape up or ship out," but, far from changing the system, he turns to the church and says, "Never tire of doing what is right" (2 Thess 3:13). If this were not enough, we discover the same

Spirit is poured out on the Macedonian churches (2 Cor 8). They lived in "extreme poverty," but had given themselves so freely to God that they begged to be allowed to share with the poor in Jerusalem. The principle, Paul argues, true even across continental boundaries, is "that there might be equality" (2 Cor 8:13; the context makes it plain that economic equality is in view). This equality due to Spirit-directed sharing is precisely the situation we observed in practice in Jerusalem in Acts.

The modern church is concerned about the power of the Spirit. Evangelism is desired; signs and wonders are called for. Given that Paul turns the third part of the precedent of Acts into principle, we should take seriously the practice of the church in Acts, expecting that a full outpouring of the Spirit in any period of history would have all three effects. While it may not take the identical form it took in Jerusalem, the presence of the Spirit will open the wallets of anyone whose heart is truly open to his presence.

Notes

[1]That is, the verb is in the imperfect tense, indicating a habitual or repeated action, not the aorist, which would have indicated a one-time action.

· C H A P T E R 8 ·

How Could You
Test the Spirit
of the Lord?

*Peter said to her, "How could you agree
to test the Spirit of the Lord? Look!
The feet of the men who buried your husband are
at the door, and they will carry you out also."*
ACTS 5:9

The story of Ananias and Sapphira is an uncomfortable one that contains a number of difficult issues. What did this couple do that was so wrong? Why weren't they simply exposed and then called to repentance? Why did they die, and why don't we see the same penalty happening in the church today?

The church after Pentecost was "filled with the Holy Spirit" (Acts 4:31), which was manifested in three ways: through (1) bold proclamation or evangelism, (2) signs and wonders, and (3) great generosity. The Spirit of God freed people from the spirit of Mammon so that they gave whenever they saw a need, selling property and belongings if necessary. There was no compulsion, no requirement. It was simply a natural response to the presence of the Spirit of the generous God within them.

Immediately before our story is that of Barnabas, who, moved by the Spirit, sold his property and gave the money to the church. Obviously, the church approved of this generosity. Ananias and Sapphira apparently wanted this same approval, but did not have the same Spirit-caused generosity within their hearts. As a result they chose to sell their property, but to give only part of the proceeds to the church. At the same time they agreed to claim that they were giving the whole amount. The text makes it very clear that the sin was not that they gave only part of the money (Acts 5:4), but that they lied (v. 3). If they gave and how much they gave was a matter between them and God. It was not a major issue. That they lied about what they were doing was a major issue—in fact, it is the issue of the rest of the story.

Before addressing Sapphira in the verse under consideration, Peter speaks to Ananias. "Satan has so filled your heart that you have lied to the Holy Spirit" (5:3). In other words, not being open to the Spirit of God, but instead living in their need for security in owning money or property, they had allowed themselves to be directed by Satan into deception. They, members of the church, had been to some extent demonized. This was a natural conclusion for Peter, for Satan is pictured as a deceiver and "the father of lies" (Jn 8:44) from Genesis 3 on. When they turned from the truth (perhaps only the uncomfortable truth that they were not secure enough to give as generously as others), they opened themselves to the arch-liar. Such a situation does not differ from that of today, for people who reject the impulses of the Holy Spirit or turn from God's truth are likewise often caught in the web of deception and falsehood that seems to descend upon them.[1] Ananias and Sapphira apparently were aware that they were telling a lie before the church, although they were themselves deceived in failing to recognize that the Spirit would reveal the truth to Peter. Peter calls this attempt at deception "test[ing] the Spirit of the Lord."

In saying that the sin is that of testing God's Spirit, Peter recalls the Old Testament testing tradition and in particular Israel's experience in the wilderness. Even before coming into the wilderness and during their years there Israel had good evidence of the reality and presence of God. He had divided the sea and defeated Pharaoh. He had provided food and water for them. But he also announced his intention to test them (Ex 15:25). He let them come into hard places to see if they responded with trust or with mistrust. In Exodus 17 they came to a place named "Testing" (Massah). Again there was no water. Again the people respond with mistrust, "Is the LORD among us or not?" (v. 7). This mistrust and demanding that God act or they will not believe that he is among them is termed "testing God." In fact, God later says that Israel "tested me ten times" (Num 14:22). It is no wonder that Deuteronomy 6:16 says, "Do not test the LORD your God as you did at Massah." The same theme is repeated later (Ps 78:18, 41, 56; 95:9; 106:14). The Jews were quite aware of this tradition, for it was picked up quite often in their literature.

Peter, then, is saying to Sapphira that in spite of the evident presence in the church of the Spirit of the Lord (the phrase picks up the idea of testing "the Lord" from the Old Testament and transfers it to Jesus, who is regularly referred to as "the Lord" in Luke's writings, and who sends the Spirit), she and her husband had chosen to attempt to "pull a fast one" on him. Their lie contained within it the assumption that the Spirit would do nothing; conscious or not, it was a challenge as to whether God was really present in the church. Will he respond, or will he turn a blind eye to their deception? As noted later in the New Testament (Acts 15:10; 1 Cor 10:9), that is a dangerous challenge. God responds, and they die.

Their immediate death without a chance to repent probably had two reasons. First, it was the first time that believers had issued such a challenge to God, so it was important for God to act clearly and decisively to prevent any misunderstanding about the reality of his presence and his willingness to hear and judge. Second, it was a time of intense spiritual presence, and where the evidence of God's presence is greater the sin of challenging that presence is more serious. There also may be mercy involved in such a judgment. While death is an ultimate penalty from the human perspective, from the divine perspective it is far less serious than a continued movement into sin and deception; the quick divine judgment prevents full apostasy (1 Cor 11:32).

The teaching of the story, then, is twofold. First, Christians are not to put God to the test. Jesus gave the proper example of endurance under testing in Matthew 4:7. Christians are to follow suit and trust God in hard places. Second, the presence of the Spirit in the church is not without its dangers. Some died for ignoring the presence of the Lord (1 Cor 11:30; the sin is a rubbing of salt in the wounds of social divisions in the church). The church was given the authority to make declarations that may have the same effect as Peter's (although perhaps not with such an immediate result; 1 Cor 5:3-5; compare 2 Cor 13:10). I have observed similar incidents in the church today, some of which were reasonably dramatic and others of which took place over a longer period of time. God is a God of holiness, and those who will not treat him as holy will experience the consequences.

The church today often prays for revival. Perhaps it should ask if it really wants what it is praying for. Obviously we would welcome the power of God in evangelism and signs among us. We might even welcome a growing presence of the Spirit in prophecy.[2] But reading this passage in the context of Acts should remind us that "in the church where the lame walked liars died." With the power of God comes his holiness, and those who are not prepared to live in his holiness will do well to fear rather than to seek his power.

Notes

[1]The most obvious parallels are the numerous pastoral leaders who have been deceived into thinking that their sin, whether sexual or not, somehow would not be discovered and that they could still go on ministering. Their public humiliation has not always broken through this deception, but it has paralleled the humiliation of Ananias and Sapphira when their sin is revealed to Peter.

[2]Clifford Hill, Prophecy Past and Present (Crowborough, E. Sussex: Highland Books, 1989), discusses this phenomenon, which surely was present in Peter in Acts and is in some people in the church today.

• C H A P T E R 9 •

All Except the Apostles Were Scattered

On that day a great persecution broke out against the church at Jerusalem, and all except the apostles were scattered throughout Judea and Samaria.
ACTS 8:1

T*he idea that one religious group would persecute another with whom they* disagreed is an all-too-familiar theme of history. But the persecution in Acts 8:1 raises some questions. Didn't a major Jewish leader call for tolerance in Acts 5? If so, what has changed? And isn't it strange that in persecuting the church the very leaders of the church would be allowed to remain? Isn't it normal in any type of political repression to arrest the leaders first of all? This calls for an explanation.

These observations do indeed show that more is going on in this passage than meets the eye. Returning to Acts 2:42 and 3:1, we note that the apostles (and the church in general) had been born within Judaism and lived their lives as pious Jews. They attended the temple at the three times of prayer (morning and afternoon sacrifices and again at dusk) and followed the other pious practices of good Jews, such as generous charity. What distinguished them was their belonging to a fellowship that believed that Jesus of Nazareth was the promised Messiah, or deliverer, of the people, a fellowship that ate meals together and followed the living direction of this Jesus through the Spirit.

Because they were a growing popular religious movement, they threatened the temple hierarchy (who were not in any way popular). The priestly leaders of this hierarchy in turn arrested and persecuted the apostles (Acts 4:1; 5:17, both of which name the Sadducees as the source of persecution). But in order to convict them before the high court, the Great Sanhedrin, the Sadducees had to convince the Pharisees, who were also part of the court, that the apostles were guilty of some major crime, such as blasphemy. The Pharisees certainly rejected the beliefs of the church, for they were a fellowship still awaiting the appearance of the Messiah, believing that Jesus rightly had been executed for his blasphemy. Gamaliel's defense of the apostles in Acts 5:34-39 shows a typical Pharisaic attitude: as long as the Christians are living like pious Jews, there is no need to attack them. Orthopraxis (right practice) rather than orthodoxy (right teaching) was the Pharisees' main issue. As they saw it, the church was not *doing* anything wrong; it was just wrong-headed. The apostles were beaten (perhaps "just for good measure"), but nothing else happened.

In Acts 6 we discover two groups in the church, the original Aramaic-speaking group, among whom were the apostles, and a new group of Greek-speaking Jewish-Christians. This group perhaps began with some of those converted at Pentecost and grew as other pilgrims were converted when they visited the city. Due to their linguistic differences such Jews went to separate synagogues in Jerusalem. Within the church they probably met in separate house churches. Stephen belonged to this Greek-speaking group.

Stephen was arrested for "speaking against [the] holy place and against the law" (Acts 6:13). In his defense he argued that Israel had at every turn rejected God and his messengers, including Moses and especially Jesus. He also argued that the temple was not where God lived, but was another example of Jewish disobedience (7:48-50). This was enough to unite the Pharisees with the Sadducees in lynching Stephen, for they saw in this statement the implication that temple worship, one of the pillars of Judaism, was not important. (In fact, another Greek-speaking Jewish-Christian, the author of Hebrews, later argued that the Pharisees' worst fears were in fact true. Jesus had superseded the old system.) Thus Christians do not need to follow Jewish customs. To the Pharisees, this was teaching Jewish-Christians to do something wrong and would lead to the defiling of the nation and the delay of the coming of Messiah; it was far worse than being wrong-headed. One of the leaders in this execution was Saul, a Pharisee (7:58; 8:1).

This background explains the persecution. In the eyes of the authorities the Greek-speaking Christians (already suspect because they came from outside Palestine and spoke only Greek) were the problem. They were persecuted and scattered, pursued as far as Damascus (Acts 8:1; 9:1-2). But the Aramaic-speaking Christians, including the apostles, were not suspect. Were they not known to be people of exemplary piety, frequently in the temple? The persecutors, principally the Pharisees, did not consider them in the same category as their Greek-speaking brothers and sisters.

Persecution would come to the Aramaic-speaking Christians about a decade later (Acts 12), but even then it would come from Herod, not from the Sanhedrin, and would not be enough to drive them all out of Jerusalem. They would remain until the Romans began to surround the city in the war of A.D. 66-70. In the providence of God, then, the Greek-speakers, linguistically and culturally equipped to fit into other areas from which many of them had originally come, were scattered to bring the gospel to the Roman world. At the same time the core of the church remained in Jerusalem to carry on the Jewish-Christian mission in the very heart of Judaism.

• CHAPTER 10 •

Baptized but Without the Holy Spirit

*Then Peter and John
placed their hands on them,
and they received the Holy Spirit.*
ACTS 8:17

Mention *"baptism in the Holy Spirit"* in a group of assorted evangelicals and you are likely to have a fight on your hands. For one group it happens at conversion with no outward experience, and to insist on a later experience is to attempt to suggest that the work of Christ was incomplete. For another group it is a necessary second work of grace after conversion that empowers one for ministry. Both groups struggle in their own way with Acts. Why didn't God give a single unitary pattern for the church to follow? How was the Holy Spirit received in the early church? What type of a historical precedent occurs in Acts 8:17? Should we be doing this today? These are just some of the issues we struggle with as we consider this topic.

The story in Acts 8 is that of the first missionary outreach of the church. The Greek-speaking Jewish-Christians were forced to flee

Jerusalem, and as they traveled to safety they "preached the word wherever they went" (v. 4). The author of Acts chooses to follow one of them, Philip, who goes first to Samaria, announcing the good news about Jesus and the kingdom of God and demonstrating through signs and wonders the reality of the message. This was a typical early Christian evangelistic pattern and typical results followed: many believed. At this point the story takes an interesting twist. As we would expect, the new believers were "baptized, both men and women" (v. 12). But none of these believers received the Holy Spirit until Peter and John arrived and placed their hands on them. This raises two questions. First, why was it necessary for the apostles to take this action? Second, how could one be a Christian believer and not have received the Holy Spirit?

It is clear that these people were true believers, the one exception being Simon Magus, around whom the story revolves. He sees the normal effects of the Spirit, recognizes that it surpasses his magic, and wishes to purchase the power (as he has all of his magical powers). Although Simon had believed (v. 13), he had failed to repent and abandon his former way of life and so had not come to true faith (vv. 21-23). He had believed in his head the story of Jesus and confessed it in baptism, but without repentance Jesus had not yet become his Lord. He was still lost. But Simon is the exception. The apostles appear satisfied with the rest and lay their hands upon them. They were fully Christian, but had not received the Spirit.

Clearly Luke considers this failure to receive the Spirit at baptism an exception. He feels it necessary to explain to his readers that "the Holy Spirit had not yet come upon any of them; they had simply been baptized into the name of the Lord Jesus" (v. 16). Normally repentance, faith and baptism were followed by just such a laying-on of hands and reception of the Spirit.[1] After all, the experience of the Spirit was the promise of the first preaching (Acts 2:38; 3:19). Paul also assumes that a believer can say, "I know I have experienced the Spirit so I know I am a Christian" (the assumption of Rom 8:9). But this experience of the Spirit is something different from the regenerating work of the Spirit (which Paul, not Luke, talks about), although the two acts of the Spirit (along with baptism) were normally joined so closely together in practice as to be distinguishable only in theory. This is so much the case that in Romans 8 Paul goes on to question the regeneration of a believer who has not had an experience of the Spirit.

A parallel situation occurs in Acts 1:8, where Jesus describes the Pentecost experience in terms of empowering for mission. Here again was a group of baptized believers (at least 120 of them). But they lacked one thing before they could be sent out on their mission: the Holy Spirit. There was no one to lay hands on them, so rather than wait for a human visit they wait for a divine visitation. In Acts 8 the order of events is the same, as are the results of the coming of the Spirit, although the waiting is for human agents.

So it is obvious from this story that it is possible to be regenerate and not to have received the Spirit's empowering presence. Since it was not the normal experience of the church, it had to be explained, but it was a possible experience. We note in this connection that Acts and Paul use the phrase "baptized in the Holy Spirit" differently as well.[2] For Acts it indicates precisely this experiential reception of the Spirit as empowerment for mission. For Paul (1 Cor 12:13) it describes the action of the Spirit in making a person part of the body of Christ, something closer to regeneration. This difference in the use of the same terminology is, of course, what one expects in the New Testament, for such phrases had not yet become technical terms but were living metaphors to describe experience. The modern discussions and controversies were not even remotely in the minds of the authors.

The discussion to this point, however, does not answer the question of the delay. If the normal experience of the early church was to join both baptism in water and the laying-on-of-hands for the reception of the Spirit to a person's confession of faith, why was there a delay in this case? There are several possible reasons for this. First, we do not have any evidence that Philip normally laid hands on new believers. It is quite possible that while the church was concentrated in Jerusalem many people took part in evangelism and baptism, but only the apostles laid hands on people to receive the Spirit. It was unique to be doing evangelism away from the apostles, for this is the first reported Christian mission outside of Jerusalem.

Second, Philip was a Greek-speaking Jewish-Christian, perhaps originally from outside of the Jerusalem area. There were some suspicions between the Greek-speaking and Aramaic-speaking groups, as Acts 6 shows. Philip may have waited for the apostles to come as a gesture of church unity. They could then approve his mission. This was no schismatic enterprise.

Third, the Samaritans were not fully Jewish. They accepted the Pentateuch and were circumcised, but they did not accept the rest of the Old Testament, and they worshiped on Mt. Gerazim, not in Jerusalem. Nor were their bloodlines purely Jewish. Furthermore, a lot of hostility existed between Samaritans and Jews. It would be no wonder, then, if Philip himself did not desire apostolic approval to see if his new church was fully "kosher." Obviously the apostles did approve, and they took the appropriate action.

Thus, while we cannot know the exact reason for the delay of the laying-on-of-hands and reception of the Spirit, there were a number of logical reasons for it. In the end, however, these baptized believers (except Simon Magus) were initiated fully, just as the believers in Jerusalem. In the process they illustrate to the modern reader the elements of the initiation process as practiced in that era. They give us historical precedent for the possibility of a delay between conversion and the experience of the Spirit, but the author has no intention of teaching that such a two-stage process is necessary. Instead, he shows that the Spirit did not guide the mission by giving a unitary pattern or set of rules, but instead personally led those under his direction into adapting the practices of the church to the needs of the local cultural and historical situation, operating relationally rather than according to a handbook.

Notes

[1]David Pawson, *The Normal Christian Birth* (London: Hodder and Stoughton, 1989), is the best source for a full discussion of this process.

[2]One good discussion of this difference is in Clark Pinnock, "The New Pentecostalism: Reflections of an Evangelical Observer," in R. P. Spittler, ed., *Perspectives on the New Pentecostalism* (Grand Rapids, Mich.: Baker, 1976), pp. 182-92.

· CHAPTER 11 ·

It Must
Be His
Angel

"You're out of your mind," they told her.
When she kept insisting that it was so,
they said, "It must be his angel."
ACTS 12:15

Ghost stories, which used to be told around the campfire and kept in the library fiction section, have now become high profile, as witnessed to by *Ghostbusters* and its successors. While another type of spiritual beings, angels, has tended to recede from literature (perhaps for the better, since the angel normally appeared as a caricature, such as the guardian angel of cartoons), ghosts have tended to come to the fore. The question that arises from Acts 12:15, then, is which of these views did the early Christians hold? Did they really picture Peter turning into an angel? Or was it more of a ghost that they pictured as walking around? What might this mean for our picture of the spiritual world today?

We are not in the least surprised that Rhoda had a problem. She was a slave in the house of Mary the mother of John Mark, and was assigned to door-keeping duty. Inside the house a group of Christians were gathered in prayer for Peter, who was chained firmly in Herod Agrippa's most secure dungeon and slated for execution the next morning. They had prayed and fasted for days, but Herod had not changed his mind. The situation looked similar to that of James son of Zebedee, who had been beheaded earlier that year. Then in the middle of the night someone knocked on the door. Rhoda went to the door and may have opened a peephole to see a man she did not recognize in the darkness. He spoke a greeting. She recognized the voice of Peter. Not bothering to unbar the door, she rushed away to the room where the others were praying and breathlessly announced that Peter was standing at the door. Verse 15 is the response she received. It is hardly surprising under the circumstances (given that they apparently did not believe their prayers for deliverance would be answered and perhaps were already praying that Peter would be faithful and calm in his execution). But it is a surprise that when Rhoda insisted that there was a man at the door and that he did sound like Peter, they responded, "It must be his angel." What does this phrase mean? If they meant "ghost" or "disembodied spirit," why didn't they say "his ghost" or "his spirit"? Isn't this a strange way of putting things?

If they meant that Peter's disembodied spirit were appearing at the door, which is what some commentators assume, they could have used other terms. For example, in Mark 6:49 (Mt 14:26) the disciples saw Jesus walking on the water at night and cried out in fear because "they thought he was a ghost" (Gk *phantasma*, "apparition"). In Luke 24:37 the disciples in the upper room were similarly terrified by the risen Christ, "thinking they saw a ghost" (Gk *pneuma*, usually translated "spirit"). But here under similar conditions they use the term "angel" (Gk *angelos*), which just a few verses earlier was used for "the angel of the Lord" (as it is five times in Acts 12:7-11). It is likely, then, that they meant something different from a ghost or a disembodied spirit.

According to Matthew 18:10 children (and presumably everyone) have angels that have direct access to God himself. They are usually called "guardian" angels, although we do not know if they guard anyone, just that they represent them before God. This "guarding" (if there is any) may be similar to what Jacob described as "the Angel who has delivered me from all harm" (Gen 48:16)—if this expresses a belief in a given angel accompanying him and caring for him. Protection through an angel also appears in Daniel 3:28 and 6:22, although it seems that these angels come for momentary deliverance rather than a continuous protection as in the Genesis account. Whatever the exact meaning of these passages, Jewish angelology developed far beyond them. While no two Jewish groups would likely have agreed in full on the topic, some Jews did believe that angels were capable of taking human form and representing particular individuals, as we can see in the Apocrypha. In Tobit 5 the archangel Raphael appears to Tobias as a human being and accompanies him on a journey, protecting and rewarding him. He has impersonated "Azarias the son of the great Ananias, one of your relatives" (Tobit 5:12 RSV), although there is no indication that Tobias or Tobit had ever met Azarias. So convincing is this angel that only toward the end of the book does Raphael find it advisable to reveal who he really is. A similar belief in angels taking human form appears in Hebrews 13:2, although there they appear as strangers, seeming to be simple Christian travelers.

This information makes the passage in Acts clear. Since Peter was known to be in prison, when a person sounding like Peter arrived the believers in the house concluded that it must be his "guardian" angel, whom they naturally assumed would act like Peter. This situation differs from those involving Jesus, where there was some reason for the apostles to believe that they might be seeing an apparition (it was a dark and stormy night, Mk 6:49) or a spirit or ghost (it was after his death, Lk 24:37). But as far as these Christians knew Peter was not yet dead, although he was surely in prison; nor would they have expected an apparition to knock before entering a prayer meeting. From their point of view Rhoda's experience could only mean that Peter's "guardian" angel had come, either to inform them of his death or in some other way to guide their prayers. Only when the door is flung open and the figure stands in the light are they convinced they are not welcoming an angel, but Peter himself—perhaps due to his having the marks and smells of a person fresh out of prison.

Interesting as this passage is, it simply witnesses to the beliefs of the Christians in that house. The author of Acts reports rather than endorses their views. Only from Hebrews and similar passages can we gather what evidence there is in the New Testament for angels in human form. And Matthew alone makes the only clear reference to "guardian" angels. Yet, taking into consideration these passages and their evidence for the real existence of angels in human form, within this context in Acts the only thing that appears to have been lacking in the world view of the Christians in Mary's home is the belief that God, who specializes in eleventh-hour deliverances, might just release Peter and that it could be him, not his angel, at the door.

CHAPTER 12

How Kosher Should Christians Live?

You are to abstain from food sacrificed to idols,
from blood, from the meat of strangled animals
and from sexual immorality.
ACTS 15:29

While I was living in Germany, a group of German-speaking Christians from Russia moved into our community. When they attended our church, there was an immediate cultural clash because some of their customs were strange to us, while some of ours, especially how the women dressed, were totally offensive to them. They wondered how people such as us could really have been Christians. We could have adopted their cultural patterns, but would that not have imposed a rigid legalism upon us that would have stifled church growth? Yet their consciences struggled with our way of life. How could we live together in one church without on the one hand compromising the grace of Christ in legalism or on the other offending the sense of decency of some good Christian brothers and sisters? That is precisely the issue that the early church is struggling with in Acts 15:29.

The cultural issue according to Acts was whether circumcision (that is, becoming a Jew) was necessary for salvation (15:1). Peter voiced the eventual solution: "We believe it is through the grace of our Lord Jesus that we are saved, just as they are" (v. 11). James agreed, referring to "all the Gentiles who bear my name" (v. 17, quoting Amos 9:12 in a form somewhat different from the Hebrew Old Testament). In other words, the Gentiles might remain Gentiles and still be saved. Circumcision was not necessary. From this it seems that Paul and the gentile mission have been victorious. But in spite of his apparent agreement, James added the stipulations found in our verse both in his advice to the council and in the letter to the gentile believers. What is more, he prefaced them with, "It seemed good to the Holy Spirit and to us," which makes them sound rather binding. Is this a case, then, in which Paul won the first round but was knocked out in the end? Does this not contradict all that Paul stood for? And if it does not, is it binding today? Must the Germans give up *Blutwurst* and the English black pudding? All of these questions press in on us in the reading of this verse.

First, we must be clear about what the council did not do. It did not require circumcision nor the keeping of the Sabbath nor tithing nor (in their full form) the kosher regulations (the Jewish dietary laws). These rules marked out a Jew from a Gentile and, in the end, they were not enforced upon gentile Christians, although James adds, perhaps as a concession to the Pharisaic party in the church, that since the Mosaic books were being read in every synagogue their teaching was available to any Gentile to whom it might commend itself. Paul surely would have been satisfied with such a situation, for his concern with "works" and "law" in Romans and Galatians is not with moral rules, but with those practices that marked out Jew from Gentile. That they were not necessary for salvation is a point of agreement between Paul and the council.

Second, we need to be clear about the nature of a worship service in the first two centuries of the church. Typically the Christians would gather in the home of one of the members, perhaps the person with the largest house. A city church would have many such cells, each with an absolute maximum of perhaps sixty people, given the size of even large rooms in those days. The central feature of the service was a meal to which every member contributed what they could. At the beginning a loaf of bread was ritually broken and shared, and at the end a cup of wine was likewise shared. But between the two a full meal was eaten.[1] This means that if they were in the same church Jews and Gentiles would eat together and share each other's food in the context of worship. Therefore the Pauline discussions of food in 1 Corinthians 8—10 and Romans 14 were not to regulate one's private behavior at home, but to assist a church in living together.

Third, while Paul never refers to the decree of the council (nor would it have been advisable for him to have done so, since he was often accused of being secondary to Jerusalem), all of the regulations are explicitly or implicitly contained in his letters. The issue of meat in Romans 14, for example, is mainly an issue over whether the animal had been properly slaughtered, that is, whether it had been strangled and whether the blood had been properly drained. The discussion in 1 Corinthians 8—10 revolves around the issue of meat that had been offered to idols. In 1 Corinthians 5 Paul discusses sexual immorality. None of these issues was foreign to Paul and on none of them does he take a position different from that of the council.

Finally, what do these rules mean in their context in Acts? All of them have to do with the Mosaic law and are drawn from Leviticus 17—18. The first issue in those chapters is the sacrificing of an animal to anything other than Yahweh—or even sacrificing it to him outside of the appointed place. Thus a Jew would find it impossible to eat meat that came from a sacrifice to a god other than Yahweh. Most meat found in pagan markets was in some way associated with sacrifices to idols. Paul does not believe that this contaminates the meat (1 Cor 8—10), although he rules out actually going to a meal in an idol temple. But in 1 Corinthians 8 he states clearly that love would make one refuse to offend a "weaker brother" (that is, a Jew) on this issue.

The second issue of Leviticus 17—18 is that of blood. Here both this regulation and the previous one are applied not only to Israelites but also to aliens, the Gentiles who might live among the Jews. There were two ways in which blood might be eaten. On the one hand, it was common in many cultures for blood to be eaten directly (as in the examples of *Blutwurst* [blood sausage] and black pudding mentioned above). On the other hand, in some cultures the manner of slaughter might lead to the retention of blood in the meat, perhaps as a deliberate means to keeping it tenderer or juicier. But neither the direct eating of blood nor retaining the blood in the meat through strangling the animal were acceptable to the Jew. The blood must be poured out.

All of these regulations have to do with meat, not with vegetables, grain or fruit. The reason for this is simple. Meat was at the core of Israelite sacrificial rites, as well as the rites of other religions. Furthermore, Jewish kosher practices had virtually nothing to say about vegetables. So one could share bread or vegetables freely between Jews and Gentiles. It was when meat was served at the Lord's Supper (as it normally was) that the issues arose, as we see clearly in Romans 14.

The third issue of Leviticus 17—18 is that of sexual relations with inappropriate women, mostly with women who were too closely related, although the same group of regulations also prohibit adultery (defined in the Old Testament as a man having sexual relations with a married woman who was not his wife), bestiality and homosexuality. Again the regulations are applied to both Israelites and aliens. This, then, is what Acts means by "sexual immorality." It would be highly disturbing to a Jew to have table fellowship at the Lord's Supper with a person and his partner if the relationship was one that God had labeled an abomination. Paul opposes just such a relationship in 1 Corinthians 5, ending with a general prohibition of sexual immorality (v. 11). In the specific case in Corinth, Paul believed that even the gentile world would disapprove of the relationship. However, many of these types of relationships would be approved of in gentile cultures but would make table fellowship in the church difficult.

What we are talking about, then, is Paul's rule of love in Romans 14, summed up in the principle, "The kingdom of God is not a matter of eating and drinking, but of righteousness, peace and joy in the Holy Spirit" (v. 17). If the Gentile Christians would keep the minimal food standards, not so much in what they did privately at home but in what they brought to church or served Jewish believers, and if they would observe minimal rules of sexual decency, then Jews and Gentiles could live and function together in the church. As long as the principles were based on love and unity, Paul had no problem. It was only when the legal rituals became a means of salvation that he put his foot down.

Are these principles binding today? It is true that we find a similar rule in Revelation 2:14, 20, which may have been written later than Acts. And there are examples of Christians in the late second and early third centuries who feel bound by the rules. But at the same time there is often an observing of the rules and an ignoring of the reasons for them. In a context in which people of differing cultures must relate in the church these or analogous rules (depending on the sensitivities of the cultures) would be applicable. But as permanent principles we should let Paul be our guide. He clearly prohibits sexual immorality for all Christians everywhere, leaving the dietary rules to our own conscience before God and our love for our fellow Christians.

Notes

[1]Perhaps the best available description of such a meeting is that of Robert Banks in his recently republished *Going to Church in the First Century* (Auburn, Maine: Message Ministry, 1990).

He
Circumcised
Him

*Paul wanted to take him along on the journey,
so he circumcised him because of the Jews
who lived in that area, for they all knew
that his father was a Greek.*
ACTS 16:3

Inconsistency confuses us, and arguing for one point of view and then turning around and acting contrary to that point of view appears inconsistent. Of course, we sometimes misunderstand the actions of others, and an inner consistency can exist behind apparently contradictory deeds. Yet when we see truly inconsistent actions we at best call the person doing them fickle; at worst we recognize him or her as a hypocrite, even a two-faced deceiver. This is the issue that appears to face us in Acts 16:3. No sooner does Acts report the Jerusalem council's decision that it is not necessary for one to be circumcised or keep the Mosaic law to be saved (Acts 15) than it mentions Paul's circumcising Timothy in order to take him along as a coworker. Doesn't this contradict Paul's principles in Acts 15? And doesn't

Galatians 2:3 state, "Yet not even Titus, who was with me, was compelled to be circumcised, even though he was a Greek"? How could the Paul who in Galatians 2:5 writes, "We did not give in to [those who wanted to circumcise Titus] for a moment, so that the truth of the gospel might remain with you," have circumcised Timothy? Was Paul himself two-faced, or is one of the accounts historically inaccurate?[1] Certainly, given the amount of space that Paul devotes in his letters to this issue, these questions are very important.

The resolution of this issue turns on a very important point. In Jewish eyes Titus was clearly a Gentile, for his parentage was Gentile, but Timothy should be a Jew, because his mother was a Jew. After all, the *Mishnah,* the Jewish legal tradition, makes it clear that children of Jewish mothers are really Jews, regardless of the race of their fathers.[2] Acts states that Timothy's father was a Gentile. It is also clear from the verb tense used that his father was dead by the time Paul selected Timothy as a coworker. Timothy's mother and grandmother (according to 2 Tim 1:5) were Jews, which fits with what we know about the laxity in the Jewish community in Asia Minor, for allowing a Jewish woman to marry a Gentile was not orthodox Jewish practice. Paul presumably converted the family during his first missionary journey, but even before that Timothy was probably steeped in Scripture and observed the religion of his mother, although she may have practiced it in secret. When his father died and what his father had felt about his religious practice is not known. He may have been a God-fearer, on the fringes of the synagogue. But neither the father himself nor his son had been circumcised. The father had not allowed his son to be fully Jewish (circumcision in the days of public baths was a public mark that would have identified Timothy as a member of a different race, the Jews).

Normally, Paul's missionary practice was to go to the local synagogue first. How could he do so with Timothy, who would have been viewed as a type of renegade Jew? And how could Timothy participate fully in the mission while being only half-Jew? With Titus a principle was involved: Gentiles do not need to become Jews.

But with Timothy the question was whether a half-Jew could fully actualize his Jewish heritage. Paul's decision is to regularize Timothy's status, perhaps to facilitate mission ("To the Jews I became like a Jew, to win the Jews," 1 Cor 9:20) or perhaps to allay suspicions ("They have been informed that you teach all the Jews who live among the Gentiles to turn away from Moses, telling them not to circumcise their children or live according to our customs," Acts 21:21). For Paul, Gentiles had no need to become Jews to improve their spiritual status, but it was not wrong for a Jew to live his Jewish culture to the fullest.

It might have appeared more consistent if Paul had not taken this step, especially in light of the issues discussed in Galatians and the fact that Timothy lived in the Galatian area. Some have suggested that troubles stemming from this action led to the writing of Galatians and the citing of the counterexample of Titus. However, it is more likely that Galatians was written before the second missionary journey and that this incident may have clarified Paul's stance. When seen as a cultural rather than a religious issue, circumcision was an indifferent practice. Where it could be used for the advantage of the gospel, it was good. Where it hindered the gospel, it was to be avoided. In no case did it make the person more or less spiritual. Analogous cultural practices can be found today. Likewise today slavish consistency may hinder mission, while apparent inconsistency may point to a deeper underlying consistency and meet the requirements of the nuanced cultural situation in which the person lives. Until this is understood, it is unwise to criticize the apparent surface vacillation.

Notes

[1]Many scholars view this text as an indication of historical inaccuracy in Luke-Acts, that is, as an unhistorical attempt to reconcile the Jewish-Christian and Gentile-Christian positions on circumcision. Yet this is in reality a surface reading of the text, for while it may save Paul from the charge of being inconsistent, it means that the author of Luke-Acts has Paul argue against circumcision in Acts 15 and the act contrary to this in Acts 16. If he were making up the story, he could have made it more consistent than that. Instead, this shows that our author is reporting history and probably understands the reasons for Paul's action, although

he reports them cryptically.

[2]The references in *m. Bikkurim* 1:4-5 show that this applied to both men and women. If one were brought up in a gentile family, one could not become fully Jewish unless one's mother was a Jew. But there would then be no difference between this person and a person whose mother and father were Jews. The same basis is recognized today in Israel's Law of Return: One is a Jew and may have automatic citizenship if one's mother was a Jew.

CHAPTER 14

Did You Receive the Holy Spirit?

> *Did you receive the Holy Spirit*
> *when you believed?*
> ACTS 19:2

Have you ever had someone ask whether you have received the Holy Spirit? That may have occurred if you have been in contact with Pentecostal or neo-Pentecostal groups, but it certainly has not been a standard question in Christian vocabulary. Rather, many of us have been told that we have received the Holy Spirit even though we have no awareness of the fact. Yet it is the question that jumps out of the text in Acts 19:2.

Paul has just arrived in Ephesus to begin a major evangelistic effort. Priscilla and Aquila have perhaps already established a house church and laid the groundwork, but Paul's arrival will trigger the major thrust. As he proclaims repentance in the face of the kingdom of God, much as Jesus did before him, he is informed that there are other "disciples" like him in the area. Upon meeting them he apparently senses something different among them, so he asks the diagnostic question of our verse. This is certainly not, however, the question we would expect to ask today. Their response, however, might not be untypical of what many modern churchgoers might give: No, we have not even heard that there is a Holy Spirit. Paul then takes a step backward and asks a second diagnostic question about their baptism, another question that sounds strange today. They had been baptized with John's baptism. Proclaiming that John's baptism pointed forward to Jesus, Paul rebaptizes them into Jesus, places his hands on them, and they receive the Spirit, prophesying and speaking in tongues. Why, we ask, did Paul rebaptize them? This is not what happened in Acts 8 when there was a separation between baptism and receiving the Spirit. Were these disciples Christians before they received the Spirit? Why this strange (to us) evangelistic procedure? What does it tell us of the role of the Spirit in the church today?

The messages of John the Baptist and Jesus were very similar. Both announced the coming of the kingdom of God but demanded repentance. Both called for baptism as the outward step of repentance (Mk 1:4, 14-15). They differed, however, because John stated that one who was coming was stronger than he, while Jesus indicated that the kingdom had come in his person (Lk 17:21). It is not until after Pentecost, however, that the mark of John's coming one is seen in Jesus. That is, John predicted that the coming one would baptize with "fire and the Holy Spirit" in contrast to his own baptizing with water, which does not happen in any of the synoptic Gospels. All of this is significant to Acts, which begins with the prediction and fulfillment of the promise of the Holy Spirit.

Paul came to Ephesus, then, proclaiming the kingdom (Acts 20:25). The mark par excellence that the kingdom had come in Jesus was the presence of the Holy Spirit.[1] When Paul meets people who claim to be disciples but do not display any of the effects of the Spirit, he asks his question. Their negative answer indicates that at the least the instruction they had received was defective, for from Pentecost onward the promise of the Spirit was part of the gospel proclamation (see Acts 2:38), especially among Jews for whom the Spirit was the sign of the coming age, the kingdom. Throughout the early church Christian initiation consisted of four discernible steps: repentance, commitment to (faith in) Jesus, baptism into his name and reception of the Spirit.[2] Having discovered that these "disciples" were defective in the last step of initiation, Paul wonders how much of the whole process was defective. By moving backward one step Paul gets the information he needs. These folk were not Christians. They had gone through the first step, repentance, but they had yet to hear about Jesus. Their baptism was a sub-Christian baptism.[3] It was then natural for Paul to lead them through the final three steps of complete Christian initiation.

This situation differs from that in Acts 8 where there was no question about the adequacy of the preaching and belief. Philip, a trusted Christian leader, had done the preaching. The baptism was clearly "into the name of the Lord Jesus," so it in no way had to be repeated, for Christian baptism is once for all. The situation in Acts 19 also differs from Acts 10, in which Peter proclaims a proper gospel, but God sovereignly gives the Holy Spirit without the usual laying-on-of-hands in order to convince Peter and the others to accept the Gentile Cornelius as a full disciple and therefore to baptize him. (One wonders if Peter would have dared to make such a step without the sign of God's acceptance in the Spirit.) Pentecost is different yet in that all of those in the upper room were believers in Christ and baptized. Only the empowering for mission in the Spirit was missing. In that situation, of course, no one could lay on hands.

The situation in Acts 19, then, is similar to the others in that the Holy Spirit is seen as the experience of normal Christian life. Furthermore, as in all Scripture, Old or New Testament, when the Holy Spirit comes something happens. The most frequent manifestation in Acts is speaking in tongues (chaps. 2, 10, 19), with prophecy second (chap. 19; in Acts 8 something observable happens but we are not told what it is). In his letters Paul does not mention any particular gift as being characteristic of receiving the Spirit, but he does indicate that the Spirit is a concrete experience, a down-pay-ment on the full experience of Christ in heaven. Thus we can safely say that Acts gives us historical precedence for the initial experience of the Spirit as evidenced in tongues or prophecy. These gifts are, of course, easy to observe. Presumably any of the gifts in 1 Corinthians 12 or Romans 12 might be similarly produced, although, for instance, a gift of healing would be difficult to manifest if there was no one around who was ill. (In Gal 3:5 Paul associates the Galatians' reception of the Spirit with their working miracles, which may be another example of gifting.) The important issue for Paul, which Acts illustrates, is not how the Spirit manifests (according to 1 Cor 12 that is under the sovereign control of God), but that believers know that they have the Holy Spirit (see Rom 8:9).

Thus, given his theology of conversion, it was natural for Paul to ask if people claiming to be "followers of the Way" or "disciples" (as the early Christians were often called), had received the Spirit. This experience, however it was manifested, was the indication that Christian initiation was complete. It was equally natural for him to lead those who had not had a full Christian experience (for instance, had not yet committed themselves to Jesus as Lord) into that experience and then to baptize them and pray that they might receive the Holy Spirit. He was simply completing the pre-evangelism that John the Baptist had begun. What would be quite unnatural would be for Christians to rebaptize individuals who had already committed themselves to and been baptized into Christ, even if their doctrine were somewhat faulty. Likewise it would be incorrect to take the historical precedent of Acts and turn it into an invariable rule of how conversion and Spirit-filling must take place. Still, Did you receive the Holy Spirit when you believed (or at least at some time after that)? is as appropriate a question today as it was then, for it is not only a historical question in Acts, but an underlying question in both Paul's letters and 1 John.

Notes

[1]See, for example, J. D. G. Dunn, *Jesus and the Spirit* (Philadelphia: Westminster, 1975) or *Baptism in the Holy Spirit* (London: SCM, 1970) for an exhaustive treatment of this theme.

[2]For a full explanation, see David Pawson, *The Normal Christian Birth* (Lon-

don: Hodder and Stoughton, 1989). This book is about the process of Christian initiation and its implications for the church today.

[3]In Acts 18:24-26 Aquila and Priscilla meet Apollos, who "had been instructed in the way of the Lord" and "taught about Jesus," but "knew only the baptism of John." While it may be that our account is very compressed, we do not hear of them rebaptizing Apollos, only of their "explain[ing] to him the way of God more adequately." If the basic commitment to Jesus is already there, even if somewhat defective, only further instruction, not rebaptism, appears to be necessary.

How Did Christians Respond to Prophetic Warnings?

In every city the Holy Spirit
warns me that prison and
hardship are facing me.
ACTS 20:23

It *is not easy to deal with prophetic words. When someone says, "Thus says* the Lord," it puts the hearer in a difficult situation, especially since the meaning of the prophetic message may not be self-evident. How does one handle prophecy? That is the issue raised by the statement in Acts 20:23, which Paul made in Ephesus on the way to Jerusalem. Even earlier Paul had some concerns about his safety in Jerusalem, for he asked the Romans to pray for him in a letter written from Corinth (Rom 15:30-32). By the time he traveled around through Macedonia to Ephesus he could cite frequent warnings by "the Holy Spirit." Since they happened "in every city" they were probably prophetic oracles given to Paul by believers in each city. These warnings continued. When he arrived at Tyre on the Palestinian

coast the believers "through the Spirit . . . urged Paul not to go on
to Jerusalem" (Acts 21:4). Again we must assume some type of
prophetic word or divine insight.

While we may wonder what, if anything, Philip's prophesying
daughters said in Caesarea (and if they said nothing, why did our
author mention that they prophesied?), another event that happened there overshadows everything else. Agabus arrived. His accurate prophecy had previously guided Paul into timely famine relief in Jerusalem (11:27-30). Now he walks over to Paul's group,
takes Paul's belt, ties himself up, and states, "The Holy Spirit says,
'In this way the Jews of Jerusalem will bind the owner of this belt
and will hand him over to the Gentiles' " (21:11). Paul's friends were
sure that this prophecy meant that Paul ought not to go to Jerusalem. Paul, however, ignored the pleas of his companions, traveled
on to Jerusalem and was in fact arrested, remaining a prisoner for
at least the next three years.

How are we to evaluate this response to prophecy? Was Paul
disobedient, receiving in his imprisonment the results of such disobedience? Were his companions, including the author of Acts (who
includes himself among the "we" who wanted Paul to avoid Jerusalem), misinterpreting the prophecy? What does it all mean for
both this passage and the interpretation of prophecy today?

We note first of all that the whole series of prophetic words,
beginning with Paul's own inner "knowledge" in Romans, indicates
trouble in Jerusalem. The messages appear to become increasingly
clear the nearer he gets to Jerusalem. All *warn* Paul, but none contains a directive. A warning can be taken in one of two ways. It can
point out a danger to avoid, or it can point out a danger to walk into
with one's eyes open. In itself a warning does not tell a person
what to do, unless one assumes that God's will is always to keep
his people out of danger. One prophecy, however, gave something more than a warning. In Tyre Paul was urged "through the
Spirit" not to continue his trip. He obviously chose to ignore this
message.

Second, while all the prophecies are accurate in indicating danger,
they are not unequivocally clear. Agabus's is the only detailed one,

but it was not fulfilled in every particular. It is true that the result of Paul's visit to Jerusalem was that he was bound and ended up in the hands of the Gentiles, that is, the Romans. It is also true that this happened because of the Jews. But it certainly was not the Jewish plan to "bind" Paul and "hand him over to the Gentiles." In fact, they were trying to lynch Paul when the Romans arrived and bound him with chains (Acts 21:31-33). An exacting historian would be correct in saying that Agabus was at least in part wrong in his prophecy. At the same time, if we did not have the story in Acts, the prophecy would have given us an accurate impression, although not in detail. Prophecy by nature is "dark speech" or "riddles" (Num 12:6-8) and partial (1 Cor 13:9, 12). Even Old Testament prophecies did not mean what they seemed to mean (Dan 9:2, 24), and both Jeremiah (17:14-15) and Jonah complained that their prophecies were not fulfilled. In what form did Agabus receive the prophecy? Was it a vision, perhaps of Paul bound, standing between Roman soldiers with Jewish accusers facing him (see Acts 21:40; 22:30)? Or did he receive words or impressions from God? Whatever he experienced, his expression of it shows some fuzziness.

Third, all prophecy needs discernment or testing. The church through the ages has already passed its judgment on the prophecies recorded in Scripture, but Paul himself taught that new prophecy had to be "weighed carefully" (1 Cor 14:29). This is not simply to determine whether it is true or false, but also to discover what it means. Paul also indicates that during this process a further revelation might clarify the meaning of the first one (v. 30). This instructional passage explains Paul's response to the prophetic words he receives in Acts. He apparently understood the words to be a warning about what would happen, preparing him for the problems facing him, rather than telling him not to go to Jerusalem. In coming to this conclusion he obviously stood against the judgment of his companions. Furthermore, he must have believed that the speakers in Tyre had gone beyond the message God was trying to communicate and had added their own interpretation, for he certainly does not obey it. In other words, he shows that in responding to a prophetic word the responsibility for discernment and decision remained upon his own shoulders. In the end he would answer to God for his actions.

Was Paul wrong in his interpretation? Different Christians may come to different conclusions on that matter. For some his three-year imprisonment indicates a failure to heed God's warnings. For others the prophecies are to be seen as preparation to endure just such a trial. God was bringing Paul to Rome in his own way. Apparently his companions concluded from their inability to persuade him that Paul had a strong inner conviction that what he was doing was right and that he ought to interpret the prophecy accordingly. They fall silent and say, "The Lord's will be done." The same principles of personal testing of a prophecy one receives, of personal decision over its meaning and of personal responsibility for that decision hold true today. We cannot tell others what to do, although we may mediate to them messages from God or give them good advice. If we hold to these principles, we will clear up some of the confusion surrounding prophecy today.[1]

Notes

[1]Several recent works discuss the gift of prophecy. The best and most practical is Clifford Hill, *Prophecy Past and Present* (Crowborough, E. Sussex: Highland Books, 1989). Also good, but somewhat weaker, are Wayne Grudem, *The Gift of Prophecy in the New Testament and Today* (Westchester, Ill.: Crossway Books, 1988) and Graham Houston, *Prophecy: A Gift for Today?* (Downers Grove, Ill.: InterVarsity Press, 1989).

· C H A P T E R 1 6 ·

Remember the Words of the Lord Jesus

In everything I did, I showed you that
by this kind of hard work we must help the weak,
remembering the words the Lord Jesus himself said:
"It is more blessed to give than to receive."
ACTS 20:35

How complete are our Gospels? Have the authors missed anything? That is the issue raised by Acts 20:35. In this context Paul is defending his ministry to the Ephesian elders. They do not doubt his ministry, but Paul knows that after he leaves false teachers will come in and will (1) seek to discredit him and (2) attempt to establish a new pattern of ministry. Paul's own example of self-giving in ministry will help them distinguish the true from the false. Having noted his faithfulness in teaching and pastoring (vv. 18-21), Paul now points out that he supported himself and his companions in ministry; he took no offerings from them nor raised money elsewhere. This was in part to teach them to "help the weak," to support poorer Christians financially. But then Paul quotes "the words of the Lord Jesus himself." The problem here is that we know of no Gospel context where these words appear. Where do they come from? What does this say about the nature and formation of the Gospels?

Jesus left no literature behind him. He taught his disciples as a rabbi would teach his students. They were expected to memorize the words and deeds of the teacher.[1] That is why the earliest rabbinic writings come from the third century, although they contain some oral traditions going back to the first century. That was, of course, a time when memory was well developed. Any scriptural scribe in Palestine would have memorized the whole Old Testament.

The author of Luke-Acts tells us in the prologue to Luke (1:1-4) that in the years after Jesus' ascension "many" collected the words and deeds of Jesus into Gospels of one type or another. He distinguishes these writers from the "eyewitnesses," probably because the eyewitnesses themselves (such as the twelve apostles) felt no need to write, for they had seen and heard enough to last them a lifetime. Furthermore, he states that he himself used careful research to sort through these accounts in writing his own Gospel. Most scholars believe that one of the written sources he used was Mark's Gospel.

In any such process of research and writing some material is discarded for one reason or another. The author of the Fourth Gospel tells us that there was a vast amount of material that he could not include in his work (Jn 20:30; 21:25). Each Gospel author had the goal of providing certain information to the church and painting a portrait of Jesus from a particular angle; what did not fit into this plan had to be dropped. Scrolls only came in limited sizes.[2]

The fact that such material was not included in this or that Gospel, however, does not mean that the stories or sayings were not genuine or were immediately forgotten. Many of them circulated in the oral tradition of the church for the first generation or two as the eyewitnesses and their first hearers told stories about Jesus. Some were later distorted and recorded in gnostic Gospels such as the Gospel of Thomas. Such second-century or later works, dug up by archaeology or found in the recesses of ancient libraries, have been heralded by some scholars as "secret sayings" of Jesus. These later heterodox gospels contain such distorted versions of Jesus' sayings that they add nothing to our knowledge of him. In the first century, however, before there was a lot of distortion, some of these sayings found their way into orthodox and even canonical works, even though they were rejected by (or unknown to) the Gospel writers. For example, James 5:12 quotes a saying of Jesus which appears in a longer form in Matthew 5:33-37. Other short sayings in James also may well be sayings of Jesus (see 1:27; 2:13; 3:18; 4:11-12, 17), but since James never tells us if he is quoting Jesus, we will never know which come from Jesus and which are his own coinage. But his readers probably knew, for in the first century when few could read the church memorized the teachings of Jesus and would have recognized them in print.

In Acts 20:35, then, Paul indicates that he knows a saying of Jesus that was not included in any of the canonical Gospels. We appreciate the fact that he tells us that it comes from Jesus, for that enables us to identify it. The author of Luke-Acts, who obviously knows the saying since he cites Paul as using it, does not include it in his Gospel, perhaps because it did not fit into his scheme or perhaps because he knew he would cite it later. His method appears to be not to repeat material if he can avoid it. So words of Jesus found in the Gospel do not appear in Acts and this one in Acts does not appear in the Gospel.

While we in the present age may lament the loss of a wealth of sayings and stories after the first century (especially given our own drive to preserve as much of the past as possible in museums, archives, libraries and on computer disks), we need to remember two things. First, orthodox Christianity believes in the Holy Spirit who oversaw getting what was necessary into the canon. What was not included might have been nice but was not necessary for us to have in written form. Second, believers in the first century had no New Testament to help them distinguish between accurate and distorted traditions. They had to rely on the personal interpretations of eyewitnesses. As the church grew and the eyewitnesses died, getting such a judgment became more and more difficult. Those first-century Christians who knew a major eyewitness would have had access to far more information about Jesus than we have today, but most Christians never met a single eyewitness and so actually had far less trustworthy information available than is contained in the New Testament.

We can be thankful for having what we do today in a form that all Christians everywhere can consult at the same time, assuming it has been translated into their language. We have sufficient fully trustworthy information about Jesus for the needs of the church, although we do not have exhaustive information or even enough to answer all of our questions or direct us in our personal lives. Yet what is needed in personal direction beyond Scripture Jesus is still quite capable of providing through his Holy Spirit in the hearts of believers, even if that does not come in canonical form and so cannot be imposed upon others.

Notes

[1]Some scholars, such as Birger Gerhardsson, *Memory and Manuscript* (Uppsala, 1961), believe that some of Jesus' disciples (such as Levi/Matthew) were literate and may have taken a type of shorthand notes. But even if some of the sayings were recorded in writing, Gerhardsson admits that memory was the major means of preserving Jesus' teaching and that such notes were at best partial.

[2]Matthew, Luke and John fill the longest scrolls available in that day. Each of them would have needed a second volume if he had wanted to include more information.

• C H A P T E R 1 7 •

Should Christian Jews Live like Jews?

They have been informed that you teach all the Jews
who live among the Gentiles to turn away from Moses,
telling them not to circumcise their children
or live according to our customs.
ACTS 21:21

A fascinating phenomenon has occurred in the Christian world in the last few decades. The Messianic Jewish movement consists of Jews who have committed themselves to Jesus as their Messiah and thus are completed, not converted. This movement is both welcomed and questioned by gentile Christians. It is welcomed because it enriches the Christian church with Jewish tradition and provides a culturally relevant path for Jews to come to Christ. It is questioned because it is a form of church to which gentile Christians can never fully belong and perhaps because of the fear that it contains overtones of superiority. The statement in Acts 21:21 raises this same question: Is it legitimate for Jews upon conversion to maintain their

Jewish culture? Or did Paul declare that any such attempt is illegitimate from the start?

The context of the passage is Paul's arrival in Jerusalem for the last time. James receives him warmly, but is concerned for the unity of the church. The Jewish-Christian mission has been very successful. "Many thousands" of Jews have believed, but upon committing themselves to Christ they expressed their faith in a very Jewish way; they have become "zealous for the law." The rumor in Jerusalem is that Paul is turning Jews away from the law, which could cause a split in the church. James reaffirms the decision of the Jerusalem council concerning gentile believers (Acts 15), but he assumes that Paul himself as a Jew keeps the law of Moses. He suggests that Paul join some of the church members who are finishing a Nazirite vow and pay their expenses, demonstrating to all that he is in favor of such observance. Paul does this, but before the process is complete is arrested by non-Christian Jews. Is this story historically accurate? Could the Paul who wrote Galatians and Romans have acted in this way? Would he have offered sacrifice in the temple and taken part in Jewish rites? Did he really want Christian Jews to live according to the law? Doesn't this contradict faith as a basis for salvation? What would Paul have said to today's Messianic Jews?

Paul clearly had no place for the observance of Jewish ceremonies by Gentile believers. He states in the strongest terms in Galatians and Romans that circumcision, sabbath observance and Jewish dietary laws are not binding on Christians.[1] In fact, he writes, "If you let yourselves be circumcised, Christ will be of no value to you at all" (Gal 5:2).

It is also clear that Paul believed that God's promises to Israel were still in effect. Therefore he expected not just a remnant of Israel to be saved in the present, but "all Israel" to be saved in the end (Rom 11:26). He could therefore also write about a separate Jewish-Christian mission with a methodology different than his Gentile-Christian mission (Gal 2:7-10).

Finally, Paul states that even though he was free he became "all things to all men," which included becoming a Jew and living under the law while among Jews, for the sake of the gospel (1 Cor 9:19-23). This means that Paul personally could take part in Jewish ritual, if for no other reason at least to forward the gospel. For him this would not be the same sort of compromise as the circumcision of Titus would have been (Gal 2:3), for Titus was a Gentile by birth and Paul was already a Jew when he was converted. Thus Jewish behavior would not have been adding anything to his Christianity, but saying that he did not have to abandon his Jewish culture to become a Christian.

The evidence of Acts along with Paul's letters confirms that James was correct about Paul: Paul did keep the law, although probably imperfectly, given what Gentile Christians must have served at the Lord's Supper (which was a communal meal for the first two centuries of the church's life). Paul, after all, was very conscious of being a Jew (Rom 11:1). As a Jew rituals such as circumcision, sabbath observance, dietary laws and tithing were part of his national and cultural identity. If Israel as a people was still important to God, then it was fitting that those who belonged to Israel racially live out their cultural identity. On the other hand, it was not fitting for gentile believers to observe Jewish customs, for they would gain no advantage in becoming Jews, since they already had Christ. What is more, such actions would put a barrier in the way of the gentile mission.

The observance of his Jewish identity must have been more than simple cultural custom for Paul. In Acts 18:18 we read that he shaved his head due to a vow. This probably indicated the start of a Nazirite vow (see Num 6) that was fulfilled when he reached Jerusalem. At the least this indicates that Paul had a place in his own personal piety for such observance, which was voluntary in Judaism.[2] It was a cultural expression of worship and submission to God that was meaningful to him, and thus there was no reason for him to have refused James' suggestion. Very likely there were many other similar private practices as well.

Thus for Paul there was no theological reason why Jews could not observe Jewish customs, as long as they were seen as signs of national identity or cultural expressions of piety, not a way of making themselves more holy than gentile Christians. At the same time it was improper for gentile Christians to follow such observances, for they were not Jews and becoming Jews would be no advantage to them. Instead, such observances would indicate that Christ was not enough for them. Finally, he insisted that Jewish and gentile Christians remain in table fellowship with one another (Gal 2:11-21; Rom 14), which meant principally the observance of the Lord's Supper together. However difficult this may have been due to Jewish dietary rules and gentile freedom from them, the rule of love was to prevail in maintaining their unity in Christ.

Within such constraints Paul felt personally free to live as a Jew whenever possible. For him returning to the temple as a worshiper was a meaningful experience in continuity with his early zeal for God that, although misdirected, had now been brought to its proper fulfillment in Christ. Likewise he would surely bless today's Messianic Jews who also find their Jewish culture meaningful in continuity with their Christian belief. What he would discourage is any tendency to separatism or elitism, for love and the unity of the faith must be preserved across cultural and ethnic barriers.

Notes

[1]Also significant is Paul's resounding silence on the matter of tithe, a fourth major mark of Jewish practice, especially since he does discuss giving extensively in 2 Corinthians 8—9. As law it can no longer be binding on Christians.

[2]It is significant that this is a voluntary practice, which means that there was no reason for Paul to do this simply to maintain his acceptance in the Jewish community. The only reason to observe such a vow was because it was a meaningful part of personal devotion.

• C H A P T E R 1 8 •

Make the Author
of Their Salvation
Perfect

In bringing many sons to glory, it was fitting that God,
for whom and through whom everything exists,
should make the author of their salvation
perfect through suffering.
HEBREWS 2:10

How could the Son of God become more perfect than he was at the Incarnation? Hebrews 2:9 says that Jesus has been made "a little lower than the angels, now crowned with glory and honor because he suffered death." Yet in the next verse we read that this same Jesus became perfect through suffering. How can this be? If Jesus was the Son of God, how could he *become* perfect through experiences on earth? Was there some imperfection in him that had to be worked out through ordeal? Doesn't this challenge an orthodox view of Christ?

The author of Hebrews implies that Jesus, as the preincarnate Son of God, was indeed perfect (1:2-3). He is greater than the prophets, heir of all things and maker of the universe. But in the passage under consideration he is not in that preincarnate role. His role here is that of "the author of [the Christians'] salvation." The preincarnate Son of God was not yet perfect *in relation to that role*. In fact, he could not fulfill that role at all until he became incarnate and died for the sins of humanity.

This brings up another aspect of the issue. Perfection is an important concept in Hebrews (5:9, 14; 6:1; 7:11, 19, 28; 9:9, 11; 10:1, 14; 11:40; 12:2, 23). The Greek term means "to bring to maturity" or "perfection" or "fulfillment."[1] The fulfillment aspect is the most important in Hebrews. Obviously the theme of the whole book is the fulfillment of the reality behind Mosaic ritual, but there is also a fulfillment coming to the lives of Christians as they go on to complete that to which they were called at their conversion. Even though Christ has done everything for them on the cross and they receive this upon committing themselves to him, there is a promise involved in this reception that is not fulfilled until they live out that to which they were called.

This same concept of fulfillment appears in Christ. At birth he is designated as Savior (Heb 1:6), but he has at that time done nothing to deserve such a title. It is a promise, a hope, but not yet a reality. He goes through life obeying the will of God and therefore experiencing suffering (2:18). The question remains: Will he keep on until the end? At Gethsemane, facing the time of fulfillment, he cries out, "Not my will but yours be done" (Heb 5:7 reflects this Gospel cry). He continues on his way to the cross and fulfills everything that is needed to be "founder" (the Greek term means "author," "founder" or "leader" in most contexts) of salvation for his followers. Before that point he was not yet perfect, for death was a requirement to bring life to his people. After his death and resurrection he was the total fulfillment of all that was needed to bring salvation.

Therefore the perfection of Christ referred to here is a functional perfection, not a moral perfection, for he was never anything less than sinless in the view of the author of Hebrews. It is an earned perfection that will show up in its other aspects three more times in Hebrews (2:18; 4:15; 5:7-9), but at this point the function is salvation, earned only through death. Thus in talking about the perfecting of Christ our author underlines the fact that it was only through death that the world could gain a Savior.

Notes

[1]The Greek terms are the verb *teleioō* and the adjective *teleios*.

• CHAPTER 19 •

Tempted
in Every
Way

For we do not have a high priest who is unable
to sympathize with our weaknesses,
but we have one who has been tempted in every way,
just as we are—yet was without sin.
HEBREWS 4:15

How could God be tempted? *Hebrews states twice that Jesus was tempted,*
for the author first writes, "Because he himself suffered when he
was tempted, he is able to help those who are being tempted" (2:18),
and now he states that Jesus "has been tempted in every way, just
as we are" (4:15). Yet many Christians argue that Christ really
could not have been tempted "just as we are." After all, he was the
sinless Son of God. Would not his very existence as God mean that
his experience of temptation was at most that of watching a strong
enemy smash himself on an impregnable castle? Was there ever any
feeling of the desirableness of sin that makes temptation so difficult
for us? Given the orthodox doctrine of the Incarnation, don't these
verses sound like nonsense?

Actually, these verses are difficult because they involve two issues, the nature of temptation and the nature of Christ. The first we have experience with; the second we as human beings have no experience with: We must rely on the simple statements of Scripture.

The Greek term for "temptation" could also be translated "test." Human beings are tested to see if we will obey God when the chips are down (see Gen 22:1, the classic example of passing a test). We are tested to see if we will remain faithful when there is nothing to win (for example, Job 1—2). We are tested to see if our hearts are truly for God or whether we are trying to serve two masters (Jas 1:14-15; compare 4:3-4). Jesus experienced all of these things, if the Gospel records are correct. In Matthew 4 Jesus faces three tests, parallel to the tests of Israel in the wilderness: (1) When he appears to be starving will he, like Israel, demand that God feed him? He passes the test and refuses, being willing to trust God to the point of death if necessary. As long as God has said "Fast," he will fast. (2) Could he be certain that God would care for him? Why not test God to be sure that he would come through? Jesus passes this test because his trust in God is unshakable. He will not put God to the test, for he has genuine faith. (3) Will God really give him the kingdoms of this world? Does that not look impossible, since Satan controls them? Is not God's way an unlikely and difficult one? One little compromise is all it will take to bring the kingdom without pain. Jesus again passes the test because he refuses to compromise with evil, however enticing or even spiritual it may seem. Thus Jesus demonstrates he is God's true Son, as Israel in the wilderness proved to be a false son. These three examples are precisely the same types of tests that we as human beings face.

But what makes us fail the test? James (1:14) and Paul (Rom 7:17) trace the cause to a principle within us that James calls "desire" and the Jews called the "evil impulse," or "yēṣer." None of the writers believe that this is guilt-producing in the sense that simply to have it made one guilty. Rather it was just "desire"—or what a psychologist might call a "drive." Food is desirable because I am hungry; shelter is desirable because I am cold. But hunger also makes my neighbors' food desirable. Likewise their house or clothing might be desirable if I were cold. As we see in observing a baby, drive or desire has no moral boundaries. Part of becoming godly is to learn when to say Yes to desire and when to say No. Err on the side of saying No too often and one might become an ascetic, refusing God's good gifts, or possibly even die. Err on the side of saying Yes too much and one becomes a libertine, breaking God's boundaries in some way or another. Satan's destructive purposes are served by either error.

Did Jesus have desire? The answer, found in Hebrews, is that he "has been tempted in every way, just as we are." Matthew 4:2 states that he was hungry. The drive or desire was present. Likewise we assume that all other normal human drives were present. He felt thirst, weariness, sexual desire, loneliness and all else that we feel. Some of these he felt to the extreme. Think of the loneliness that he felt when he cried out from the cross, "My God, why have you forsaken me?" Jesus was, according to our text and the witness of the New Testament in general, fully human.

The one exception to human experience we find in Jesus is that he did not sin. In Matthew 4 he never gives in, but passes each of the tests. In Gethsemane he struggles mightily, but in the end says, "Not my will, but yours." At the cross he surely felt the impulse of pain and anger as he was stripped naked and nailed to the crossbar, but his response is, "Father, forgive them." To each situation, Hebrews asserts, he gave the proper response in the sight of God. He was without sin. Could he have sinned? Scripture never enters into such philosophical speculation. But it certainly implies that there was virtue in not sinning and that the test was real, which seems to imply the possibility of failing. One point, however, Hebrews makes crystal clear: whether Jesus could sin or not, the issue in the end is academic. He did not sin.

Although the church through the ages often practically has denied the humanity of Christ, picturing him as more divine than human, it has refused to allow that distortion doctrinally. The creeds assert that there were not two natures, as if the human nature would feel something and the divine nature would give the right response. There was also no attenuation of the human nature so that he experienced human feelings in some less intense manner than other human beings. He was, the creeds assert, fully incarnate, everything that we as human beings are, except that he never sinned. While the creeds are not Scripture, they safeguard what the author of Hebrews is attempting to express: Jesus experienced testing just as all of us do.

The reason for this dogmatic statement is important. According to Hebrews 4:15, Jesus can "sympathize with our weaknesses." He can do this, the argument runs, because he has experienced the same type of weaknesses. He may be exalted at God's right hand now, but he fully and experientially understands all that human beings are going through.[1] "Because he himself suffered when he was tempted, he is able to help those who are being tempted" (Heb 2:18). One must have experience with a situation to be helpful in the situation, but even then one will not be helpful unless the experience is successful. A person who failed a test is hardly the one to coach another on how to prepare for the test. Jesus took the very same test as we do, indeed, a more intense form of the very same test. But he passed. He "was without sin." He did not fail in any way. As a result he can in fact respond with true sympathy to human beings now suffering under testing, for he truly "feels with," having himself felt the same pain and impulses. He can also show by example the successful way through the test.

The Incarnation is a mystery, but the witness of Hebrews is that it was real. There is no way Jesus was not like us, except in our sinning. Offensive as this may be to the mind, which prefers a Greek view of a God untouched by real human feelings and testings, it is comforting to the heart, which is precisely why the author of Hebrews taught it.

Notes

[1]One might object that a major part of human experience is that of guilt, which Jesus could not share because he did not sin. Such a response would be correct when one considers Jesus' life, but it breaks down at the cross. There Jesus did take sin upon himself—even if it was not his own—experiencing fully what it means to be guilty before God. In fact, because he knew God so well, it is likely that he experienced our guilt far more keenly than we do. Therefore there is truly no human experience other than the act of sinning with which Jesus cannot identify.

• C H A P T E R 2 0 •

He Learned
Obedience from What
He Suffered

During the days of Jesus' life on earth,
he offered up prayers and petitions with loud cries and tears
to the one who could save him from death, and he was heard
because of his reverent submission. Although he was a son,
he learned obedience from what he suffered and,
once made perfect, he became the source
of eternal salvation for all who obey him.
HEBREWS 5:7-9

When we read this passage we are keenly aware of Jesus' emotions, his "loud cries and tears," and we appreciate this look into Jesus' humanity. But then the passage grates against our sensitivities when we read that Jesus "learned obedience." Wasn't Christ already obedient in becoming incarnate? Was there anything that the Son of God had to learn? Can *God* learn? Again, as in the last chapter, we struggle with the implications of this passage for Christology. Can we hold an orthodox view of the divinity of Christ and still accept Scripture?

The context of our passage is that of the high priesthood of Jesus.

Immediately after describing the exalted nature of this call, the author turns to the qualifications of Christ. The main qualification of a true priest is that he must obey God. Jesus was obedient to God. The author then makes it clear that obedience was learned in the context of suffering.

The example of suffering given here appears to be that of Gethsemane; it is the only occasion we know of when Jesus prayed intensely while facing death. The author does not describe a serene Jesus calmly facing the cross, but rather paints a vivid picture of a deeply distressed Jesus wailing out loud prayers to his Father. This in itself shows a genuinely distraught human being, not an individual who minimizes the cross because he knows it will turn out all right. What is interesting, however, is that God saved him from death, not because of the intensity of the prayer, but because of his reverence or piety (what the NIV translates as "reverent submission").[1] That is, even in the most intensely trying situation Jesus maintained reverential submission toward God. And his prayers were heard, not in the sense that he did not die, for Hebrews is very aware of the death of Christ, but in the sense that he was "delivered out of death" (an overliteral translation that makes the intended point) or raised from the dead.

This information, then, instructs us about what it means to learn obedience and be made perfect. The obedience Jesus learned was the obedience of suffering. It is one thing to obey when there is no resistance; it is another thing to obey when that very obedience will bring you pain. Before the Incarnation who resisted the Son? Only in his life on earth did he suffer for his obedience. In other words, there are some things that even God can experience only by becoming a human being with all of our human limitations.[2] Obedience in the face of suffering is one of them. This in turn brought Jesus to perfection, which has the sense of "maturity" or "fulfillment." That is, through obedience in the face of intense suffering, Jesus was able to complete or fulfill his mission, namely to become the source or basis of eternal salvation (versus a temporal deliverance) to those who in turn obey him. This completed mission is the basis for his present high priesthood.

This whole passage, then, turns on obedience in the face of suffering. Jesus was the Son, heir of all and exalted above the angels (Heb 1). But as a good Son Jesus submitted to the will of the Father. This will included intense suffering, and yet he obeyed to the end. The result was that he was eternally delivered from death and so is now a high priest forever. The believers Hebrews is addressing are experiencing suffering, although so far no one has died (12:4). They, like Jesus, will also obtain eternal salvation by obedience to the end, obedience to Christ.

Thus, Jesus does learn, although it is not a theoretical learning but an experiential learning of what it is to obey in the face of intense suffering. He also experiences a perfecting through this obedience, a perfection in the sense of a completion of his work as Savior, making him in reality what he was by God's declaration. Any Christology that has a place for genuine humanity must also have a place for such a learning (with "loud cries and tears") and such a perfection. Furthermore, it is just such a Christ that is worthy of trust when we are ourselves facing suffering.

Notes

[1]Some translations prefer "he was heard [delivered, set free] from his fear." This has a good basis in the use of the Greek term in the Greek Old Testament, but given the fact that (1) the author of Hebrews is a literate person and (2) classical Greek literature uses the Greek term used here for "piety" and (3) the context of our verse, the meaning used here is more likely.

[2]This is similar to the difference between our experiencing a hurricane by means of a computer model and living through a real hurricane. The first might give one a tremendous understanding of a hurricane, perhaps a far better one than could be obtained by the person in the middle of the storm, but it is the second type of experience that makes it possible to empathize with the terror of those living through the storm.

• C H A P T E R 2 1 •

Is Repentance
Ever
Impossible?

It is impossible for those who have once been enlightened,
who have tasted the heavenly gift, who have shared
in the Holy Spirit, who have tasted the goodness
of the word of God and the powers of the coming age,
if they fall away, to be brought back to repentance.
HEBREWS 6:4-6

Most Christians know of individuals who for one reason or another have left the faith. They may not have actually denied the faith, but they are certainly not practicing the faith. For such people this is a very troubling passage. Is there anyone who cannot be brought to repentance? Can a person have shared the Holy Spirit and then be lost? And are these people really eternally lost? Is this really a description of a Christian? All of these issues crowd in upon one another as we read this passage. It is important to sort out the issues and proceed carefully as we deal with a problem with which personal feelings are so tightly bound.

First, this passage is not unique, but rather is part of a group of passages concerning people who cannot be forgiven or brought to repentance. Mark 3:28-29 refers to blasphemy against the Holy Spirit, which will never be forgiven. The context is that of people observing the work of the Spirit through Jesus and calling it the work of the devil. This is a rejecting of the evidence of their own experience. In 1 John 5:16 (discussed in a later chapter) the author speaks of a "sin unto death" about which, the elder implies, prayer is useless. Finally, the verse under consideration here refers to a class of people who cannot "be brought back to repentance." The issue is not whether God would forgive them if they repented, but whether there is any way to bring them to repent at all. The answer is No. They are like farmland that produces nothing useful. "In the end it will be burned." This is surely what our author believes is in store for such people. Painful as it may be to contemplate, it is one of the realities of life that people can so harden themselves against God that nothing will keep them from hell.

Second, the people under discussion are fully initiated Christians. In the preceding passage, the author contemplates whether he should discuss Melchizedek, a difficult teaching, or return to the basic teachings of the faith. He lists these foundational experiences as repentance, faith and teaching on (a) baptism (differentiating the Christian baptism from other types of cleansing rituals), (b) reception of the Spirit (laying on of hands), (c) resurrection of the dead and (d) eternal judgment. If the instruction they received had been defective, there would be some reason to go over it again. But he will not return to these teachings, for he knows these readers. They are fully initiated Christians. There was nothing defective in how they were brought to Christ, so there is no use in going back over the basics.

How do we know they are fully initiated? We know it by looking at the description in our verses. They are "enlightened" (often a reference to baptism, but at the least meaning that they have received accurate teaching about God), "have tasted the heavenly gift" (often a reference to participating in the Lord's Supper, but at the least meaning salvation or reception of the Spirit), "have shared in the Holy Spirit" (who except Christians receives this?), and "have tasted the goodness of the word of God and the powers of the coming age" (probably indicating their experience of prophetic words and miracles, for healing and similar events were seen as a present experience of what would be fully realized in the coming age; see Gal 3:1-5). These are people with a full Christian experience, defective in no way. In fact, this is one of the clearest descriptions of Christian initiation in the New Testament.

Third, what is the author's concern about these people? Hebrews 6 is an excursus the author inserted into the argument because he is afraid that when he gets to the difficult subject of Melchizedek the readers will "turn him off." He is not afraid that they will not understand or go to sleep while this section of the book is read, but that they will reject the teaching and with it their commitment to Christ. Throughout the book he is concerned that they will leave their Christian faith and return to Judaism. The concept of an order of priests after Melchizedek (namely Jesus, the only one he cites as being in that order) contrasts with, and is an implicit criticism of, the Aaronic order that served in Jerusalem, which is something the readers may not have wanted to hear. The author is warning them before he brings the difficult teaching not to apostatize, because the consequence of such an action is damnation.

His warning comes as a description of what it would mean to apostatize. That he is talking about full-blown apostasy is clear, for he uses the phrase "they are crucifying the Son of God all over again and subjecting him to public disgrace" (6:6). That is, they once confessed that Jesus was Lord and Messiah, which means they repented of the injustice of the crucifixion. Now in rejecting the faith they are declaring that the crucifixion was correct after all—Jesus was a blasphemer and not Messiah. Such a public recantation exposes Jesus to public disgrace.

Is it possible that the author is simply writing about a hypothetical situation? If so, there are two possible ways to understand it. The first is that both the author and his readers know that this can not happen, so it is hypothetical for all of them. In that case one wonders why the author wasted his ink. His purpose clearly is to exhort them not to return to Judaism. If his warnings are only hypothetical, how would they keep people from apostatizing? The second possibility is that the author knows this is hypothetical, but he believes his readers will take it seriously. In that case it would serve as a warning, but it would also be deceptive. Is the author of Hebrews likely to defend the truth with deception? Would he scare his readers with a situation he knows could never happen? Neither of these possibilities makes any sense in the context, so it would appear to be a counsel of desperation to claim that this passage is hypothetical.

What, then, is the author of Hebrews saying? He is refusing to return to basics on the grounds that there is no use in doing so for people who have been accurately initiated into the Christian faith. His arguments to keep them in the faith must come from deeper truth, not from a clarification of the foundational truth. He then points out by way of warning that if fully initiated Christians, like they are, turn their backs on Christ, they will so harden themselves that nothing anyone can do will bring them back to repentance. Their end result will be eternal damnation. But, he concludes, while this is a real possibility for some, "we are confident of better things in your case" (6:9). If he were not, at least for some of them, there would have been no use in writing the letter at all. They may be on the verge of apostasy, but they have not made the decision and crossed the line. To what degree this is a charitable assumption and to what degree this is sober reality could be determined only if we knew the full facts about the community to whom our author is writing.

But in so writing our author strikes the balance found throughout the New Testament. The New Testament authors write out of an experience of the grace of Christ and a firm conviction that they are on their way to a greater inheritance in heaven. At the same time, they write with a concern that they or their readers could apostatize and thus lose what they already have. So long as people are following Christ they are supremely confident about them. If their readers turn back to the world, rejecting the rule of Christ, then the New Testament authors never express any hope that without repentance such people will enter heaven. This is a sobering, but not a fear-producing, type of tension, seen in Paul (1 Cor

9:27; Gal 5:2, compare 7-10; Phil 3:12; 2 Tim 4:7, sometimes speaking of the tension in his own life and sometimes speaking of his concern for others), James (5:20, the purpose of the letter being to "save [a sinner, meaning a believer who has turned to the world] from death"), Jude (23), and John (1 Jn 5:16-17, the emphasis being on praying for people before they commmit the "sin unto death"). The call to the modern reader is to pay attention to the warning and "to imitate those who through faith and patience inherit what has been promised" (Heb 6:12) so that the author would say of us as well, "we are confident of better things in your case—things that accompany salvation."

• C H A P T E R   2 2 •

Who Was
"This
Melchizedek"?

This Melchizedek was king of Salem
and priest of God Most High.
He met Abraham returning from the defeat
of the kings and blessed him.
HEBREWS 7:1

The historical Melchizedek and his deeds occupy three verses of the Old Testament, Genesis 14:18-20. The comparison of Jesus with this figure occupies a whole chapter of Hebrews, beginning with Hebrews 7:1. What is more, the author of Hebrews has some strange things to say about King Melchizedek: "First, his name means 'king of righteousness'; then also, 'king of Salem' means 'king of peace.' Without father or mother, without genealogy, without beginning of days or end of life, like the Son of God he remains a priest forever" (7:2-3). Who was the historical character Melchizedek? How is Hebrews using the Old Testament? Is this use legitimate? Was it legitimate only for the author of Hebrews or is it still legitimate today? All of these questions spring to mind when we reflect upon this passage.

Little is written about the historical figure. Palestine in the Middle Bronze Age (the period before 1500 B.C.) was divided into numerous city-states. Melchizedek is identified as the priest-king of Salem, which many scholars identify with Jerusalem. There they worshiped *El Elyôn*, or God Most High. While this term is frequently used in the Psalms for Yahweh, it is not recorded as a name by which the patriarchs knew God. Still, Abraham must have recognized an identity between this one and the God he worshiped, for he later takes an oath by God Most High (Gen 14:22). Perhaps he had previous contact with Melchizedek or he and his allies had paused to pray and worship in Salem on their way north. But from the explicit information we have, Melchizedek remains one of the shadowy non-Israelite figures of the Old Testament, including Balaam, which show that God apparently was known to people other than to Israel.

Melchizedek fades from view after this incident, presumably returning to Salem and living out his days. Some scholars point to the sudden appearance of the Zadokite line of priests after David captures Jerusalem, suggesting that they descended from Melchizedek (the ZDK in Zadok and Melchizedek are forms of the same root) and merged with the Aaronic line. Whatever the case, later Judaism did speculate on Melchizedek. There is some evidence that the Hasmonean priest-kings of Judah (164 B.C.—63 B.C.), from which the Sadducees probably came, looked to Melchizedek for a precedent of a person who was both a priest and a king. In response, rabbinic Judaism (and presumably Pharisaic Judaism earlier) named Melchizedek as one who would "not inherit the age to come" because he blessed Abraham first before he blessed God! A third Jewish view is found in the Dead Sea Scroll 11QMelchizedek, in which he appears as an archangel warrior. None of this speculation is taken up by the author of Hebrews, although his caution in speaking about Melchizedek may be related to the low view taken of him in Pharisaic circles.

What the author does is look at what the text does and does not say and draw historical correspondences to Christ. He first looks at his name. *Melek* is the standard Hebrew for "king," and *zedek* comes from the same root as "righteous" or "righteousness." Originally the name probably meant "my king (= god) is righteous" or "my king is *Zedek*," but our author reads it as one might normally read what is called a Hebrew construct state, "king of righteousness." He then looks at his being king of Salem and notes that Salem comes from the same root as *salôm* (often *shalom*), the Hebrew for "peace" or "well-being." Thus he derives the meaning "king of peace." It is clear that he wants the readers to draw a parallel between Melchizedek and Jesus, whom he has argued is without sin and therefore righteous (4:15), in contrast to the Aaronic priests. He also has called Jesus the bringer of God's true rest (4:1-11), which might be comparable to peace. But the author never makes either of the comparisons explicit. Nor do we discover if calling Melchizedek "king of righteousness" has any implications for the low view we presume was taken by Pharisaic Judaism. Presumably our author knows the background of his readers and expects them to draw the proper conclusions.[1]

Then our author notes that Melchizedek is not called "son of" anyone. That several other individuals in the Abraham stories are also named without their parents (such as Abimelek) is immaterial, for he is only interested in the parallel with Melchizedek. He is not talking about history. He then points out that Melchizedek also has no descendants named in the text, nor is there any mention of his birth or death. Historically we expect none of this for a figure who makes only a cameo appearance in the narrative. But for our author they are a parallel with Jesus. He has already indicated that Jesus pre-existed before his birth (1:2-3), but his real interest is that Jesus exercises his priesthood in heaven as a resurrected being. Thus it literally has no end, just as no end is reported of Melchizedek's life. This contrasts with the repeated changes of ministry due to death of high priests in Aaron's line, even under ideal circumstances.[2]

The author of Hebrews, then, demonstrates a way of interpreting the text that is foreign to our modern methods of exegesis. That is, he sees Melchizedek and each detail of the Genesis text as a

"type" or historical precedent for Jesus, the "antitype." This form
of exegesis is frowned upon today, but such a typological interpretation was quite moderate according to the standards of the author's age. We argue that neither etymology (explaining the meaning of the names) nor typology (noting the correspondences in
history in what the text does and does not say) bring out the meaning that the original author (the author of Genesis) had in mind
when he wrote the text. Therefore they are not appropriate means
of interpretation if we are interested in *biblical* authority being behind our interpretation.[3] This was not the point of view of the
biblical writers, who believed that there were deeper meanings than
the historical to be discovered in texts, a view that they shared with
their contemporaries. Furthermore, the New Testament writers
believed that they were under the inspiration of the Spirit and had
in Jesus the key to the deeper meaning of the Old Testament. The
surprising thing is not how they interpreted Scripture, but how
conservative they were in doing it.[4]

How can the modern reader evaluate this? Orthodox Christians
believe that the writers of Scripture did have the inspiration of the
Spirit. Therefore it would be the prerogative of the Spirit to give
whatever message he wanted through his Scripture, even if it
might not be the historical message. But can the same be done
today? Certainly the New Testament expects that the Spirit will
remain in the church, but any speaking under the inspiration of the
Spirit, according to Paul, cannot be a claim to absolute truth but
must be "weighed carefully" (1 Cor 14:29). Scripture, of course, has
already been weighed carefully by the church as a whole and found
fully of the Spirit. No present speaker can claim such credentials.
Thus, exegesis such as we find in Hebrews could be appropriate and
helpful for the church so long as the speaker (1) did not claim the
authority of the scriptural text for it and (2) did not expect his
words to be accepted without careful sifting and weighing (and
perhaps correcting and revising). The only exegesis that can claim
a higher level of authority is that in which the speaker points his
or her finger to the text and is aligned with its message clearly
enough for all to see.

Notes

[1]For a fuller study of the interpretation of this passage, see Bruce Demarest, *A History of Interpretation of Hebrews 7.1-10 from the Reformation to the Present* (Tübingen: J. C. B. Mohr, 1976).

[2]The circumstances in the first century were not ideal, for since 170 B.C. when the Seleucid king had deposed the last Zadokite high priest, Onias III, rulers of Palestine had frequently stepped in and changed high priests, except during the relative independence of 164—63 B.C. Under the Romans the high priest was often changed every year or two as a deliberate policy to limit their power. The author of Hebrews quietly ignores these facts, for he wants to look at ideal Judaism, not the actual situation.

[3]See, for example, Walter Kaiser, *Toward an Exegetical Theology* (Grand Rapids, Mich.: Baker, 1981).

[4]For further information, see Richard N. Longenecker, *Biblical Exegesis in the Apostolic Period* (Grand Rapids, Mich.: Eerdmans, 1975).

A Copy and Shadow of What Is in Heaven

They serve at a sanctuary
that is a copy and shadow
of what is in heaven.
HEBREWS 8:5

I*n a college philosophy course I learned that Plato believed that what we call* realities on this earth are really only shadows of the eternal ideals, which are not physical at all. Likewise Buddhist thought looks on the phenomenal world as unreal. If we read Hebrews 8:5 with this in mind, we are quite likely to be somewhat confused. The verse quite clearly refers to the tabernacle in the wilderness, which it claims was a copy of something in heaven, as the rest of the verse points out: "This is why Moses was warned when he was about to build the tabernacle: 'See to it that you make everything according to the pattern shown you on the mountain.'" In what way, we might ask, was this a copy? Is there a sanctuary in heaven? And if so, could it be made out of goats-hair cloth and sea-cow skins? If not, has the author been influenced by Plato (since it is unlikely that he had ever met a Buddhist)? Or, to put the question another way, is there a New Age influence in Hebrews?

Hebrews does have a great concern with the tabernacle. In fact, the author never once mentions the temple, either Solomon's temple or the second temple (later enlarged and beautified as Herod's temple), which Jesus knew. Some see this as an indication that the temple was destroyed before Hebrews was written, while others note that if this were true, the author could have pointed the fact out, strengthening his case for the inadequacy of Judaism by showing that sacrifices were no longer being offered. Therefore it is more likely that our author views the temple as irrelevant, whether or not it was standing. God never commanded the building of the temple (2 Sam 7:5-7); he never gave a blueprint for it. He certainly did not say anything about Herod's version of the temple. But he did command the building of the tabernacle in the wilderness. Our author, who shares with Stephen (Acts 7) a rather negative evaluation of the temple, therefore points to the ideal, to the tabernacle. In fact, in every way he points to Judaism at its ideal, as if it were actually running the way the Old Testament said it should. In this way he can clearly point beyond reform (cleaning up the present wrongs) to replacement (Jesus as the end of the old system).

There was probably a variety of belief in Judaism concerning the tabernacle itself, but clear evidence exists that at least some Jews believed that it corresponded to a heavenly sanctuary. For example, 2 Baruch 4:5 states, "And again I showed [this building . . .that was already prepared from the moment that I decided to create Paradise] also to Moses on Mount Sinai when I showed him the likeness of the tabernacle and all its vessels" (compare Josephus, *Antiquities* 3.123; *Wars* 5:212-13; *Martyrdom and Ascension of Isaiah* 7:10). We do not know how far back this tradition goes, but it was a common idea in the ancient Near East that the temples on earth were models of the homes of the gods.

Yet before we jump to the conclusion that Hebrews is Platonic, we need to contrast this belief with the Platonic Judaism of Philo. Philo also used the language of "shadow," but for him what was in heaven was not a structure, but ideas and principles. These were metaphorically expressed in the physical structure on earth. The real is the world of ideas. This is not the position of Hebrews. In quoting Exodus 25:40 the author's stress is on "the pattern shown you," something that Moses saw (a more literal translation of the Hebrew reads: "that you were caused to see"). There is a correspondence between heaven and earth, but it is that of two physical realities in different spheres, not that of the ideal and the material. Heaven may be a better form of the material, a spiritual material, so to speak, for the New Testament, but it is viewed as real and solid, unlike Platonic and Buddhist thought.[1]

The belief in a heavenly sanctuary is also found in Revelation. The altar in heaven (perhaps the altar of sacrifice) is mentioned (6:9), as well as the altar of incense (8:3). Both the temple and the altar are mentioned in Revelation 14:18. That the temple contains "the ark of his covenant" is noted in 11:19. Finally, the temple is called "the tent of testimony" in 15:5 (in the context of the singing of the "song of Moses the servant of God"). In other words, in the prophet John's vision there exists in heaven a temple that is the original of the tabernacle. To the extent that it is described, its furniture corresponds to that of the Mosaic tabernacle. While Revelation is an apocalyptic vision, there is no indication that the author did not believe that what he saw was real, as real as God, the Lamb, and the events he saw on earth. Hebrews, then, is far from alone in this belief in a heavenly sanctuary.

What this means for our author is that Moses saw the heavenly tabernacle while on Mount Sinai. He copied the pattern by divine command—not that he used the same materials (after all, he had to make a portable earthly shrine), but that he translated the plan into the available materials of the wilderness. That this was a tabernacle and not a temple was probably deliberate, since a tent or tabernacle is a temporary dwelling, while a house or temple is a permanent dwelling. The permanent was in heaven; the temporary (or as Hebrews puts it, the "copy and shadow") was on earth.

The point our author is making is twofold. First, just as the copy is inferior to the original, so also all the features of the earthly tabernacle and its worship are inferior to the heavenly. Jesus' ministry is in the heavenly tabernacle, not the earthly. Second, just as the earthly tabernacle was set apart as holy by sacrifice, so must the heavenly be cleansed. But its sacrifice must be superior to earthly sacrifice. "It was necessary, then, for the copies of the heavenly things to be purified with these sacrifices, but the heavenly things themselves with better sacrifices than these" (Heb 9:23). This better sacrifice was none other than the blood of Christ, brought into the Holy of Holies, not of the earthly tabernacle, but of the heavenly.

In other words, the presentation of the earthly tabernacle as a copy is not a downgrading of the material world, but an exaltation of the work of Christ. His work is complete and final, superior to anything that could have been done on earth, because it was done in the very dwelling of God, in the heavenly tabernacle itself.

Notes
[1]This fits with the belief in the resurrection of the dead, which is repugnant to the Platonist and something from which the Buddhist would attempt to escape. Throughout the New Testament the resurrected dead have bodies. They are not just spirit. So while Paul in 1 Corinthians 15 can speak of a transformed body, a spiritual substance, he is clearly talking of something other than mere spirit (otherwise there would be no need for a resurrection at all). The Gospel narratives also speak of the physical properties of the resurrected body of Jesus, even though some of his abilities appear to transcend normal physical activities.

· C H A P T E R   2 4 ·

He Has Made
Perfect Those
Being Made Holy

*Because by one sacrifice he has
made perfect forever those
who are being made holy.*
HEBREWS 10:14

The men who wrote the Dead Sea Scrolls used to call themselves "the perfect of way," but Christians have not wanted to call any human being (other than Jesus) perfect. In fact, when people intimate that they are in any way perfect, we call them proud, not perfect, and believe that they are self-deceived. Thus it does not surprise us that Hebrews glorifies the work of Christ, but it does surprise us when we read in this passage that Jesus has "made perfect forever" a group of human beings. Who are these people? How could a living human being be perfect? Furthermore, how can they be perfect if they are still "being made holy"? Aren't the two expressions contradictory? We wonder if the author of Hebrews is confused.

When we turn to look at the verse in question, the meaning of the first part is clear in context. Hebrews 10:11-12 contrasts the daily offerings of the Aaronic priests, "which can never take away sins," with the completed once-for-all sacrifice of Christ. The Aaronic priests still stand, working at a job that will never be finished, while Christ sits "at the right hand of God," his work completed. From this perspective he has made all who believe on him "perfect forever." The author then quotes Jeremiah 31:34, a passage about a new covenant, arguing that according to this new covenant in Christ, "their sins and lawless acts I [God] will remember no more" (Heb 10:17). He then adds, "And where these have been forgiven, there is no longer any sacrifice for sin" (v. 18). In other words, perfection here does not mean that people are free from moral error, but that they are completely forgiven for their moral error. This sense is possible because the Greek term for "perfect" can mean "complete" or "fulfilled" or "brought to a conclusion." For the author of Hebrews, Jesus has brought the work of forgiving sins to a conclusion or to completion. He has fulfilled the new covenant. Those who commit themselves to him are perfect in that there is nothing remaining in them that God has to forgive.

How does this fit with the concept of "those who are being made holy"? In Hebrews 10:10 the author uses the same Greek term (for making something holy) in another tense. There he refers to a work completed in the death of Christ, a holiness given to the believer on the basis of what Jesus has done. "And by that will [of God in establishing the new covenant], we *have been made holy* through the sacrifice of the body of Christ once for all." Four verses later he changes the tense, using the same one as in Hebrews 2:11, which refers to a process.

We can interpret this in two ways. The first is that individuals are made holy as they commit themselves to Christ. Thus our verse would indicate that the work of Christ is once-for-all, but as individuals repent and commit themselves to Jesus they enter into this completed work, being made holy, that is, fit to enter the presence of God—forgiven of their sins. The progressiveness of making people holy is in this interpretation that of spreading the gospel so more and more people enter into the holiness available in Christ.

This is one possible explanation of the tension between the already perfected and the being-made-holy.

The second way of interpreting the phrase is that there is a tension in the Christian life. On the one hand, we have been forgiven. Nothing else is needed. No further work of Christ is necessary. On the other hand, sanctification is a progressive action in the Christian life. We are not yet completely free from sin. Our past sins may have been forgiven; the power of sin in our lives may have been broken; but we keep sinning and God must continue to confront us and bring us to repentance over and over again. We are in the process of being made truly holy, not just forgiven for our failure to be holy.

While both explanations are possible, I personally prefer the second, because it appears most fully to take into account the change in tense in the verb and reflects the fact that the spread of the gospel is not a topic in this chapter. Furthermore, it expresses a tension that is frequently found in the New Testament. Christians are not to walk around feeling guilty, but forgiven. They stand before God in an attitude of gratitude for forgiveness, not cringing because of guilt. Yet the more they appreciate the sacrifice of Christ, the more they become aware that they are not yet holy in the sense that they still sin. Indeed, that which they might not have viewed as sin before they now see as sinful. God is producing holiness in each believer, but it is a process that takes discipline (as Heb 12 will argue). Losing sight of either side of this tension is disastrous. On the one hand, we might so focus on the perfection accomplished on the cross that we neglect to cooperate with God in growing in holiness. On the other hand, we might so focus on the process of becoming holy that we lose the relief of knowing that Christ has done all that is necessary, and so wallow in guilt and feel alienated from God. Both sides of the balance are necessary, and both are found in this verse.

◦ C H A P T E R 2 5 ◦

If We Deliberately Sin, There Is No Sacrifice Left

*If we deliberately keep on sinning after
we have received the knowledge of the truth,
no sacrifice for sins is left.*
HEBREWS 10:26

All who examine their lives according to Jesus' standards discover sin;
it may not be a frequent event or a flagrant sin, but none of us has
lived up to what Jesus has revealed of the Father's character. We
are also forced to admit that some of our sin is deliberate. That is,
we do not deliberately set out to sin, but we know in ourselves that
some deed or activity is wrong (at least for us, if not for everyone),
yet we stifle our consciences and do it anyway. At times we may
even recognize that we planned our sin quite carefully, or at least
planned to walk into temptation, knowing full well (in our hearts,
if not in our minds) that we would give in. If this is an accurate
description of the human condition, then Hebrews 10:26 is very
disturbing. Is this verse making the distinction that the Old Testa-

ment does between deliberate and accidental sins? Is it saying that there is forgiveness for accidental or unknowing sins, but not for the other type? And if this is the case, are all of us who have knowingly sinned after our conversion lost? If that is in fact the meaning, this verse should cause terror and despair rather than mere concern.

The Old Testament makes a clear distinction between willful or deliberate sin and inadvertent sins.[1] After discussing the procedure for obtaining forgiveness for inadvertent sins in Numbers 15:22-29, the author adds, "But anyone who sins defiantly, . . . that person must be cut off from his people" (v. 30). The example that follows this passage tells of a person who gathered wood on the sabbath, presumably because his fire was going out and he had neglected to gather enough wood the previous day. Surely this was a small act, unlike murder or even theft. But it was also clear that he had consciously gone out to do work on the sabbath and was not ignorant of the law against work on that day. It was a deliberate sin. He was stoned to death at the command of the Lord. A deliberate sin is not to be taken lightly.

Although the Old Testament makes a distinction between deliberate and accidental sin, that does not appear to be the point being made in Hebrews, which looks at life from a perspective of Jesus' already having come and died for sin. If Jesus understands human weakness and helps those who are tempted (2:17-18; 4:15), he is hardly going to fail to understand our failure. Similarly, Paul's response to failure was to restore the person (Gal 6:1), even when the sin was quite serious (2 Cor 2:5-11).[2] Hebrews is not a Pauline writing, but it comes out of the same circle of acquaintances (13:23). We would therefore expect similar attitudes toward forgiveness of sin.

The point Hebrews is making can best be seen by following the author's progression of thought. Having noted the adequacy of Christ's sacrifice in 10:1-18, he urges the readers to draw near to God with confidence (vv. 19-22). This is expressed in (1) holding on to the hope that we have in Christ, (2) encouraging each other to live the faith in practice and (3) gathering together (vv. 23-25). The opposite of these would be to withdraw from the Christian gatherings, to stop doing public expressions of faith, and to give up commitment to Christ and hope in him. In other words, the opposite would be apostasy.

That this is the point of the passage is clearly seen in Hebrews 10:29, where the "deliberate" sinners are described as those who have "trampled under foot the Son of God," treated the "blood of the covenant" as something common (in other words, looked upon Jesus' death as just any common criminal's death) and "insulted the Spirit of grace." This is deliberate sin, but deliberate in the sense that a person willfully is renouncing Christianity and rejecting Jesus, his death and the personal experience of the Spirit (which is the slander against the Holy Spirit condemned in Mk 3:28-29).

It is not that such deliberate sinners (or apostates) did not know the truth. The author is clear on that point. Only "after we have received the knowledge of the truth" is such an action so serious. Like those mentioned in Hebrews 6:4-8, they have been fully initiated into Christianity, for the phrase "knowledge of the truth" is common in the later New Testament writings for having come to full Christian conversion (Jn 8:32; 1 Tim 2:4; 4:3; 2 Tim 2:25; Tit 1:1; 1 Jn 2:21; 2 Jn 1). But they have chosen to reject their experience of Christ. Had they received a distorted picture of Christianity there might have been hope, for one could correct the distortion. But they have developed a "sinful, unbelieving heart that turns away from the living God" (Heb 3:12). For such people there is no sacrifice for sin remaining; they have rejected the only one that exists. What remains is the judgment of God.

This does not mean that the early church took sin lightly, deliberate or accidental. Any sin called for rebuke and restoration or, if unrepented of, discipline (see Mt 18:15-20; 1 Cor 5:1-5). And sinning could lead to sickness (Jas 5:15) or death (1 Cor 11:30). Furthermore, deliberately hardening one's conscience and disobeying God could start one on the way to this outright rejection of the faith. It might also indicate that the person remains outside the faith, for Jesus is not yet Lord to the one who disobeys him (1 Cor 6:9-10; Gal 5:19-21). Yet serious as their condition is, the possibility remains that all such people can be brought to repentance in one way or another. There are still arguments to be put forward and evidence to be shown. For the people our author is talking about, however, nothing of the kind is possible. They knew the truth fully, but have deliberately renounced what they once embraced. There is no new evidence or arguments to present. We can only tremble at the thought of the judgment awaiting them and take care that we stay far away from the slope that leads down into that pit.

Notes

[1]With the possible exception of the Day of Atonement, the Old Testament required no sacrifices for what we call sin. The unintentional sins mentioned there are situations in which a person or the community does not know the law. Only after doing something do they discover that God has prohibited it. Other types of sin and guilt offerings that were required were for such things as the healing of leprosy (restoring the former leper to the community) and the blood of childbirth, neither of which involve any moral failure. Old Testament offerings were primarily for ritual impurity and had almost nothing to do with what we call sin.

[2]The sinner here is probably not the person mentioned in 1 Corinthians 5, but a leader who had opposed Paul and forced him to withdraw from the church during the "painful visit" (2 Cor 2:1). Paul wrote his "letter of tears" after this, and the church responded by disciplining the rebel leader (2 Cor 2:3-4). So the sin was rebellion against God's apostle, perhaps even expelling the apostle from the church he had founded.

• C H A P T E R   2 6 •

See to It That No Bitter Root Grows Up

See to it that no one misses the grace of God
and that no bitter root grows up to
cause trouble and defile many.
HEBREWS 12:15

We all know the truth that "*suffering produces perseverance*" and other Christian virtues (Rom 5:3), but at the same time we know people who have experienced suffering or sickness (which are treated as quite different categories in Scripture)[1] and have become bitter rather than better due to the experience. Bitterness, to be sure, is no Christian virtue, even if it is at times overlooked in people of faith (see Ruth 1:20-21 for the example of Naomi). It is not addressed directly in Scripture except in one possible verse, Hebrews 12:15. Yet this text still raises a number of issues. What is a "bitter root"? Does it have anything to do with the vice of bitterness? Why is it connected to missing "the grace of God"? And how does it "defile many"?

A frequent interpretation of this verse is that it simply warns against bitterness or "bitter root judgments." Since the term "bitter" appears in the verse and all of us know individuals who have for one reason or another become bitter, such an interpretation sounds reasonable. The verse, then, would rightly point out that such attitudes (and the judgments of others that flow from them, like poison seeping out of a festering wound) can injure those who hold them, blocking these people from the many good things God has for them (which we may witness in a person who has had a similar experience but has allowed it to work for holiness rather than bitterness). In addition, it can injure the whole Christian community, infecting it with a fractious negativity and smearing the character of its leaders. Such observations have been made by most pastoral leaders. The question is whether the author has these observations in mind.

Unfortunately, the answer to that question must be No. The context of the passage in Hebrews 12 is that of holding onto the faith despite difficulties. Where commitment has grown weak, it is to be strengthened; the "lame" in the community are to be healed; "level paths" are to be made for their feet (vv. 12-13). The "level paths" (from Prov 4:26) are the ways of holiness without which no one will see God (v. 14). Having called for a firm commitment, the author continues with a series of warnings. Esau, an irreligious man,[2] had an inheritance and lost it, being unable afterward to regain what he had so lightly sold. Israel was disciplined severely at Mt. Sinai for her disobedience, but the Christians to whom Hebrews is addressed have come to an even more glorious place and therefore will be so much more severely disciplined if they reject God. What might they be in danger of rejecting? They might reject the message of our author, who is calling for them to hold fast to Christ and not abandon him in apostasy.

Looking more closely at verse 15, we see that this interpretation fits. The phrase "bitter root" is an Old Testament allusion, for it is very similar to a phrase in the Greek version of the Old Testament, the version normally quoted by the author of Hebrews. In Deuteronomy 29:18 we read, "Make sure there is no [person] among you today whose heart turns away from the LORD our God to go and worship the gods of those nations; make sure there is no root among you that produces such bitter poison." By comparing the two contexts, we see the point our author is making. To miss or fall short of the "grace of God" is the equivalent of turning away from the Lord in the Old Testament. Simply put, it means apostasy, a failure to commit oneself to God's grace. Such an apostate is a "bitter root" or, to use the Old Testament phrase, a "root that produces bitter poison." Just as one apostate in Israel could influence many neighbors to serve other gods than Yahweh, so one apostate among these Christians could lead others to forsake their faith. This, then, is the meaning of the text within its context.

Bitterness is not good. It is, in fact, a form of anger (that is, a nursed anger that has been allowed to smolder within), a topic about which the New Testament has much to say (see Gal 5:20; Jas 1:19). It can also be a characteristic of jealousy, which is condemned in James 3:14. Thus, if bitterness is broken down into its root vices, one will discover that the Scripture has a lot to say about it. But our passage is not about bitterness; it is about apostasy. If bitterness is not good, apostasy is devastating. It means missing the grace of God and coming into judgment before the God who is "a consuming fire" (Heb 12:29). It cannot be tolerated in the church, for it not only destroys the individual apostate, but it can infect others, weakening if not destroying their faith, and so defile many.

Notes

[1]See Peter H. Davids, "Sickness and Suffering in the New Testament," in C. Peter Wagner and F. Douglas Pennoyer, eds., *Wrestling with Dark Angels* (Ventura, Calif.: Regal, 1990), pp. 215-37.

[2]While the biblical Esau was not, strictly speaking, a fornicator, he did marry Hittite wives (Gen 26:34-35), which is commented upon negatively. Both intermarriage with non-Hebrew people and the use of temple prostitutes connected fornication to apostasy, the serving of other gods. In extrabiblical traditions both Esau and his wives are viewed as sexually immoral: see Jubilees 25:1, 8; Palestinian Targum on Genesis 25:29; *Genesis Rabba* 70d, 72a; *Exodus Rabba* 116a. Whatever the connection (or lack of it) to Esau, our author is clearly against all sexual misconduct (Heb 13:4).

Are Christians Masochists?

Consider it pure joy, my brothers,
whenever you face trials
of many kinds.
JAMES 1:2

No one considers "trials" to be something pleasant. If we were asked, "Would you like to have a few tests or trials?" we would certainly quickly decline. In fact, the term "trials" used in this verse means a "test," and often is translated "temptation" in other contexts. As we will note below, the trials in this case are the tests of faith that come from low-grade persecution from outside the church and from conflict within it. This is hardly a situation in which one would expect to have joy. How can James argue that we should consider it "pure joy" then? Is James some type of masochist? Are Christians to become masochists if they obey the New Testament? Is it necessary to deny pain and smile all the time, as some Christians seem to imply? Our humanity cries out for an honest explanation of such questions, for to deny the reality of pain is a denial of our being human.

James 1:2-4 does not stand alone. It parallels similar sayings in Romans 5:3-5 ("we also rejoice in our sufferings") and 1 Peter 1:6-7, all of which are "chain sayings" that link together virtues, one leading to the next. The situation pictured in all three of these passages is that of persecution. James and 1 Peter picture the persecution as a test of faith, a trial or temptation (the two authors use the identical phrase). Romans simply calls it "suffering" or "affliction" or "tribulation" (the term, like all terms for suffering, indicates persecution or hardship endured because of the faith, not illness). We know something about the type of persecutions that Paul endured; James's community appears to be experiencing low-level economic persecution; 1 Peter's readers have apparently been ostracized from their society and subjected to some violence (although not death). None of these are pleasant situations. None of these would ordinarily make us rejoice.

The call to rejoice, however, is not masochistic. Masochism is taking pleasure in pain. The masochist wants to experience pain because it is the pain that gives this person pleasure. In these passages, however, we are not to rejoice in the pain, but in the future reward beyond the pain. For example, why does James believe we should rejoice? Because trials give us an opportunity to develop the virtue of perseverance, which will in turn lead to a mature Christian character. We rejoices like an athlete in a practice session. Athletes may run or lift weights to the point of pain, but all the time their eyes are set on the big race or game. They rejoice, not in the enjoyment of the stress but in the knowledge that their muscles are growing stronger and therefore they will do better when it counts. James is probably dependent upon Jesus: "Blessed are you when people insult you, persecute you and falsely say all kinds of evil against you because of me. Rejoice and be glad, because great is your reward in heaven" (Mt 5:11-12). Here we see why character is important: it will be rewarded in heaven. In other words, faithfulness under pressure today earns eternal reward tomorrow. This is what Jesus lived, according to Hebrews, because he was the one "who for the joy set before him endured the cross, scorning its shame" (12:2). This is what Christians are to live. As one writer puts it, James is talking about "eschatological anticipated joy."[1] It is joy, not in the present feelings but in the anticipation of praise when one finally stands face to face before Jesus. The joy of that day is tasted in part already in the painful present. Thus Paul and Silas sing in the Philippian jail, not because they enjoyed the beating (although it may have been one reason why they were awake) but because they knew their Lord would more than adequately reward their suffering (Acts 16:25). It is a privilege to suffer for Jesus (Acts 5:41).

This is not to say that we cannot call pain, pain. Paul makes it very clear that he could recognize pain, call it what it is, and experience it with the full depth of human anguish (1 Cor 4:9-13; 2 Cor 4:3-12; 11:23-29). He also left us the example of fleeing from persecution when it was appropriate (Acts 17:10, 13-14). Yet even in such situations he, with James, could look beyond them to "an eternal glory that far outweighs them all" (2 Cor 4:17). We may know less of James's life, but from the passion in his letter there is no reason to believe that on this point he would have disagreed with Paul. His is a real humanity and depth of feeling, but at the same time he looks beyond the present experience to a transcendent reward.

James, then, is no masochist, but he points to an important truth. Only those who are heavenly-minded will suffer for their faith in the present. Those who do not have this anticipated joy invest themselves in the present and avoid disgrace and suffering for Christ, for it could cost them all they have invested themselves in. Those who do have James's perspective can be reckless in their obedience to Christ, for any price they may pay today will be paid back with interest by their Lord. And it is that smile of pleasure on his face when he greets them that they rejoice in, for they already see it dimly down the halls of time as the Spirit makes it real in their hearts.

Notes

[1] J. J. Thomas, "Anfechtung und Vorfreude," *Kerygma und Dogma* 14 (1968): 183-206. We have translated the term *eschatologische Vorfreude* as "eschatological anticipated joy."

• CHAPTER 28 •

God Does Not Tempt Anyone

When tempted, no one should say,
"God is tempting me." For God cannot
be tempted by evil, nor does he tempt anyone.
JAMES 1:13

When *a person is suffering, it is always a temptation to blame God.* After all, is God not sovereign? Does not everything in some sense come from him? Thus James 1:13 pictures a situation in which a person is suffering (being persecuted or experiencing disadvantage due to a commitment to Christ), and this suffering is testing the commitment to God. The question is, Will this person remain faithful to God, or disobey him? (The Greek term that is translated "tempted" also can be translated "tested"; therefore, I will use the two terms interchangeably.) Precisely in such a situation the person might want to blame God. "God, you sent this situation, and it is too hard for me. It is your fault if I give in." Paul speaks to just such a concern in 1 Corinthians 10:13. Yet the problem for modern readers is not the situation, but James's response. How can he say God does not tempt anyone when Genesis 22:1 says, "Some time later God tested [same word as tempt] Abraham"? Furthermore, if God cannot be tempted, how could the Scripture speak of Jesus' being tempted, assuming that the writers believed that he was God? Isn't this a clear situation of one scriptural author contradicting another? And doesn't James contradict Genesis in such a way as to question the sovereignty of God himself?

These problems are related, for both the issue of whether God tests (tempts) anyone and the issue of whether God can be tested call upon the Old Testament testing (tempting) tradition. This tradition begins with Abraham, who is presented as one who is tested and passes the test, God concluding, "Now I know that you fear God, because you have not withheld from me your son, your only son" (Gen 22:12). Later in the Pentateuch, however, Israel is presented as the group that when tested "disobeyed me and tested me ten times" (Num 14:22). This means that their response to the testing of God in the wilderness (Ex 15:25) was not that of trusting obedience, but that of blaming and demanding (this is what happened at Massah, a name that means "testing" or "tempting"; Ex 17:2, 7). This resulted in commands such as that in Deuteronomy 6:16, "Do not test the LORD your God as you did at Massah." (Pss 78, 95 and 106 reflect upon this tradition.)

James sees the testing situation occurring in his community in these Old Testament terms. His concern is that the believers should be trusting like Abraham; they are not to be as Israel and fail the test by blaming God. James gives two reasons for not blaming God. We can translate the first reason, "God ought not to be tested by sinful people," instead of the traditional translation, "God cannot be tempted by evil." The Greek word *apeirastos*, translated "ought not to be tested" (or "cannot be tempted"), is found only once in the New Testament and nowhere else previously in Greek. Later it is found only a very few times in the church fathers. In those later contexts our translation fits as well as or better than the traditional translation. Furthermore, our translation makes better sense in the context in James. It would be hard to see why the fact that God cannot be tempted would make it wrong to claim that he is behind a test, but it is easy to see that "God ought not to be tested" meets the situation, for then the phrase paraphrases Deuteronomy 6:16 and tells them not to blame God as Israel did at Massah, which is the very thing James pictures them doing. This also solves the problem of Jesus' testing (or temptation), for he was in fact tested by an evil being, which this translation allows to be possible, even if it is a sinful act.

But what about "God does not tempt [test] anyone"? To deal with this problem we must consider the development of doctrine within and between the testaments. Old Testament Hebrews, at least in their earlier period, traced all events directly back to God. Whatever happened, God caused it. This level of revelation was quite appropriate, since God's first task with Israel was to convince them that there was only one God for them to worship. Beginning late in the Old Testament, however, and continuing into the intertestamental period, it became clear that other beings often actually caused the test. While God, since he is sovereign, could have prevented a given situation,[1] he did not instigate every event. This development is seen clearly in Scripture by comparing pre-exilic (or early exilic) 2 Samuel 24:1, which reads, "[God] incited David against them," with the postexilic 1 Chronicles 21:1, which says, "Satan . . . incited David." The later book shows a more complex picture. It does not deny the previous model, but it admits that the model that traces all events directly to God leaves out details and complexities that later revelation fills in.

The Jews took their clue from such examples of development in Scripture and understood many other Old Testament Scriptures in this same way. For example, in Jubilees 17:15—18:16 the story of Abraham is retold in terms similar to Job. (Job is a later book that, with Chronicles, fits into the period when Judaism knew more about Satan than it did before the exile.) In Jubilees the Prince Mastema (Satan) comes to God and demands that he test Abraham (whom God knows has already proved faithful in many tests). The test, then, does not originate in God, but in Satan.

This appears to be James's position. In his concluding call to remain faithful to God under pressure, James says, "Resist the devil" (4:7). Satan is the one who is behind the test. This belief is simply stated, not argued. Even in his earlier passage (1:13) James does not have to explain this to his readers, for they share with him the same theology. So he can simply remind them of the fact in one line, "God does not test [or tempt] anyone." It is not God who wills ill to people and tries to make them fall; it is Satan. It was not God who wished to do evil to Abraham, but the devil. Therefore rather than blame God (who gives only good gifts, 1:17), Christians should look within at their own desires, which make them vulnerable to the Satanic test and lure them to fall (1:14). Having seen this, they should stand firm, thus resisting the devil, the ultimate mastermind behind all temptation. This position is not only good for James's day, but it warns against the same danger of blaming God and gives the same strategy for standing in the test that is appropriate for today.

Notes

[1]The Scripture never asks why God does not prevent certain situations, except in statements such as 2 Peter 3:9, which suggests that his desire for the salvation of as many as possible keeps him from intervening in a drastic way. We human beings, of course, do not know which events God does not prevent because he has some hidden purpose in them and which he does not prevent because to do so would mean to bring the end of the age prematurely. We can speculate on this, but Scripture does not enter into our speculation.

CHAPTER 29

A Person Is Justified by What He Does

You see that a person is justified
by what he does [works]
and not by faith alone.
JAMES 2:24

Ever since Martin Luther, Christians have struggled with putting James 2:24 together with such statements of Paul's as "we maintain that a man is justified by faith apart from observing the law" (Rom 3:28). It appears at first glance that James is advocating a justification through works and Paul one through faith. This impression grows when we realize that each cites the example of Abraham to support his argument. Are these two authors opposed to one another? Must we choose between the two for our theology? Was Luther correct that James is an "epistle of straw" that contradicts Paul's essential insight into the gospel?

The answer to all of these questions is No. A surface reading of James and Paul fails to understand what either author was saying.

Therefore, we must examine each of the critical terms in the verse in James: "faith," "works" and "justified."

The first term James and Paul have in common is "faith." In James 2:19, the author gives a clear definition of what he means by "faith alone": "Do you believe that God is one?" This is not only the basic creed of Judaism (Deut 6:4) but also a truth about God that Jews believed Abraham discovered. It is orthodoxy, but in James it is an orthodoxy totally separated from obedience ("You have faith; I have deeds," 2:18), an orthodoxy that demons have as well. Elsewhere James gives a different definition of faith. The faith of James 1:6 and 2:1 is that of personal commitment, which includes trust and obedience; in contrast, the faith that James sees his opponents claiming in 2:14-26 is orthodoxy without action.

Paul also has a definition of faith, which he gives in Romans 10:9-10. Faith means a commitment to a living Lord Jesus and a confession that "Jesus is Lord." This is similar to the relational trust type of faith that James refers to in chapter 1. In Galatians 5:6, Paul goes on to state that in Christ the issue is not one of Jewish rituals (circumcision), but of "faith working through love." This faith-love pairing is not accidental, for it occurs repeatedly in Paul (see 1 Cor 13:13; 1 Thess 1:3; 3:6). Love, of course, is not a feeling or emotion, but loving action, that is, deeds or works. For Paul, then, faith is a commitment to Jesus as Lord that results in a life of love. If the love is lacking (as "the deeds to the flesh" or "unrighteousness" show), then such a person is no heir of God's kingdom (1 Cor 6:9-10).

Since James (in 2:14-26) and Paul are using different definitions of faith, it is not surprising that they use the example of Abraham differently. For Paul (in Rom 4 and Gal 3), the critical issue is that Abraham was declared righteous in Genesis 15:6, which comes chronologically before the institution of circumcision in Genesis 17. Since ritual law is the issue for Paul, as we will see below, the fact that Genesis 15 comes after significant acts of obedience by Abraham (such as leaving Haran to journey to Palestine) is no problem. For James, on the other hand, the critical issue is that the declaration of actual righteousness in Genesis 22:12 shows that the faith referred to in Genesis 15:6 is not mere orthodoxy but a trust leading to actual righteous deeds, so that "[his] faith worked together with his deed and the faith was completed by the deeds" (Jas 2:22). In other words, the two men come at the Abraham narrative from different directions, using different definitions of faith, and as a result argue for complementary rather than contradictory conclusions.

The second term James and Paul share is "works" or "deeds," the Greek word *ergôn*. In the verse cited above (seen against the wider context of Jas 2:14-26), James is clearly arguing for *certain* works. The two deeds he cites are (1) Abraham's offering of Isaac and (2) Rahab's hospitality to the spies. Within the Epistle he mentions other acts of charity and the control of language. These fit well with Abraham's act, for in Jewish eyes this offering was the culmination of a lifetime of obedience to God and charity toward others. The fact that Isaac was not sacrificed was seen as a declaration of Abraham's righteousness.[1] Furthermore, Rahab's hospitality, like some of Abraham's actions, was viewed as an act of charity. We are not surprised, then, to discover that charity is the issue that begins the argument leading to our verse (2:14-17). Thus the works James is arguing for are good deeds (charitable acts, generosity).

Paul is clearly against certain works as a means of becoming righteous, but the works he is against are "the works of the law," a phrase also found in the Dead Sea Scrolls, but never used by James. The "of the law" is always present, at least in the near context, when Paul speaks negatively of works. What are these deeds? The principal one Paul mentions is circumcision, although he also speaks of the observance of (Jewish) holy days and (Jewish) dietary laws. In other words, while Paul never mentions charity and other good deeds in these negative contexts, he is against those cultic acts of the Mosaic Law that set apart a Jew from a Gentile. This fits the context of the Pauline letters, for the issue he is facing is that some Jewish-Christians are demanding that the Gentile believers become proselytes to Judaism to be saved. Paul denies there is any such need to become Jewish, although there is a need to become godly.[2]

There is, then, no real conflict between James and Paul on the issue of works. Just as his use of "faith" is different from James's, so is Paul's use of "works" different. Not only does Paul always use a phrase James never uses, but in places such as Galatians 5:19-21, he can list evil deeds (similar to James's list in 3:14-16) and then say, "I say to you [now] and I said to you [earlier] that those doing such things will not inherit the kingdom of God." Paul will not separate moral righteousness from eternal salvation.

Perhaps the most misunderstood of the three terms used in common by James and Paul is the Greek word group including *dikaiosynē* ("righteousness"), *dikaiōsis* ("justification") and *dikaioō* ("declare righteous," or "justify"). The usual meaning of these words in the Septuagint is for actual righteousness or a declaration of such righteousness (for example, Rom 1:17; 2:13). James invariably uses these traditional meanings (he never uses *dikaiōsis*). Paul, on the other hand, often writes of God's making a sinner righteous (justifying a sinner, Rom 2:24) or of a righteousness obtained by Christ's being given to the sinner (5:17) or of the resulting state (justification, 4:25; 5:18).

Unfortunately, the Pauline meaning (of which James may well have been ignorant) has dominated Protestant thinking since the Reformation and has been read into James by many translations (as the KJV, RSV and NIV all do in Jas 2). This creates an artificial conflict between James and Paul. James, on the one hand, is asking how God knew Abraham was righteous when he made the statement in Genesis 22:12, and how the reader can know that the faith in Genesis 15:6 was a trust that actually made Abraham righteous. The answer is, from his deeds. And without such deeds any claim of righteousness or of faith is empty. Paul, on the other hand, is pointing out that both Jews and Gentiles are equally short of God's standard of righteous judgment, and thus the issue is how God will make the unrighteous righteous. The answer is, not through cultic ritual but through commitment to (faith in) Jesus Christ. The two authors use their terms in different ways because they address different issues.

It is clear, then, that James and Paul are moving in two different worlds. In James's world Jewish ritual is not an issue (perhaps because all of those in his church are Jews), but ethics is. His problems are with those who claim to be right with God on the basis of their orthodoxy, although they are ignoring obedience issues, especially charity. Abraham and Rahab, in contrast to the demons, demonstrate that saving faith is seen in its deeds. Paul, on the other hand, is concerned about the relationship of Jews and Gentiles in the church. His concern is that commitment to Jesus as Lord is all that is necessary for salvation. A Gentile does not have to become a Jew to enter the kingdom; those ritual deeds that marked the Jew are unnecessary. In the places where Paul does address the issue of whether a person can enter the kingdom while living in sin, he emphatically denies this is possible, agreeing with James.

Paul himself realized that he was at times misunderstood. Some misinterpreted his denial that legal ritual was needed for salvation, making it into an argument that ethical issues were irrelevant to salvation (Rom 3:8; 6:1; 1 Cor 6:12). Paul strongly repudiated these people. It is unclear whether James was contending with an orthodoxy-without-deeds rooted in Judaism (such as rabbis would later attack) or a misunderstood Paulinism (such as Paul himself attacked). Both are possible backgrounds. It is clear that James is not attacking any actual belief of Paul's, but that Paul could endorse everything James wrote, although given his differing use of vocabulary Paul would not have said it the same way.

This verse, then, remains hard, but it is hard because its teaching is uncomfortable. God is concerned with our deeds, and they are related to whether or not we enter the kingdom. It is not hard because there is any conflict between this teaching and Paul's. The two merely *sound* contradictory rather than *are* contradictory. In fact, a lot of the apparent contradiction is due to the misunderstanding of Paul found in Luther and perpetuated by those who fail to put Paul into his proper Jewish background.

If James is dealing with a misunderstood Paulinism, then, it is probable that the sermon in 2:14-26 comes from a period before he met Paul, for it is likely that once they discussed the gospel together James would have cited Paul's own words against anyone who claimed Paul as an authority for such a twisted doctrine as James is countering.

The James-Paul issue, then, is partially a misunderstanding of Paul (stemming, as we noted, from the fact that Luther was concerned with earning his salvation through penance and pious deeds rather than with Jewish ritual, thus a reading of Luther into Paul) and partially a problem of reading Paul into James. In reality, the writings of James and Paul demonstrate a relative harmony, combined with differing spheres of ministry and thus differing perspectives (which are apparent in Galatians and Acts).

Notes

[1]For further information on this, see R. B. Ward, "The Works of Abraham: James 2:14-26," *Harvard Theological Review* 61 (1968): 238-90, and Peter H. Davids, *Commentary on James*, New International Greek Testament Commentary (Grand Rapids, Mich.: Eerdmans, 1982), pp. 126-32.

[2]See further, J. D. G. Dunn, "The New Perspective on Paul," *Bulletin of the John Rylands University Library of Manchester* 65 (1983): 96-122, or the discussion of the relevant passages in J. D. G. Dunn, *Romans 1—8*, Word Biblical Commentary (Dallas: Word, 1988).

CHAPTER 30

Friendship with the World Is Hatred Toward God

You adulterous people, don't you know
that friendship with the world is hatred toward God?
Anyone who chooses to be a friend of the world
becomes an enemy of God.
JAMES 4:4

What is it like to be publicly called an adulteress by the main leader of your church? James is given to strong statements, and the one in James 4:4 is one of them. Not only does he appear to be insulting his readers, but he also seems to be arguing that one cannot love God and at the same time, for example, have a career. Is this any way for a Christian leader to behave? Does this not create some type of otherworldly Christianity? Does not the Scripture teach that God loves the world? If so, what is wrong with Christians doing what God does? What does James mean when he says this?

The language of our verse is very direct. James does literally call his readers "adulteresses" (a fact obscured by the NIV translation). This does not mean that he is addressing only women, but that he wants us to see it as our clue that he is borrowing language from the Old Testament. The Old Testament pictures Israel as God's bride, who at the same time wanted to enjoy other "lovers," finding security in other gods and imperial powers (see Is 1:21; Jer 3: Hos 1—3). Given the New Testament bride-of-Christ language (2 Cor 11:2; Eph 5:22-24; Rev 19; 21), borrowing this language for the New Testament is quite appropriate. The "other lover" in this case is "the world," that is, the values and goals of their culture.

The Christians whom James is addressing wanted to be successful and gain status in the world's eyes, while at the same time they were followers of Jesus. This parallels what Israel did in trying to serve both Yahweh and Baal. Israel, and especially the Kingdom of Judah, never planned to give up the worship of Yahweh. All of his feasts were duly celebrated, his sacrifices made. The priests were employed to ensure this. But at the same time the people served Baal (and other gods), even erecting their altars in the courts of Yahweh's temple. Likewise these Christians were struggling for worldly status even within the church (Jas 4:1-2; compare 2:2-4).

Jesus pictured a similar situation when he said, "No one can serve two masters. . . .You cannot serve both God and Money" (Mt 6:24). The issue is not *how well* one can serve this or that master, but that one *cannot* serve them both. It is impossible. It is impossible first of all because one has only so much emotional energy. If you are deeply invested in the values of your culture, you cannot have enough energy left over to have a similar investment in God and his values. If you are invested in God,[1] you do not at the same time have the energy left to value what the surrounding culture values. Therefore we display what we value in our use of time, energy and money. All are in limited supply. All are placed at the disposal of what one is emotionally invested in. If these treasures go to one place, they cannot go to another.[2]

Second, it is impossible to serve two because both are jealous lovers. Throughout the Old Testament, God presents himself as the one who demands exclusive loyalty. He is a husband who will not share his wife with anyone else, even if the sharing only happens when he is off at work! Likewise Baal (or whatever other god) demands more and more. What begins as a both-and arrangement slowly erodes into a Baal-only arrangement as Baal takes so much energy that the worship of Yahweh begins to be neglected. In the New Testament Jesus points to God's exclusive demand when he speaks about taking up one's cross and following him (see Mt 10:38). The person going out to execution on the cross has invested all—wealth, reputation, even life itself—in the cause for which he is dying; there is no future separate from that cause. It is this same total commitment to which Jesus calls all of his followers. For this reason the New Testament does not talk about a tithe—God wants it all (see 2 Cor 8:2-5).

James is doing nothing more than calling his readers to a similar total commitment. In the preceding verses we discover that the readers have been using two means to get what they want. First, they struggle with each other, perhaps including vying for power within the Christian community. Second, they pray. But, adds James, they receive no answers to their prayers. This is because they are trying to use God to gain their own ends. God becomes the "sugar daddy" to fulfill their desires, but it is desire, not God, that they are really serving. Both strategies, that of struggle and that of manipulative prayer, show that they are invested in the world. The one is clearly a direct and open struggle, while the other sounds very pious; the underlying commitments and results are the same. When push comes to shove they are committed to their cultural values, not to God.

Our verse, then, is a warning. They have become God's enemies by their commitment to the world. Is there any hope? The next verse tells us that God is indeed jealous, but then James goes on to point out that God gives grace to the humble. Yes, there is hope if they will humble themselves and repent. God is ready to give them grace.

Can one have a career and serve God? James's answer is No. The career or vocation of every Christian is to serve God. One might serve God *within* a given career, but the career must not be where one's heart is invested if the person is indeed serving God (and not God's enemy). How can we tell the difference? Watch what happens when there is a conflict of values. (The conflict can come over issues of personal morality, but more often comes over issues of corporate morality and goals or over the issue of commitment to the job, such as whether one will agree to a transfer.) Does the person compromise and do what is expected by the corporate (or academic or professional) culture? Or does the person lose status on the job by refusing to compromise? This decision shows clearly whom they are really serving. Is this, then, an otherworldly lifestyle? James's answer is Yes. By this he would not mean that one does not have a very down-to-earth practical effect on this world (especially since caring for the poor is a very important part of his message), but that all of one's life and lifestyle is determined by a commitment to Christ. The only reward that really counts is that which comes from Christ. The values that a person values are Christ's values. For James this is not a special level of Christianity; it is Christianity pure and simple.

This saying in James is hard, but not because it is that difficult to understand. It means just what it says. The problem is that we with our divided hearts find what it means very uncomfortable. Here, however, James is just as uncompromising and just as realistic as his master, Jesus.

Notes

[1]Being invested in God does not necessarily mean being busy in church work. It would mean spending enough time in the presence of God to learn from him what priorities he has for one's life. See Joyce Huggett, *The Joy of Listening to God* (Downers Grove, Ill.: InterVarsity Press, 1986) and Peter Lord, *Hearing God* (Grand Rapids, Mich.: Baker, 1988). Church work itself often can be simply more worldly business, a way to gain status or one's personal ends in another sphere.

[2]For further reading, see John White, *Magnificent Obsession* (Downers Grove, Ill.: InterVarsity Press, 1976, 1990), especially chap. 2.

• C H A P T E R 3 1 •

You Rich People, Weep and Wail

*Now listen, you rich people, weep and wail
because of the misery that
is coming upon you.*
JAMES 5:1

Picture a person walking into an exclusive restaurant near Bay Street or Wall Street where the corporate elite dine and crying out, "Hey, you rich folk, weep and wail because of your misery!" Picture him somehow breaking into a gathering of national leaders in the White House or of religious people of means and stature meeting with the prime minister and saying the same thing. This is the incongruity that appears in James 5:1, which begins a six-verse condemnation of the rich. Such a condemnation immediately raises the question "Why are these rich people condemned?" Does not God love the wealthy people as well as the poor ones? Are not many wealthy folk just as Christian as their poorer brothers and sisters? Is this condemnation not rather unfair and arbitrary?

James already has mentioned the rich, referring to them specifically in 1:10-11 and 2:5-7, and in general terms (without using the word "rich") in 2:2-3 and 4:13. In none of the references does he say anything good about them. Interestingly, in these latter passages (2:2-3; 4:13) the individuals are members of the Christian community; in the passages where he uses the term "rich," the people are not Christians. James apparently finds the terms "rich" and "Christian" mutually exclusive.

Why, then, does James not connect the term "rich" to Christians? He is certainly free in calling Christians "the poor" (1:9; 2:2-3, 5-6). The reason is probably that James is following the teaching of Jesus, who said, "Blessed are you who are poor," and also, "But woe to you who are rich" (Lk 6:20, 24). In fact, Jesus indicated that wealth was a stumbling block to entering the kingdom of God—it is only God's ability to do the impossible that gets wealthy people in (Mk 10:23-27). It is incorrect to try to soften this by saying, "It is impossible for anyone to enter, poor as well as rich. All enter through a miracle of God," for Jesus does not say this. He notes that he came especially to preach the gospel to the poor (Lk 4:18), and he tells the poor whom he blesses, "Yours is the kingdom of God." He never says anything like this to the rich.

The key to this distinction is found at the end of his major discourse on wealth in Luke 12:34, "For where your treasure is, there your heart will be also." Given that human beings have only a limited amount of emotional energy to invest in anything, to the degree that one is earth-invested, one's heart is not set on heaven or the love of God. To have a heart set on heaven will mean placing one's "treasure" or investments there as well, which normally means giving earthly wealth in charity. Thus when we see God's miracle in the saving of a rich man, Zacchaeus announces his newfound freedom from wealth before Jesus announces his salvation (Lk 19:1-10).[1] Likewise, when the Spirit comes in Acts, the Christians begin to share their possessions with the poor. James is very aware of this gospel tradition and bases his teaching on that of his older brother Jesus.

Up to this point we have seen why James does not use the term "rich" for Christians and that therefore the people he is speaking about are not believers. That, of course, would be enough to condemn them to hell. But there is another reason that James singles out these particular rich people for such strong condemnation, and that is their treatment of the poor.

There is a progression in James's argument in 5:1-6. First, he notes the uselessness of their wealth, described in terms of garments and money. Stored goods deteriorate, as Jesus pointed out (Mt 6:19-20). Since James's church knows the words of Jesus, James is implying that these people could have had lasting investments had they shared their goods with the poor and thus obtained wealth in heaven. But of course they do not do this, for they are not followers of Jesus and so do not have his values. (Although the wealthy in James's day would have included the political and religious leaders of the Jewish people, who should have had spiritual values similar to those of Jesus.)

Second, their failure to obey the gospel (the teaching of Jesus) will witness against them in the last judgment. Here we find the parable of the rich man and Lazarus (Lk 16:19-31) condensed into two clauses. The rich man was probably an observant Jew, but he failed to submit to God in that he had plenty and yet did not help the poor beggar lying at his very gate. So these rich have stored up goods, but it is the "last days," or end of the age, and the final judgment is coming. Their failure to use their goods for God's purposes will "eat [their] flesh like fire," the fire of hell.

Third, they have practiced injustice. The other charges were bad enough, but now we discover that these absentee landlords (a typical rich person in first-century Palestine) have withheld the pay of the reapers. Leviticus 19:13 states, "Do not hold back the wages of a hired man overnight" (compare Deut 24:14-15). The reason for this law was that the poor laborer would immediately spend his wages for food for himself and his family. No pay meant no food. But even though they were reaping and therefore had a harvest to sell, these wealthy people found some reason not to pay their workers, perhaps arguing that they could not afford to sell the crop and pay them until the price was higher. They surely had a "legal" reason, justified by the "rabbinic" interpretations of their day. But God condemned such people in Isaiah 5 (especially vv. 9-10), which also uses "the Lord Almighty," and he continues to do so. (Contrast Job in Job 7:1-2; 24:10; 31:13, 38-40.)

Fourth, the rich have been self-indulgent. Feasting is fine if there is enough to go around, but self-indulgence when there are those without is a horrible crime before God. Again we think of the parable of the rich man and Lazarus, but we should also note that in the laws for the feasts of the Lord (Deut 16) no one was to appear empty-handed; the typical poor (Levite, widow, orphan, alien) were to feast with those who had means. In his condemnation of indulgence, James sounds like Amos.

Indulgence, of course, was viewed more seriously in James's world than in ours of the recent past. The first-century Mediterranean cultures believed that there was only a limited amount of goods in the world, so if someone collected more, someone else would have less or go without altogether.[2] The Western world has behaved as if goods or wealth were limitless and all could be rich if they worked hard enough or were smart enough. Only recently has Western society begun to face limitations and see that when viewed on a global scale, and especially when the environment and future generations are taken into account, the first-century view is probably more realistic than ours.

Fifth, these people have oppressed the righteous ("innocent men" in the NIV). In the phrase "condemned and murdered," James probably does not mean that they carried out an illegal activity, but rather they used the courts to kill. Probably even this killing was not done directly, but through taking away the means of support of the poor through fines or giving judgments in favor of the rich. A peasant who loses his farm or is thrown out of work will soon starve if no other force intervenes. It is all the same to God whether the death is direct or indirect, whether the proceeding is legal or illegal in human terms. In his book it is all murder. That these people were his poor Christians (the most likely ones being referred to) makes his judgment that much more certain.

Therefore, James is hardly arbitrary in his condemnation of the rich. Not only are they not Christian, but he has a number of charges against them. Furthermore, prophetic warnings like this one call people to repentance (although the repentance of wealthy people is less likely than that of the poor, according to Scripture), so these people, like those of Nineveh whom Jonah warned, are not outside of God's love. Yet, before we shake our heads sadly about the rich, we must remember that *any one* of the five charges is serious enough to bring God's condemnation. It is not enough to avoid judicial murder and legal oppression if we are living in self-indulgence and storing up what might have been shared. The Christian response to such a condemnation should not be to continue to point the finger, but to "stand firm" in obedience to Christ (Jas 5:8) and pray to be so filled with the Spirit that we will joyfully join with those in Acts who laid up treasures in heaven by sharing with their poorer brothers and sisters. This will provide a model of the virtue that God desires in a world that still practices (and even extols) the vices he condemns.

Notes

[1]This matches John the Baptist's call to repentance in Luke 3:7-14, which also has an economic focus and also demands repentance before acceptance by God, in his case symbolized by baptism.

[2]See B. Malina, *The New Testament World* (Atlanta: John Knox, 1984). Not all of his arguments are equally convincing, but his demonstration of the concept of "limited goods" is well founded.

• CHAPTER 32 •

The Prayer Offered in Faith Will Make the Sick Person Well

And the prayer offered in faith will make the sick person well;
the Lord will raise him up. If he has sinned,
he will be forgiven. Therefore confess your sins
to each other and pray for each other
so that you may be healed.
JAMES 5:15-16

Faith healing" is a dirty word for much of the church. Many of us have known people who have been mishandled by others who believed in healing. I personally can remember one person who died and whose widow was told that the only reason he had died was that either he had failed to have enough faith or he had sinned; in other words, to protect their own egos they blamed the victim. Others who have not been abused to that extent have been confidently promised healing, but have not in fact been healed. With this background, James 5:15-16 concerns us, for it appears to many to give support to the very situations that have emotionally or physically abused us or our friends.

This particular passage does indeed raise a number of issues for

the careful reader. James has given us the picture of a person sick
in bed. The proper response to this situation, he instructs us, is to
call for the elders of the church; they will pray over the person,
anointing him or her with oil in the name of the Lord. But how can
James say so matter-of-factly that "the prayer offered in faith will
make the sick person well"? Did he not have failures in prayer?
Does he really mean that elders will have no such failures? And
why does he bring in the issue of sin? Did not Jesus deny that sin
had anything to do with sickness (Jn 9:1-3)? Isn't James giving people a basis to load guilt for supposed sin on top of the illness that
is already afflicting the person? This passage looks more dangerous
than it does pastoral.

Prayer for healing is mentioned frequently in the New Testament. Jesus, of course, healed many (although we never hear him
using prayer as a means), and he sent his disciples to do the same.
It is they, not Jesus, who anoint with oil (Mk 6:13). Acts continues
the acts of Jesus (now being done through the Holy Spirit) and
notes numerous healings, beginning just after Pentecost (chap. 3)
and continuing to the end of the book (28:7-10). Paul's mission and
preaching likewise were characterized by miracle (Rom 15:18-19;
Paul's miracles appear to have been mainly healing miracles and
demon expulsions), and his converts experienced the same (Gal 3:5).
Furthermore, he mentions "gifts of healing" among the gifts of the
Spirit (1 Cor 12:9). It is not surprising, then, to find James writing
about healing prayer in the close of his letter where a pagan writer
would have put in a health wish. (A normal Greek letter of this type
characteristically ended with a summary, an oath, a health wish and
a purpose statement; Christian versions of all of these occur in
Jas 5.) He is not introducing something unfamiliar to his readers
(one did not do that in the closing), but underlining a practice they
knew about and shared in common with others in the early church.

While anointing with oil is mentioned in the context of our passage (5:14), probably as a type of acted prayer,[1] it is clear that the
operant force in healing is God's activity in response to prayer: "the
prayer offered in faith will make the sick person well." But this
prayer is to be a "prayer offered in faith." Of course, we would

expect the elders to be able to pray in faith, for they were supposed to be the most mature spiritual leaders of the church and should have the most faith. Notice that it is the *elders'* faith, not the person's faith, that is mentioned; there is absolutely no basis for blaming a person's lack of faith for not being healed. If anyone is to be blamed it is the elders, the people who prayed. Faith itself is a commitment or trust in God, like the asking in faith of James 1:6.[2] It is a personal relationship, not simply an intellectual conviction. It is also a gift of the Spirit (1 Cor 12:9).

So we are not talking about prayer based on an intellectual conviction that God heals; we are talking about praying out of a relationship with God in which the conviction has grown that God will heal, not in the sense that that is the general will of God (which it always is),[3] but in the sense that it is the specific desire of God now. George Müller, famous for his prayer for funds for his orphanages but also known in his day for his prayer for the sick, noted that while he always had faith (in the sense discussed here) for funds, only until 1836 did he have faith for healing the sick.[4] He still continued to pray for the sick and people were often healed, but apparently he no longer did so with the certainty and success that he continued to experience in praying for funds. It was no longer the prayer of faith in that sense. James, like Jesus (Mk 11:22-24), promises that a prayer of faith will be answered. His statement is a straightforward expectation, which must have been the experience of his community.

This prayer does not appear to be of the five-minute variety, for not only is it likely that such prayer would take time, especially time for listening to God, but there appears to have been some discussion of the person's sins. James is clear that sin is not always the cause of illness. He says, "*If* he has sinned." Like Jesus in John 9:1-2, he apparently knows of situations, perhaps many situations, in which sin was not involved. But like Paul in 1 Corinthians 11:30, he knows of other situations in which it was involved. If James 5:16 is any guide to the practice of his community, an opportunity was given under the wise guidance of the elders for self-examination and confession, with prayer for forgiveness (if needed) being included in the prayer for healing. Most modern people who pray regularly for the sick can give many illustrations of times when resentment or anger or bitterness or other sins were at the root of an illness. It is important to James to promise that the sin will be forgiven, not just the sickness healed, for without knowing that the sin (which could not be seen directly) was also removed, the person might fear that it would reappear in yet a worse illness. In fact, the experience of forgiveness itself has been known to lead to healing without any further prayer about the disease. Conversely there are examples of healing that was short-lived because the person returned to the root sin.

Finally, James notes, "Confess your sins to each other and pray for each other so that you may be healed." Nowhere in his discussion has James mentioned a gift of healing. Perhaps he expects such gifts of the Spirit to show up when needed in people filled with the Spirit. The focus of his interest is different from Paul's. But up to this point he has been discussing the activity of the elders called to the bedside of a person who is ill, probably too ill to go to church. Now he broadens the scope of his teaching. Before a person becomes so ill that the elders must be called, Christians should confess their sins and pray for one another. Confession of sin keeps the slate clear and prevents sin from being able to cause illness. Confession to another Christian (presumably one who has some spiritual wisdom and does not gossip) makes the repentance and confession concrete. It also makes it much harder to rationalize the sin. And it makes the prayer for forgiveness just as concrete. James does not mention these reasons; he just states the command. Likewise, prayer for each other before the illness becomes serious is in order. Why wait until the elders must be called? Why should the elders do all of the pastoral ministry? And how else will Christians gain the experience in prayer and the faith that will make them good elders? In case the believer says, "I'm not an elder and so God would hardly listen to me," James adds, "The prayer of a righteous man is powerful and effective" (v. 16). All that is needed is to be in harmony with God (righteous) and any Christian can pray with the effects of Elijah.

James is not giving a full treatise on prayer for the sick. There was no need to do so in the early church, for such prayer was their practice. It could be observed everywhere; they had not yet learned not to do it. James is just giving a reminder, encouraging them when the Greek letter form gave him opportunity. In doing so he presents a challenge to the modern church to learn what it is to pray the prayer of faith and so to pray effectively in such a way that people are healed, not abused.[5]

Notes

[1]The oil is certainly not a medicine, for (1) ancient peoples knew of more types of medicine than oil and would not prescribe a single medication for all ailments, and (2) there was a perfectly good term for "medicine" in Greek, so there was no need to use "oil" to substitute for a more general term. It is also not sacramental if this term implies virtue in the oil itself, for it is the prayer, not the oil, which heals, although the oil may be part of the praying.

[2]The point in James 1:6 is that one is to ask in childlike trust in God, confident of his character as the God who gives generously. The doubter or "double-minded" person is the person who prays but at the same time has their real confidence in their own skills or ability to manipute others. They pray more to "make sure" or to "get God's blessing on our plans" or because it is the pious thing to do than because they really trust God. In James 4:1-5 James points out that these people are really friends of the world and even such prayers are motivated, not by a call of God, but by an attempt to manipulate God to fulfill their own desires.

[3]See Peter H. Davids, "Suffering and Sickness in the New Testament," in C. Peter Wagner and F. Douglas Pennoyer, eds., *Wrestling with Dark Angels* (Ventura, Calif.: Regal Books, 1990), pp. 215-37.

[4]The reason for this appears to have been a conflict within the Christian Brethren movement, of which he was one of the leaders, over the place of spiritual gifts. Until the late 1830s the Brethren actively sought and expected spiritual gifts. However, around 1836, after J. N. Darby (another leader) reacted negatively to Edward Irving (a pastor who was what we might call a "proto-charismatic"), they abandoned this expectation. Darby then developed the concept of the cessation of spiritual gifts, which has characterized later dispensationalism.

[5]Perhaps the best contemporary book on prayer for healing is Ken Blue, *Authority to Heal* (Downers Grove, Ill.: InterVarsity Press, 1987).

• C H A P T E R 3 3 •

He Will
Save a Person
from Death

*Remember this: Whoever turns a sinner from
the error of his way will save him from death
and cover over a multitude of sins.*
JAMES 5:20

We are brought up short when we read James 5:20, the very last verse
in the epistle. Instead of ending with a greeting or blessing, James
ends with a strange statement. For us it raises some questions. Who
is the "sinner" to which James is referring? We know that all of us
are sinners, so does it mean us? Who will be saved from death? Is
it the sinner (in which case we may be in trouble) or the one saving
him or her? And from what type of death will the person be saved?
Are we still in danger of eternal death if we sin, or is James saying
that sin can lead to physical death? Unless we can answer these
questions, the epistle ends with a muddle rather than a clear message.

The verse is in fact very significant. James is written in a typical

Greek letter form. It was customary to end such a letter with a summary (5:7-11), an oath (v. 12), a health wish (vv. 13-18), and a purpose statement (vv. 19-20). Our verse, then, should be part of the statement of the purpose of the whole letter. That in itself is reason enough to assign its understanding a great importance.

The condition our verse speaks to is described in James 5:19. A Christian ("one of you") has erred. James gives us plenty of illustrations of this in the letter. The errors he addresses are those of partiality and greed, of anger and jealousy. All of them are found within the church. Such error calls for another Christian ("someone") pastorally to point it out so that the person can repent and be restored ("bring him back"). That, of course, is what the entire letter is about, bringing the Christians he addresses back to proper Christian behavior. This is indeed the purpose statement of James. Therefore the sinner in our verse is a Christian who has fallen into sin, such as greed or criticism of others.

This Christian brother or sister has erred or gone the wrong way—the text is not talking about an individual sin, however "serious" we may consider it, from which the believer quickly repents. As Jesus points out in Matthew 7:13-14 (which may be the word of Jesus that James is applying here), there are two ways. The way that leads to life is narrow and difficult, while the one leading to death is broad and easy. Unfortunately there are many ways to get from the narrow to the broad way. This Christian (the sinner) has taken one of them and is observed by another, whom we shall call the rescuer. The question is, Who is saved from death—the sinner or the rescuer? Ezekiel 3:18-21 is a discourse on the responsibility of the rescuer. If someone sees a person fall into sin and sits by and does nothing, the sinner will indeed receive the results of the sin, but the potential rescuer will be held guilty of the sinner's blood. In the Old Testament such guilt usually cost the person his life. On the other hand, the rescuer who tries to warn the sinner is free of any guilt, whatever decision the sinner makes. This is certainly the message of Ezekiel (33:9; compare 1 Tim 4:16), but is it the message of James?

It seems to me that James's message is that the sinner is the one

rescued from death by the rescuer's efforts. There are four rea-
seons for this. First, the fact that sins are covered (an adaptation of
Prov 10:12: "Love covers a multitude of sins") seems to refer to the
sinner's sins, not the potential sin of the rescuer. Only the sinner
has erred in the context. Second, the word order in the Greek text
makes it more likely that it is the sinner who is delivered from
death. Third, the very picture of turning a person from his wan-
dering way (a rather woodenly literal translation that brings out
James's imagery) suggests that it is the error that is putting the
individual in danger of death. The rescuer is presumably safe (although potentially in error, if he or she fails to help the erring
Christian).

What, then, is the death that the person is saved from? Certainly
sin can lead to physical death in the New Testament, as shown by
the deaths of Ananias and Sapphira (Acts 5:1-11), as well as by
Paul's statement in 1 Corinthians 11:30 (compare 1 Cor 5:5). More-
over, in James 5:15-16 we discover that sin may be involved in the
illnesses of Christians, and the sickness of 5:14-15 appears to be a
serious, perhaps even life-threatening, illness. Could this be what
James is referring to? By turning a sinner from their error a person
is saved from physical death, their sins being forgiven?

Attractive as this solution is, it is not the most likely interpretation of the passage. The fact that each of the units of James 5:7-
20 is separate and dictated by the letter form means that we should
look to the body of the letter (and the call to repentance in 4:1-10)
rather than the "health wish" (5:13-18) for the meaning of "death"
in our verse. Both testaments view death as the end result of sin,
usually referring to death in terms of eternal death or condemnation at the last judgment (Deut 30:19; Job 8:13; Ps 1:6; 2:12; Jer
23:12; Jude 23; Rev 20:14). James has already mentioned this in 1:15:
desire gives birth to sin, which results in death. That death is con-
trasted with the life that God gives (1:18). Since death and life are
parallel ideas, it is likely that they are not physical but eternal (or
eschatological, to use the more technical term). This parallel, plus
the seriousness of the tone in chapter 5, indicates that it is this sort
of death, the ultimate death that sin brings about, which is in view.

What James is saying, then, is that a Christian may err from the way of life.[1] When another Christian attempts to rescue him or her, it is not a hopeless action. Such a rescue effort, if successful, will deliver that erring person from eternal death. That is because the sins will be covered (the language is that of the Old Testament sacrifice; when atonement was made the sin was said to be covered as if literally covered by the blood). It may be one simple action of rescue, but it can lead to the covering of "a multitude of sins." In stating this, James shows his own pastor's heart and encourages all Christians to follow in his footsteps, turning their erring brothers and sisters back from the way of death.

Notes

[1]Neither James nor the rest of the New Testament is concerned to answer the speculative question "How could a Christian who had eternal life lose it?" All of the theological answers given are based on various theological assumptions and either deny the meaning of the various texts (such as "The Christian does not really die eternally, but simply loses his or her reward") or explain the texts according to their theological beliefs (such as the Calvinist "They appeared to be Christian, but their lack of perseverance shows that they were not really regenerate," or the Arminian "Yes, people can fall away from the faith and be lost"). James, like all New Testament writers, is not interested in theological neatness, but in pastoral concern. He simply sees the situation (a Christian on the wrong way), recognizes the danger (death) and goes to the rescue, rather than asks how it fits into his theology. So while theological responses are appropriate in their place, we ought not to expect a New Testament writer to select among them.

CHAPTER 34

The Goal of Your Faith, Salvation

*For you are receiving the goal
of your faith, the salvation
of your souls.*
1 PETER 1:9

Evangelical Christians frequently speak of "being saved." In other words, it is easy for them to speak of having received salvation at some point in the past when they committed themselves to Jesus as Lord. But does this language fit with that of 1 Peter? In 1:9 Peter appears to be speaking of salvation as a goal, an end result, not something already possessed. Does this mean that a revision of language is in order? And, more important, does this mean that salvation is uncertain?

Peter uses the term "salvation" four times in his first Epistle (1:5, 9-10; 2:2); he refers to being saved three more times (3:20-21; 4:18). One of these references is to a present process of salvation (3:21, the subject of a later chapter) and the rest refer to a future salvation (except 3:20, which refers to Noah's salvation). In 1 Peter salvation will not be revealed until the last time (1:5). It comes after the end of the present process of suffering for Jesus (4:18). Therefore it is something that one can grow up *into* (2:2; not "in" as NIV). In other words, Peter is relatively consistent in viewing salvation as something future.

It is true that the New Testament sometimes speaks of salvation in the past tense. Jude 3, for example, speaks about "the salvation we share," and Titus 3:5 states, "He saved us through the washing of rebirth." Acts 15:11; Rom 8:24; Eph 2:5, 8; and 2 Tim 1:9 also speak of salvation in the past tense. But these are a minority of the references to the term in the New Testament. It is far more common to speak of salvation as a present process (1 Cor 1:18; 2 Cor 2:15) or a future event (Rom 5:9-10; 10:9; 11:26; 13:11; 1 Cor 3:15; 15:2; 2 Cor 7:10; Phil 1:28; 1 Thess 5:8-9; 1 Tim 4:16; Heb 1:14; 9:28; 10:39). While some may argue with the categorization of this or that verse, the general trend is evident in these lists of passages. Salvation may be thought of in terms of a past event, but normally it is viewed as a future event.

This focus on the future has to do with the very nature of salvation. All of the verses that speak of salvation as past focus on *the basis* for salvation, which is Jesus' death appropriated by commitment to him (faith), not human rituals, even those in the Old Testament. But most of the verses speak of *the reality* of salvation, and that is future. Salvation means deliverance from some danger. When the term is used theologically, it means the danger of condemnation in the final judgment (Rom 5:8-9). Since that is the nature of the danger, then the salvation cannot become actual until the final judgment happens. Until that point the Christian has hope of salvation (1 Pet 1:3), but not the salvation itself. By "hope," of course, Peter does not mean an "I hope so" type of hope, but a confident expectation that something will happen. It is the type of hope one has for graduation when the registrar of the school has already indicated that the requirements have been met and one's place in the graduating party reserved.

Salvation, then, is a goal. It is what Christians are moving toward.

According to 1 Peter it begins with baptism (3:21), but it is finally revealed only in "the last time" (1:5). The mark of those who are "being saved" is their remaining firm in the faith under pressure (4:18).

Should evangelical language be revised? It would not be a bad idea to regain the balance of Scripture. In speaking of salvation almost exclusively as a past event there is a loss of two things. First, there is the loss of a sense of the last judgment. That creates a lack of seriousness about judgment, which no New Testament author had. Second, there is a loss of the sense of tentativeness. It is not those who "make a decision for Christ" (which is not a New Testament term), but those who "stand firm to the end" (Mt 10:22; 24:13; Mk 13:13) who will be saved. Historically, theologians have expressed this in two ways. In the Wesleyan tradition, salvation is truly tentative and may be lost, while in the Reformed tradition, God assures that those whom he has truly regenerated will in fact endure (persevere). But both traditions accurately reflect the biblical stress that it is not a one-time decision long-ignored that brings salvation, but a commitment to Christ lived out through obedience to the end of life. Salvation is fully certain, but only for those who are now living life in obedience to Christ. While we must not forget the basis for our salvation and totally stop referring to our having been saved (past) by the death of Christ on the cross, it would helpful for language about salvation to reflect the tentativeness and sense of the final judgment observed in the New Testament. Then, with 1 Peter, people will look forward to salvation more as a goal than as a past event.

• C H A P T E R 3 5 •

She Called
Her Husband
"Master"

---

*Like Sarah, who obeyed Abraham and called him
her master. You are her daughters if you do
what is right and do not give way to fear.*
1 PETER 3:6

We live in an age of the emancipation of women. *The New Testament,*
then, appears to us offensive when it suggests that something less
than full emancipation is the case. Isn't this the situation with
1 Peter 3:6? Isn't 1 Peter teaching that women should refer to their
husbands as if the women were the slaves and the men were their
owners? Isn't such an expression itself offensive and demeaning?
And what does *not giving way to fear* have to do with such a situation?
Is Peter setting women up for second-class status and abuse?

The passage in 1 Peter is referring to Genesis 18:12, in which
Sarah laughs and says to herself, "After I am worn out and my
master is old, will I now have this pleasure [of having a child]?" The
point is that Sarah (perhaps even in her thoughts) refers to her

husband as "my lord" (not "my master"),[1] showing a proper respect toward him. The irony is that in the context, while appearing to respect Abraham, she is laughing at the words of Yahweh himself; Peter, however, like most New Testament authors, is not concerned with the context, only with the single use of the term.

But what is the context in 1 Peter? The passage is addressed to upper-class Christian women with unbelieving husbands (a far more common situation in that culture than that of Christian husbands with unbelieving wives). These women are advised to be subject to their husbands, for it is their virtuous behavior that will convert them, not their arguments for Christianity nor their fancy dress (the fact that fancy dress was possible points to their being upper-class women; peasant women typically had one decent set of clothing and virtually no expensive jewelry). Such submission was also the mark of "the holy women," that is, the Old Testament women, of whom Sarah is the chief. This submission will mark these Christian women out as being themselves holy (Sarah's children).

We notice, then, what is not being said. First, it is not being implied that this submission extends to giving up the practice of their Christian faith or compromising the standards of holy living laid down by Jesus. These women are to continue to "hope in God" and "do what is right." Their husbands, being unconverted, may in fact threaten them with punishment or divorce, demanding that they not go to the church gatherings or that they practice something Christ has forbidden, but these women are not to "give way to fear." Suffering for the name of Christ is honored in 1 Peter. Yet like all of those to whom 1 Peter is written, they should suffer because they are committed to Christ, not because they have broken cultural standards of which Christ would approve.

In other words, what we see here is that the submission of these women is not to be absolute. They have submitted to Christ first of all. That is the one absolute submission. Now they follow him and submit to their husbands. Their culture demanded absolute submission to their husbands, including in matters of religion. This epistle is calling for them to take an independent stand on religion and morality, but to be model wives in every other way, which means that Christ would not be blamed for what was not truly the result of obedience to him.

Second, this pattern is not presented as the ideal for Christian marriage. Only in 1 Peter 3:7, as we shall see in the next chapter, does the author get around to discussing Christian marriage. Given that he has so little to say about it, it is likely that either such marriages were not a problem or that they were relatively rare in the communities he is addressing. In a Christian marriage the wife is an heir with her husband "of the gracious gift of life." In other words, she is an equal partner in the gospel. The husband is to take action in giving her honor and treating her with consideration, even though he warns the husbands to do so, "so that nothing will hinder your prayers." This, then, is Christian marriage, in which the husband, using the power granted him by his culture, treats his wife as a full partner and equal. But of course this is not normally possible in pagan marriage.

Thus, Peter is doing three things. First, he is presenting an evangelistic strategy. People are won to Christ, not by words alone and certainly not by rebellion, but by living to the fullest pagan virtue (when it is consistent with Christian virtue), so that the non-Christian will see that the effect of Christ in one's life is to make one able to live the ideals that pagans could write about but rarely live.

Second, he is noting that the normal Christian position is the way of submission. No New Testament writer has a problem with submission, for it is what Jesus practiced, as Peter points out in 2:23. Liberation in the New Testament comes from the powerful giving up power, the wealthy sharing their wealth, not by the oppressed demanding their rights or the poor their support. The effect of the Spirit is seen in the act of giving up, not that of demanding. Thus Sarah's action shows an attitude consistent with New Testament virtue. This was especially important, given the role possibilities for women in that day.

Third, he is following the pattern Paul described in 1 Corinthians 5:12-13 (and illustrates in 7:12-16), that Christians should not try to impose their standards upon non-Christians. After all, such peo-

ple do not have the power of the Spirit to follow Christian standards. Thus our passage does not address the behavior of the unbelieving husband, only that of the wife. She alone can show Christian virtue. She can hope that her husband will in fact come to faith
and, filled with the Spirit, in turn begin to treat her as an equal as
instructed in 1 Peter 3:7.

This passage illustrates the fact that the concept of marriage as
an intimate relationship between husband and wife is a relatively
modern concept. The Mediterranean culture did not expect emotional intimacy between husband and wife. A man was closest to
his mother and siblings; he might also have male friends (the father-
son relationship generally was not an emotionally close one). A
woman was closest to her children and her siblings, perhaps having
other women friends (although women were generally expected to
stay at home). The emotional distance between husband and wife
in this passage (which the term "lord" certainly indicates) would not
have bothered Peter, for while there are a very few examples in
Scripture of marital emotional intimacy, it was not a cultural expectation. Likewise, although it may be culturally desirable today, it
cannot on biblical grounds be made the essence of marriage. The
essence is the publicly sanctioned covenant or commitment of each
spouse to the relationship.[2]

Notes

[1]The translation "my master" in the NIV is unfortunate in that it implies
that Peter is thinking about women as slaves. In fact, he is following the
Greek translation of the Old Testament in using *kyrios,* or "lord," which
may mean simply the respectful "sir" or could imply superior status such
as "my lord" would imply in traditional British usage. When Peter refers
to the master of a slave, however, he uses another term, *despotēs* (2:18),
which shows that that is not what he is thinking about in this verse.
[2]See B. Malina, *The New Testament Word* (Atlanta: John Knox, 1984), for a
description of Mediterranean culture, and R. Paul Stevens, *Married for Good*
(Downers Grove, Ill.: InterVarsity Press, 1986), especially the first four
chapters, on the concept of what marriage is (the rest of the book works
out these and other issues in the context of the marriage pattern of the
Western world).

• C H A P T E R 3 6 •

The Weaker Partner

*Husbands, in the same way be considerate as you
live with your wives, and treat them with
respect as the weaker partner and as heirs
with you of the gracious gift of life,
so that nothing will hinder your prayers.*
1 PETER 3:7

Does the Bible talk down to women? In the previous chapter we looked at 1 Peter 3:6 and discovered that it concerned Christian women married to non-Christian husbands, a fact that explained some of its more difficult features. The same explanation will not work for this passage, although it raises some of the same questions, since it is addressed to Christian husbands. In what way is the wife "the weaker partner"? Isn't this a condescending term? Doesn't it imply the inferiority of women? And then what does being "considerate" mean? Is this the consideration of a master taking a slave's desires into account? Finally, why would a failure here hinder people's prayers? All of these issues demand explanation.

The interesting thing about questions based on this verse is that several translations have interpreted the Greek term in different ways. What is translated "weaker partner" in the NIV in a more literal translation of the Greek would be "weaker vessel" (as KJV; compare RSV: "weaker sex"). The translation "weaker vessel" is almost as confusing as the use of the term "vessel" in 1 Thessalonians 4:4. A study of this vocabulary reveals that most likely the author is thinking of the person either as a body that is the vessel for the Spirit (a meaning found in the apostolic fathers) or as a creature created by God (a meaning coming from the parable in Jer 18:1-11). Either of the two meanings declares that the man and the woman are both creatures, but one of them, the woman, is weaker and more vulnerable.

Unlike the later church fathers, Peter is not thinking of the woman as being weaker morally (Rom 5:6 says that all human beings are weak this way, and 1 Peter is close to Paul in its thought) or weak in conscience (Rom 14:1, something Paul never links to sex), for neither of these applies to woman as "vessel" or "creature," and neither of these applies to woman as over against man. Instead, Peter's idea must be that the man experiences the woman in the context of most cultures as weaker both physically (and therefore we hear so much of the abuse of women by men) and socially. Physical weakness is clear in that males are on average larger and stronger than women. Social weakness is illustrated in 2 Corinthians 10—13, in which Paul repeatedly speaks of being socially weak because he was neither imposing to look at nor spoke good Greek (due to his foreign origin); this put him at a social disadvantage and often required that he have a local sponsor. A woman is likewise often disadvantaged the moment people realize that they are dealing with a woman rather than a man, a fact even more true in first-century culture than today.

It is obvious that this weakness, whether physical or social, gave (and still gives) the husband a great advantage in the marriage; he could abuse his wife's vulnerability. But the topic of this section in 1 Peter, understood from 1 Peter 2:13, is that of submission. The husband, argues Peter, shows his proper submission by not taking advantage of his wife's weakness. Instead he is to "live with" her "considerately" or "according to knowledge." The knowledge referred to is not theoretical knowing about her but personal knowledge, which could form the basis either for exploiting her or for considerate care. The latter is what the Christian husband is to exhibit. This considerate care based upon personal knowledge of one's wife is to extend to the whole marital realm, for "live with" includes the sexual as well as other areas of the marriage.

Another way Peter expresses this idea is to say that the husband is to treat his wife with "respect" or "honor," which means that even if the culture does not honor women, he will honor his woman. His honoring her gives her the advantage of his strength in a culture that may be physically abusive and of his status in a culture that might look down on women. Like Christ, he takes (and even gives up) what he has and bestows it upon the one who lacks it.

The culture may look at the woman as "weaker," or inferior—in fact, that low view of women was very true of the Mediterranean culture of Peter's day—but 1 Peter says that she is a "joint heir" (the "heirs with you" translation in the NIV may disguise the strength of the phrase). In other words, in the realm that counts, the spiritual, she is an equal. The New Testament perspective is that marriage itself and sexual differences in particular are temporal and will not continue in heaven (see Mt 22:30). Thus from the heavenly perspective it is not the weakness of the woman that is ultimate, but her equality. Since this is the reality of the future, the Christian husband is to recognize this in the present in the way he respects or honors his wife. There is, as Paul argued in Galatians 3:28, no *real* (in the sense of ultimate or lasting) difference between male and female. Fully Christian marriage lives this out, being more determined by the fuller reality of the future (the eschatological reality) than by the legal and social givens of a culture.

Therefore, we can now see why this would affect prayers. Several New Testament passages (Mt 5:23; 6:12, 14-15; 1 Cor 11:33-34; Jas 4:3) indicate that relational differences with others will hinder one's prayer life. How much more would this be the case if one's wife were complaining to God of her husband's mistreatment of her? Even if she did not complain, would not God see her tears?

Isn't he a God of compassion and justice? Doesn't he stand in for the weaker and the oppressed? On the one hand, then, we have the promise implied in Matthew 18:19-20 that husband and wife make the smallest church, a place in which Christ can be present; therefore prayers made in unity with him will be heard. On the other hand, when they are estranged and especially when the more powerful is oppressing the weaker, no prayer will be heard, for God will put the relationship and living like Christ in self-giving ahead of any request—except that of repentance.[1]

Is Peter then condescending to women? No, he is not condescending; he is realistic. He recognizes that in the cultures with which he was dealing (and to a large extent today as well), the wife was disadvantaged in the relationship, almost always physically and often legally and socially as well. He therefore counsels the husband to live like Jesus and to take his physical and social advantage and use it to make his wife the equal she really is in God's eyes. This type of relationship, 1 Peter argues, will lead to the situation in which prayer can be answered. Any exploitation of one's wife, however, blocks the way between the husband and his God.

Notes

[1]It is unclear whether the "your" (plural) in "your prayers" refers to the husbands' prayers only (since husbands are addressed as a group) or both the husbands' and the wives' prayers. Probably the former is meant, but we must remember that bitterness and resentment in the wife will also block prayers as surely as the husband's oppressiveness.

CHAPTER 37

Baptism That Now Saves You

And this water [of the flood] symbolizes baptism that now
saves you also—not the removal of dirt from the body
but the pledge of a good conscience toward God.
It saves you by the resurrection of Jesus Christ.
1 PETER 3:21

Most Christians have been baptized, but they disagree about how to baptize, when to baptize, and what baptism means. This passage speaks to this latter issue (and perhaps by implication to the others), but for many Christians it complicates the problem rather than solves it. In fact, the whole paragraph of 1 Peter 3:18-22 is difficult. However, the problem on which we are going to focus is only that of baptism, for while several statements in the paragraph may be confusing, this appears to have major doctrinal issues at stake. If baptism saves a person, how does it do this? Isn't it Jesus who really saves? Doesn't such a doctrine as this verse teaches contradict the idea that salvation is by grace through faith? This seems to add a ceremonial work, much like circumcision. And what, then, is the

state of people who are not baptized? Should our opening statement be modified to say that "all Christians have been baptized" and
that those who believe themselves to be Christians but are not
baptized have not in fact been saved? Surely some explanation is
needed.

The point of this paragraph (1 Pet 3:18-22) is to give a reason for
suffering for doing good. The reason is found in the example of
Christ. "For Christ died for sins once for all, the righteous for the
unrighteous, to bring you to God. He was put to death in the body
but made alive by the Spirit" (v. 18). Christ also was righteous, but
he still suffered. He was condemned to death in the arena of the
world (better than "in the body" of the NIV). Yet this was not the
end of him. Instead God raised him from the dead, no longer in the
arena of this world, for death and evil can no longer touch him.
Jesus was raised in the arena of the spirit, just as Paul taught in 1
Corinthians 15:42-49. And he has been exalted so that all beings in
the universe are subject to him. Since he is an example for the
Christians to whom Peter is writing, the implication (brought out
clearly in the next chapter) is that also for them suffering for righteousness is not ultimately an evil, but the door to a resurrected life
in which they too will be beyond the grasp of all evil and will reign
with Christ.

Within this context Peter says several difficult things. First, he
mentions that in his resurrected form Christ proclaimed something
to certain "spirits in prison" who had disobeyed in the days of Noah.
"Through [which Spirit] also he went and preached to the spirits in
prison who disobeyed long ago when God waited patiently in the
days of Noah while the ark was being built" (vv. 19-20). While more
ink has been used in writing about this passage than about any
other in 1 Peter, the meaning of it is now relatively clear. The
"spirits" are the fallen angels of Genesis 6:1-6, who were disobedient to God in the days of Noah. They are also mentioned in 2
Peter 2:4-5 and Jude 6, which are themselves dependent upon stories such as those recorded in the pseudepigraphical book 1 Enoch,
the first section of which has a lot to say about these angels, or
"Watchers." They disobeyed by forsaking their proper realm and

marrying human women. As punishment, they were imprisoned. According to 1 Peter, Jesus "preached" to them in his resurrected state. His proclamation was not of the gospel but of his victory and their condemnation (much as Enoch proclaims in 1 Enoch), the theme that is picked up in 1 Peter 3:22.

The passage, then, may imply that the powers of darkness thought they had destroyed Jesus, but that in raising him from the dead God turned the tables on them (symbolized in the result of the one angelic rebellion mentioned in the Old Testament) and Jesus himself proclaimed their doom. Likewise the Christians may appear to be on the losing end as the powers of darkness unleash persecution against them, but they with Jesus will rise and end up in triumph.[1]

In mentioning this triumph of Jesus, Peter is reminded that Noah built the ark and that "in it only a few people, eight in all, were saved through water" (v. 20). Why would this fact be important to Peter and his readers? The believers in Asia Minor to whom he is writing were once pagans, very much part of their culture, fully accepted in their cities and villages. Now they are being ostracized and slandered because they are Christians. The whole world appears to be against them. True enough, Peter reminds them, but the world was also against Noah. He looked a fool building the ark, but the majority were wrong and drowned in the flood. The minority of eight people (Noah, his three sons and their wives) were the only ones saved, although they were saved through water, and it must have been a rough voyage at that.

This has set the stage for 1 Peter's drawing an analogy to the Christian experience. The concept that an Old Testament event symbolized a New Testament one is common in Scripture. It is found in Paul (Rom 5:14; 1 Cor 10:6, 11) and in Hebrews (8:5; 9:24).[2] This is not surprising, since the same God operates in both testaments and his character is consistent. One would expect corresponding actions. There are, however, some differences; Paul sees a correspondence between baptism and the crossing of the Red Sea and the covering cloud in Exodus (1 Cor 10:2), while Peter draws his parallel with Noah. Neither interpretation is wrong since we are moving in the world of analogy, not of literal meaning.

As Noah was saved through water, so is the Christian: "Baptism now saves you." How does baptism save a person? The answer is, "by the resurrection of Jesus Christ." In other words, baptism is a union with Christ, and, united with Christ, we are carried with him to resurrection life. Paul has similarly used baptism as the point of union with Christ (Rom 6:4-11; Col 2:12). The key is that, as in 1 Peter 1:3, it is being joined to Jesus that saves. Without Jesus and his resurrection, baptism would be useless.

Peter goes on to argue this when he explains his point in more detail. Christian baptism consists of being immersed in water (in fact, at least in the third and fourth centuries it was done naked to be sure that one came in full contact with the water). The amount and type of water is never mentioned, although by the second century cold running water was preferred. (See Didache 7:1-4 in the apostolic fathers to see the order of preferred types of water in Asia Minor between A.D. 100 and 150.) The point in 1 Peter is that the outward washing is not the important part. That is simply "the removal of dirt from the body." Without something more one would go into the water a dirty sinner and come out a clean sinner. The water has no magic properties nor does the ritual itself save. If it did, baptism would be like circumcision was for the Jew, and Christians would indeed be saved by works (which in Paul means ritual acts), although not works of the Old Testament law.

What does save in the baptismal experience is the "pledge" or "answer" to God from "a good conscience." For some scholars this means a request made to God for a good conscience; in other words, it is a request made in baptism that God would purify one and forgive one's sins (see Heb 10:22). This certainly is a possible interpretation, for it makes the expressed commitment to Christ, not the ritual act, the point of salvation. More likely, however, is the interpretation based on parallels with Jewish rites and the use of the term "pledge" in other literature. This sees the candidate for baptism being asked a series of questions, such as "Do you pledge yourself to follow Jesus as Lord?" (perhaps reflected in Acts 8:37 and 1 Tim 6:12). The response of commitment to God and identification with Christ is what saves, *if* it comes from a good conscience. In other words, a hypocritical response will have no effect. An honest pledge of commitment, however, will result in salvation, for it joins the person to the resurrection of Christ.

However, this leaves many questions open for us, such as "What about people who are never baptized and yet make a commitment to Christ in another setting?" For Peter this would be a strange question, though, for after adequate instruction in the faith, baptism in the name of Jesus was the first thing done to all converts in the New Testament period. The idea that a person would confess Christ and yet would not be baptized would be absurd to Peter. Therefore he does not consider it a question needing an answer. He would surely have admitted that the thief on the cross had been saved without being baptized (Lk 23:43), but why should that be the norm for people who are not on crosses or otherwise inhibited from baptism? Are they trying to avoid a command of Christ? If so, have they ever committed themselves to Christ at all? These are the type of questions Peter would have wanted to ask had the question been put to him. In short, rather than ask such a question (unless we are concerned about a thief-on-the-cross type we know), why not simply get baptized? Yet all of this is unstated, an assumed part of New Testament teaching.

What Peter does say is clear enough, however. Christians are saved through their being joined to Christ and his resurrection. This should make them unafraid of what any human persecutor can do to them, for Christ has triumphed over all that sphere of life and the spirit world that operates behind it. The normal point of salvation for Christians in the early church was baptism. Even here it is not the ritual itself or the water that saves, but the commitment that one makes to Jesus as Lord. (Or the forgiveness one asks from Jesus the Lord, taking the alternative interpretation.) As in Paul, salvation is a relationship. Ritual in Christianity, just as a wedding in marriage, is simply the way of entering into that relationship.

Notes
[1]I have argued this position in detail in Peter H. Davids, *The First Epistle of*

Peter, New International Commentary on the New Testament (Grand Rapids, Mich.: Eerdmans, 1990), pp. 124-47. Further literature is cited there to support this argument.

[2]See further on this type of interpretation, Leonhard Goppelt, *Typos: The Typological Interpretation of the Old Testament in the New* (Grand Rapids, Mich.: Eerdmans, 1982).

He Who Has Suffered in His Body Is Done with Sin

Therefore, since Christ suffered in his body,
arm yourselves also with the same attitude,
because he who has suffered in his
body is done with sin.
1 PETER 4:1

Which of us has not suffered in his or her body? Which of us has stopped sinning? At first glance 1 Peter 4:1 does not appear difficult. That Christ has suffered in his body is a given of the Christian faith, for how else would one describe the cross? Likewise it is a very common idea in the New Testament that Christians should be prepared to follow Christ, including following his example of suffering. One need only read Philippians 2:5-11 to get an example, or 1 Peter 2:21. But in our present passage something else is added, namely the idea that "he who has suffered in his body is done with sin." In what way is this true? Does it mean the same as Romans 6:7, "Anyone who has died has been freed from sin"? Or does it have another meaning, especially since it uses "suffered" rather than "died" and "is done with" rather than "has been freed from"? At the bottom of this discussion is the crying question, If "done with sin" means "stopped sinning," why am I still sinning? Does it mean that I have not suffered enough?

There are five different explanations of this passage. First, it might refer only to Christ (the "he" is Christ and no one else). Second, it may refer to a Christian's identification with Christ at his or her conversion-initiation (especially baptism). That is, when one identifies with Christ's death, sin has no more power over that person (Rom 6:1-12; 1 Jn 5:18-19). Third, it may mean that when a Christian decides to suffer for Christ, that believer has chosen decisively to break with sin and its compromises. Fourth, it may mean that when Christians suffer, they break the power of sin over their life. Finally, it may mean that when Christians die, they will be freed from sin as Christ was.

In choosing among these we notice, first, that Peter, unlike Paul, never uses "sin" as an abstract principle or power. Peter is always thinking of concrete acts of sin. This makes the second and third options unlikely. Furthermore Peter speaks of the suffering as a completed action, which also makes the concept of identification or decision (both of which are ongoing) unlikely.

Second, when we consider the remaining options, we see that while 1 Peter is about persecution, it is not about martyrdom. Naturally, one can hardly say that the prospect of dying for one's faith was totally absent from Peter's consciousness, yet the types of suffering that he mentions are those of social ostracism and abuse, not the official proceedings that could lead to execution. This makes the last option unlikely.

That leaves two options remaining, and both are probably in Peter's mind. The source of the saying is Christ, who is pre-eminently the one who "suffered in the body"—or better, "suffered in this physical world"—right up to the point of death (which is more than these Christians have been called to do yet). The result was not a loss for Jesus, but rather a freedom that he has from the whole realm of sin and death. He is no longer subject to those things which he endured while living on earth. So likewise the

Christian who has suffered has made a decisive break with sin. This happens totally when the Christian goes to the extent of Christ and dies; but it happens in part when the Christian suffers in any way. The act of suffering for Christ makes the attractiveness of sin hollow. The believer has put all his eggs in one basket, that of Christ, and has paid too great a price to turn back now.

This explains why it is an *attitude* with which believers are to arm themselves. It is the attitude seen in Christ and expressed in the saying "He who has suffered in the body [or flesh] is done with sin." If they have this attitude their own suffering will result in their "not liv[ing] the rest of [their] earthly life for evil human desires, but rather for the will of God." That is, if Christ is really the one they are following, their great example, then suffering will separate them more and more from sinful acts, making them increasingly invested in heaven, until they come to that point when they die like Christ, and, like him, are totally finished with sin and all its effects in this world.[1]

We can now answer our questions. We may in fact still be sinning because we have not chosen to suffer and thereby have done with sin. Perhaps when we come to the point of choice, we choose compromise and then wonder why we cannot overcome temptation. On the other hand, we may still be sinning because we have not suffered enough. While we have chosen Christ and against sin and are making good progress in the battle, we have not yet died. We may be longing for a perfection that will only be ours in resurrection, not that very real maturity that is possible in this world.

Notes

[1]For further explanation, see the comment on this verse in Peter H. Davids, *The First Epistle of Peter*, New International Commentary on the New Testament (Grand Rapids, Mich.: Eerdmans, 1990).

The Spirit
of Glory and
# of God

If you are insulted because of the name of Christ,
you are blessed, for the Spirit of glory
and of God rests on you.
1 PETER 4:14

No one likes being insulted. *It is certainly not the time in life when a* person usually experiences either God or glory, yet 1 Peter seems to associate the two. In 4:12-18, Peter encourages his readers to be faithful under persecution and not to think of it as something foreign to their Christian experience. In the middle of that section is the strange verse that is the subject of this chapter. It seems strange because it makes us wonder if the Spirit "of glory" in any way differs from the Spirit "of God." Also, why should the Spirit rest on people just because they are insulted? Isn't this a rather unusual way of making a point? What point precisely is he making?

This phrase in 1 Peter *is* unusual. In fact, it is so grammatically difficult that some of the scribes tried to "clean it up" by making various "corrections" to the text. Yet the context is clear, and it is this context that enables us to understand what Peter is getting at.

Immediately before this verse the author has called the sufferings that these Christians are experiencing a participation in the sufferings of Christ (v. 13). They have identified with Jesus and are experiencing sufferings (such as persecution) on earth parallel to those he received. But this participation in his sufferings will lead to participation in his glory. Suffering is not virtuous in itself, but when it is endured because of one's faithfulness to Christ it is the path to glory.

Now Peter makes the nature of some of those sufferings clear; they are being "insulted because of the name of Christ." These Christians claim to be serving Christ, and their neighbors are making fun of them or perhaps slandering them (with all types of rumors about what Christians *really* did in their services). That enduring such rejection brings a blessing is something Jesus made clear when he said, "Blessed are you when people insult you, persecute you and falsely say all kinds of evil against you because of me" (Mt 5:11; compare Lk 6:22). The world around them is rejecting them, but Jesus is accepting them. He has called them blessed.

It is also clear that the only persecution that will result in this blessing is that which results from their faithfulness to Christ. In the next verse Peter notes that suffering as a criminal or a meddler in the affairs of others will not bring a blessing (unless, of course, the accusation is false, an excuse for punishing them for being Christians). Sometimes Christians are persecuted because they are obnoxious, not because they are faithful. At the same time, we recognize that true faithfulness to Christ will bring the genuine type of persecution.

When this persecution happens, 1 Peter promises that the Holy Spirit will rest upon them. This may recall Jesus' promise "When they arrest you, do not worry . . . for it will not be you speaking, but the Spirit of your Father speaking through you" (Mt 10:19-20; compare Mk 13:11; Lk 12:11-12). At times this glory could be visible to the Christian (Acts 7:55) or to others (Acts 6:15; compare Stephen's term for God in Acts 7:2). Yet note that this "glory" did not always get the person out of trouble; it was the vision of glory that led to Stephen's being stoned! In other words, through the Spirit of God, the Christians undergoing persecution for Christ will experience in the present a taste of the glory they will have in its fullness later (1 Pet 1:7; 5:4 refer to the coming glory).

There is another reason for the dual name for the Spirit. The people insult the Christians; God causes his Spirit of glory to rest on them. Instead of insult they receive glory in the eyes of God. The people persecute because of the name of Christ; it is the Spirit of God himself that rests upon them. They have been faithful to Christ, so God is happy to let his name be identified with them. The balance in this passage is impressive.

What, then, is Peter saying? The call to Christ is a call to come and die. Part of the dying with Christ includes persecution for Christ. But the Christian is not alone in persecution. While the world is heaping up insult and shame, God is placing his Spirit of glory upon them. It is no surprise that this is the reported experience of many of the martyrs of the first centuries of the church. And because they have identified with the name of Christ, God identifies with them through his Spirit. Thus Peter can say, "Praise God that you bear that name [for which you are suffering]" (4:16). Rejection is never pleasant, nor is it to be sought, but when it comes out of faithfulness to Christ it brings with it the presence of the Spirit. It is this idea that our strange expression brings out. And it is in this, not in the suffering itself, that a Christian can truly rejoice and praise God.

• C H A P T E R   4 0 •

It Is Time for Judgment to Begin with the Family of God

For it is time for judgment to begin with the family of God;
and if it begins with us, what will the outcome be for
those who do not obey the gospel of God?
1 PETER 4:17

I do not enjoy thinking about judgment of anyone; I especially dislike con-
sidering my own possible judgment. Thus, it bothers me when the
author of this Epistle suddenly begins to refer to the persecution
of Christians (the context of this passage) as judgment. Now it
would be no surprise for a New Testament author to talk about
judgment coming upon unbelievers, but this passage is speaking
about *believers*. Can that be right? Did not Christ take the judgment
of believers? How can Peter take such a dark and gloomy perspective, if he really believes in grace? Does that mean that if I am
persecuted I am a sinful Christian in need of judgment? Wouldn't
that perspective add guilt to my suffering, rather than allow me to
rejoice in suffering for Christ?

The answer to our questions is relatively easy, although it is not comfortable to contemplate. The topic of our passage is "the judgment" (the Greek text has the definite article). What judgment could this be? Peter has already referred to judgment (1:17; 2:23; 4:5-6), and in every case it is God's judgment and therefore probably the final judgment. Given the use of the same phrase in other New Testament passages (Acts 24:25; Rom 2:2-3; Heb 6:2; 2 Pet 3:2; Jude 4; Rev 17:1; 18:20), this conclusion becomes firm. Thus 1 Peter is saying that the final judgment is beginning, not with the pagans or the unbelieving Jews, but with the family of God, the church. The persecution they are experiencing is a phase of that final judgment.

How this is the case becomes clear when we examine God's judging in Jewish tradition. In an Old Testament tradition, judgment begins at God's house. For example, Ezekiel 9:5-6 reads, "Follow him through the city and kill. . . . Begin at my sanctuary." Jeremiah, in speaking to the nations, says, "See, I am beginning to bring disaster on the city that bears my Name, and will you indeed go unpunished?" (25:29) The nations will not go unpunished, for judgment has begun with God's own people. Likewise, at the end of the Old Testament period, Malachi 3:1-6 speaks of the Lord coming to his temple and purifying the Levites. He concludes, "So I will come near to you for judgment." Does the Lord judge his people? The answer of the Old Testament is Yes, and if so, how much more severely will he judge the pagan nations.

In Malachi and continuing in the intertestamental period, this judgment is interpreted as a purifying judgment, which will bring God's people to repentance. "Therefore, he did not spare his own sons first. . . . Therefore they were once punished that they might be forgiven" (2 Baruch 13:9-10).[1] The New Testament shares this position. Not only is the story of Ananias and Sapphira (Acts 5) a graphic example, but Paul clearly states this teaching. Speaking to Christians who were ill because of their sin, Paul writes, "If we judged ourselves, we would not come under judgment. When we are judged by the Lord, we are being disciplined so that we will not be condemned with the world" (1 Cor 11:31-32). Hebrews 12:7-11 also speaks of the suffering of Christians as discipline, although discipline can come for two reasons. Soldiers go through the discipline of training programs to harden themselves so that they may stand in battle; children are disciplined when they have done wrong. Both appear to be in the mind of the author of Hebrews, although the latter is foremost for Paul.

There is, then, a New Testament teaching that God will judge his church, his people. This judgment is a discipline to harden them so that they will not sin or to turn them from the sin into which they have already fallen. It is therefore grace, for God disciplines so that he will not have to condemn Christians in the concluding phase of the final judgment (that is also the hope of church discipline; 1 Cor 5:5). It is based on grace, for we never hear of God judging Christians for sins that they have repented of. Yet, gracious as it is, such a judgment is very real and very painful, a point upon which all of the New Testament authors agree.

Part of the graciousness of God's act is seen in Peter's question "What will the outcome be for those who do not obey the gospel?" If the beginning of the final judgment, the purifying action of God within his church, is so severe, despite the fact that they are God's own family and have obeyed the gospel, what will the conclusion of the final judgment be like when he turns his attention to those who have refused to obey him? It is a mercy that God turns his church to repentance and spares it from the fate of the unbeliever. That is precisely what Peter concludes, citing the Greek form of Proverbs 11:31, "If it is hard for the righteous to be saved, what will become of the ungodly and the sinner?" (4:18). Faith will be tested (1:6; 4:12), for Jesus said that the way to life was narrow (Lk 13:23-24), but for the unbelievers, "It is a dreadful thing to fall into the hands of the living God" (Heb 10:31).

In this passage, then, Peter has three ways of looking at persecution. First, it is a test of faith, showing if the commitment of the professed Christian is genuine or not (4:12). Second, it is an identification with the sufferings of Christ, which will not only result in glory in the future, but leads to the Spirit of glory resting upon them now (vv. 13-14). Finally, it is a discipline or judgment, which shows that they are in fact God's family and yet purifies them to live more in the character of the family. The final judgment has begun, but it has begun with the purification of God's church, God's people, just as it happened in the Old Testament. It will be consummated, however, not in condemnation for his people—they are his family and will be saved after being purified—but in terrible conclusive judgments upon unbelievers, which Jesus described so graphically (for example, Mt 24—25) and Revelation pictures in visions (Rev 15—16; 20).

I still do not like the idea of judgment, but my suffering does not necessarily mean that I am specially sinful. Since I am committed to Christ, the persecution I suffer is a sign that I am part of the household of God. He, as a good father, is purifying his family for our good. It is a sign of belonging. I may not enjoy the experience, but I can rejoice that I am among those facing judgment now, being purified in preparation for heaven, rather than among those who will face the full force of divine judgment later.

Notes
[1]The same teaching is in 2 Baruch 13:1-12; Testament of Benjamin 100:8-9; and the Dead Sea Scrolls 1QS 4:18-21; 1Qh 8:30-31; 9:10; 11:8-10, all of which are Jewish writings that are available in English.

• C H A P T E R   4 1 •

You May
Participate in
the Divine Nature

---

*Through these he has given us his very great
and precious promises, so that through them
you may participate in the divine nature
and escape the corruption in the world
caused by evil desires.*
2 PETER 1:4

I can see the headlines now: "Well-known New Age Expert Declares 2 Peter a New Age Tract!" That is, while no one who reads the New Testament can be unaware that God has given his people many "very great and precious promises," it is quite surprising to read in 2 Peter 1:4 that the goal of these promises is that we might "participate in the divine nature." Surely this has to be something written by a New Age guru? It is as bold as anything written by a medieval mystic and far more radical than most things written by Christians who are today accused of being "New Age." Even without this association we ask, How can a human being participate in the nature of God? Furthermore, we wonder for our own benefit, if this participation is in fact possible, what in the world does it look like?

It is quite true that if 2 Peter had been penned today, such a phrase most likely would have caused some readers to accuse the author of being at least a covert spreader of "New Age" teaching. Fortunately, the book was canonized long before the modern witch hunt began, and it is not considered proper to attack biblical authors, no matter what they say. Yet this observation, as salutary as it is, does not explain what this verse means. Until we grasp that, it will be difficult for us (if we dare) to use similar language in a proper way today.

There is a clear progression in Peter's thought in this passage. First, he present's Christ's divine power (his first use of the adjective "divine") as providing Christians with everything needed for a godly life (1:3). Christ mediates this power to us human beings through personal knowledge of (not simply theological knowledge about) God, who is the one who has called believers to Christ. Therefore the movement in this passage is from a call to Christ through the power and glory of the Father to a life of godliness through Christ's divine power revealing the Father to human hearts.

This glorious power of God forms the basis of his promises. What are these promises? They are surely the promises, found in many New Testament presentations of the gospel, of a place in Christ's eternal kingdom (2 Pet 1:11) and the rewards that go along with it (such as those described in 1 Pet 1:3-5). Then why were these promises given? So that Christians might become "partakers in the divine nature." The phrase "divine nature" itself is well known from Greek philosophical literature, but it is also found in the Jewish-Hellenistic literature of the New Testament period. In this first-century literature, to "participate in the divine nature" does not mean merging into God or union with deity (which is the sense equivalent language has in true New Age thought). In other words, neither the Greeks (for the most part) nor the Jews, even the most Greek of them, were pantheists. They all expected a continuing personal existence beyond death, not a uniting with the Eternal or a becoming part of the One. What "partaking of the divine nature" does mean for Greek and Jewish authors is to take part in the immortality and incorruption of God (or "the gods" in pagan Greek literature). One who has so participated will, like God, live in the immortal sphere and like him will not be tainted with any corruption. Certainly Peter means at least this much. And if this is all that he means, then he is indicating what will happen at death (or the return of Christ). That is, the promises of God lead us on and direct our life until we obtain the inheritance of what they promise, the divine nature, at death.

This presentation of the goal of the Christian life contrasts with the lifestyle of the false teachers against whom 2 Peter is written. God's goal is that we set our eyes on his promises and head toward heaven, thereby escaping "the corruption in the world caused by evil desires." The false teachers, on the other hand, are involved in these evil desires. In fact, it is their lifestyle, not their doctrine, that shows them to be corrupt. Desire, of course, can be good. We desire food so as not to be hungry, for example. But desire needs to be controlled by God's goals and principles. When desire itself rules us, it is indeed evil (for it desires the bad as well as the good), and it leads us to corruption. Those whose goal is really the divine nature will not be turned aside or controlled by such evil desires.

It is possible that Peter means more than this. Paul, for example, can speak of the Holy Spirit being within Christians. Therefore the divine nature (a term Paul does not use, but could have) is within, giving life (Rom 8:11; compare 2 Cor 3:18). James (1:18) and John (Jn 3:5-6) speak of being born of God and therefore having something of God's nature. In fact, 1 John 3:9 describes new birth so literally that it says God's "sperm" (usually translated "seed," but the same word is used for the sperm or semen of a male) remains in the child of God. According to 1 John, because this or that person is born of God he or she does not sin. This is because the nature of the Father is in them. Unfortunately, in this letter Peter does not speak about the Holy Spirit as Paul does, nor does he use the new birth terminology that John uses, so we cannot know if he would have included any of these ideas in his concept of partaking of the divine nature, although it is possible that he would.

What can we say, then, about our passage? The author is a writer who boldly uses the terminology of Greek philosophy and culture and redefines them in a Christian sense. He points to the Christian's supply of all that is needed for a holy life in the divine power of Christ. He also points to the goal of the Christian life as a participation in the divine nature, at least at death, when—like Christ—the Christian will live immortally in the incorruptible heavenly realm. He may be indicating that this participation is an experience that the Holy Spirit mediates to Christians in the present life, although his language is not clear enough to be certain of this. In saying what he does, Peter actually says less than some of the other New Testament writers about the joining of human beings to God, even if his language is more striking. At the same time he clearly calls Christians to use the provision of Christ and fix their eyes on the promises of God so that they will in fact escape the corruption in the world and in the end receive the promised divine nature. It is this drawing on Christ's power and focus on the future, which includes allowing that future to determine present lifestyle, which is all the Christian need do to receive the glorious hope of participating in the nature of God.

• C H A P T E R 4 2 •

Make Your
Calling and
Election Sure

*Therefore, my brothers, be all the more eager
to make your calling and election sure.
For if you do these things, you will never fall.*
2 PETER 1:10

Because Christians take salvation seriously, we are often plagued with doubts about it. Even if the problem does not afflict us, most Christians have had friends who were fearful that their salvation might be in doubt. Therefore the exhortation to ethical duty in 2 Peter 1 is not in itself an issue, for similar exhortations occur throughout the New Testament. But what does the author mean in verse 10 in exhorting us to make our "calling and election sure"? Does this mean that if we do not live the type of lifestyle that he is suggesting, we may not be elect? Does it mean that we might not be saved? Or does it mean that we might lose the salvation that we already have? Even if such thoughts have not bothered us, 2 Peter raises these troubling questions for us.

The passage is certainly calling for moral effort. The call for zeal in the phrase "be all the more eager" tips us off to that fact. If that were not enough, this verse comes right after another exhortation to moral living. In 2 Pet 1:5-7 we discover a chain of virtues that Christians are strongly encouraged (using a phrase similar to "be all the more eager") to develop. Developing them will make us effective and productive in our relationship to Christ, while the failure to develop them means that we are blind and have forgotten the cleansing from past sins that we have experienced. We are not surprised at this encouragement to moral effort, for the false teachers in 2 Peter are false precisely in that they are not living morally (false teaching in 2 Peter and in many other New Testament writings is false because it sets a wrong moral example, not because it teaches wrong doctrine). They apparently claim to see, but in Peter's eyes they are blind.

To make one's "calling and election sure," then, is to guarantee or confirm or ratify (the term has those meanings in various contexts) the calling one has received. The calling, of course, is the calling to Christ referred to in 1:3. The ideas of calling and election are closely associated. Paul in Romans 8:30 puts election before calling, which is a logical order (God would decide and make a choice, or elect, before he called the person to Christ, or so it would seem to us), but other New Testament writers, including Paul himself, often pair the two concepts as virtual synonyms (see 1 Cor 1:26-27; 1 Pet 2:9; Rev 17:14). The point is that this word pair (and Peter is fond of word pairs) indicates God's action in bringing a person to Christ. This is what needs to be confirmed or ratified by the ethical obedience of the Christian. However, the author is not saying that moral effort can *produce* election to Christ's kingdom. The calling and election are first (the grace of God appears in 1:3), just as faith comes first in his list of virtues in 1:5. Everything else is to be a fruit of faith. What he does believe is that without moral living one will not enter the kingdom, which is precisely what Paul also believed (1 Cor 6:9-10; Gal 5:21).

Peter makes his point clear in the second half of the verse. To confirm one's calling is not to "fall." This term can mean to sin, as in James 2:10 and 3:2. But if this were all Peter had in mind, the sentence would be so obvious as to be meaningless: If you live ethically (do these things), you will not sin (fall). That is as obvious as saying, If you are running, you are not standing still. Biblical authors did not waste valuable papyrus on such statements. Therefore Peter is using the term as it is used in Romans 11:11, to "fall" in the sense of "come to grief" or "fall disastrously." In Jude 24 a related term refers to God's grace in keeping people from falling in this way, meaning "leaving the faith." The opposite of falling, then, is to "receive a rich welcome into the eternal kingdom of our Lord and Savior Jesus Christ" (2 Pet 1:11). In other words, the author pictures Christians on a journey begun with the calling/election of God. If they fall on the way, they will never reach the goal of the kingdom (salvation). But if they do not stumble, and instead develop the virtues he has already listed, they will in the end arrive at the kingdom and be warmly welcomed into it.

This teaching is important within the context of 2 Peter. As noted above, the false teachers in the church were not living according to Christian standards, yet they were claiming to be elect and on their way to Christ's kingdom. The author is denying this claim. While the whole New Testament witnesses to forgiveness of sin for all who repent, and acknowledges that Christians do sin from time to time, no author in the New Testament, whether Paul or James or Peter or John, believed that a person could be living in disregard of Christian standards and still be "saved" (or still inherit the kingdom). As Jesus said, a good tree bears good fruit (Mt 7:17). You cannot consistently get "unsaved" fruit from a "saved" tree.

The call in 2 Peter, then, is to move onward. There is no attempt to solve the question as to whether one can be "lost" after being "saved." Peter's concerns are much more practical. "Make sure that you are in fact saved!" That is, if you have experienced the call of God, you are to ratify it by your obedience to him, your moral submission. If you do this, there will be no doubt of your salvation nor of your eventual welcome into the kingdom. What about those who are concerned that they might not be truly elect? Their lifestyle of obedience to Christ, which flows from trust in him, should be convincing proof of their state of grace; if they lack this evidence, they would do well to repent and to make their "calling and election sure."

CHAPTER 43

The Word of the Prophets Made More Certain

And we have the word of the prophets made more certain,
and you will do well to pay attention to it, as to
a light shining in a dark place, until the day dawns
and the morning star rises in your hearts.
2 PETER 1:19

When I was ordained I took an oath, "I believe that the Holy Scriptures of the Old and New Testaments are the Word of God." What could be a better or firmer basis on which to build ministry? Yet one may wonder when reading 2 Peter 1:19. Isn't this a strange thing to say about Scripture? How can Scripture be "made more certain"? Is there some of Scripture that is not certain or is less certain? If it is not certain, or not fully certain, can Scripture be trusted? Even if it applies only to the Old Testament, the passage raises the question of how this scriptural author understands his Bible.

The teaching that 2 Peter sees to be at issue (and which therefore triggers this whole discussion) is the doctrine of the Second Coming of Christ (or the *parousia*),[1] "the power and coming of our Lord Jesus

Christ" (1:16). This is precisely the doctrine denied by the false teachers (3:3-10), which may be the basis for their loose living (especially if it included a denial of final judgment). In 2 Peter 1 the author argues first that the apostles have in the transfiguration actually seen a foretaste of the return of Christ (1:16-18). At this point he brings in Scripture to strengthen his case.

The NIV translation that we have quoted (along with the RSV and NEB) appears to state that the eyewitness report of the apostles confirms and thus makes more certain what the Old Testament says about the Second Coming of Christ. But that probably is not the best translation of the text. The Greek idiom Peter uses normally meant "to have a firm hold on something." If that is the case, then we should translate it, "We place very firm (or firmer) reliance on the prophetic word."[2] What Peter is saying, then, is that, yes, the apostolic eyewitness report is certain and reliable, but that Christians (including himself) place even more reliance on what the Scriptures say about the return of Christ.

That he is talking about Scripture when he speaks of "the word of the prophets" is virtually certain, for with one minor exception in the apostolic fathers, all other occurrences of this phrase refer to the Old Testament. For the early Christians, of course, the whole Old Testament was viewed as messianic prophecy, speaking about Christ, even if they normally used only certain passages. The concept that "the word of prophecy" equals the Old Testament is reinforced in the next verse, in which Peter discusses the origin of the "prophecy of Scripture." Unlike the false teachers who are presenting their own ideas, the Old Testament writers (while 2 Pet 3:15-16 refers to Paul's writings, it is doubtful that the author thought of them as "prophecy" like the Old Testament) spoke from God. That is, they spoke God's ideas taught to them by the Holy Spirit.

Peter, then, is calling on his readers to hold onto Scripture and its meaning until "the day dawns and the morning star arises in your hearts." The morning star is Jesus (Rev 22:16) and the dawning of the day is his coming. The dawning is "in your hearts," for the context is speaking about revelation, not about government or judgment or other aspects of Christ's return. When Christ returns the full revelation of God will be revealed in the hearts of the believers. Until then they need to hold onto the confident expectation of his return on the basis of the apostolic witness and especially the word of Scripture. These, of course, are partial, "a light shining in a dark place," but they are accurate and true—they are light. The dawn will come and the full light of the sun will overwhelm the small light of the lamp, but it does this by giving more light, not by giving something other than light.

Thus, Peter is not implying that Scripture is at all uncertain. What he is saying is that there are two bases on which one can know that Jesus will return. The first is the apostolic witness of the transfiguration, when the glory of Christ was revealed in part. The second is the word of Scripture. More reliance is put on this second basis than on the first. Yet both are true. Therefore for Peter Scripture is the firmest basis on which to establish one's faith. Nothing more certain can be found until the presence of Christ himself at his Second Coming makes the limited light of Scripture unnecessary.

For Christians this is a helpful reminder. We are to value Scripture, depend on Scripture and support our faith through Scripture. Yet Scripture is not eternal nor what our faith is placed in (unlike some of the rabbinic writings, which did teach that the Law or Torah was before the world and was in fact the reason for the creation of the world). We worship our Lord and his Father, not Scripture. Scripture simply points us to them. It is a true light shining in the darkness. What we ultimately long for is not a fuller knowledge of the book, but the blazing brightness of the presence of the One of whom the book speaks and who even now the book directs us to experience in our hearts.

Notes

[1]*Parousia* is the Greek word for "presence," translated "coming" in the NIV in 2 Peter 1:16, and it has become the technical term for what Christians refer to as the Second Coming of Christ in the language of New Testament scholarship.

[2]See R. J. Bauckham, *Jude, 2 Peter*, Word Biblical Commentary (Waco, Tex.: Word, 1983), pp. 223-24.

Which Celestial Beings Are Not Angels?

Bold and arrogant, these men are not afraid to slander celestial beings;
yet even angels, although they are stronger and more powerful,
do not bring slanderous accusations against such beings
in the presence of the Lord.
2 PETER 2:10-11

Media fantasy worlds are filled with all types of fantastic beings, spiritual as well as material. Yet we expect the Scripture to be more down-to-earth (which it often is). In 2 Peter 2 the author is condemning false teachers, specifically their pride and presumption. We would understand it if he then aimed some verses against their slandering angels in some way, but what we find is that suddenly he refers to "celestial beings" that are not angels, for the angels are presented over against them in the very next clause. Who could these celestial beings be? Have we in fact entered some science-fiction world of dark monsters? Are these simply mythological, or a figment of Peter's imagination? And if they are real, what is their meaning for Christians today?

The false teachers of 2 Peter were known for their immorality. The author says they will be condemned, for they "despise authority" or, better, "despise the authority of the Lord" (2:10). Not surprisingly, then, these people have nothing but contempt for other beings too.

The concept of celestial beings of one type or another has already been mentioned in 2 Peter. In 2:4 the author mentions the sinning angels of Genesis 6:1-4. Jude 6 refers to them as "the angels who did not keep their positions of authority." They are kept in prison, waiting for the final judgment, a picture we also see in 1 Peter 3:19-20. Now in the passage under consideration, Peter refers to "glorious ones" (a more literal translation than "celestial beings"). While some commentators believe that these are church leaders, the language appears too exalted for that. They could, of course, be good angels, but a natural reading of the passage shows a contrast between these "glorious ones" and the angels mentioned in the next clause. Also, the parallel passage in Jude 9 refers to the archangel Michael's dispute with Satan, which our author has generalized into the behavior of angels in general over against that of evil angels (perhaps because he did not think his readers would know the story to which Jude refers). Therefore we conclude that by "glorious ones" or "celestial beings" Peter is referring to evil angelic beings of some description.

That such beings exist is clear elsewhere in the New Testament. Paul refers to "rule and authority, power and dominion" (Eph 1:21) and "thrones or powers or rulers or authorities" (Col 1:16). He also mentions that Christians fight against "the authorities, against the powers of this dark world and against the spiritual forces of evil in the heavenly realms" (Eph 6:12). Furthermore, Revelation 12 and Daniel 10 refer to battles among spiritual forces in the unseen world. In other words, there is plenty of evidence in the New Testament for the existence of evil celestial beings, either in terms of fallen angels or other types of celestial beings. Nowhere is this terminology explained to the church nor is detailed information about these realms offered (perhaps to prevent our entering into the speculation and fascination evident in some intertestamental Jewish writings), but it is everywhere assumed that they exist.

The false teachers 2 Peter opposes, then, speak disrespectfully, even slanderously, of such beings, even though they are far weaker than these spiritual beings. But the angels, who are more powerful than these beings (our author may be thinking of archangels, since an archangel is mentioned in Jude) would not make such an accusation against them before the Lord. The contrast shows the magnitude of the foolishness of the false teachers.

Why would they slander celestial beings? We do not know. Perhaps they had been warned that if they continued in their licentious ways they would fall under the power of such beings. (We do not call them demons, for we do not know if demons are the same as or different from such beings; they may be far more powerful than demons, who appear in the New Testament to attack or control single individuals and so may be low-level evil spiritual beings.) They may have scoffed at their existence or boasted of being able to control them. All such presumption is dangerous.

What does this mean for the church? The church is called to take the existence of an infernal hierarchy seriously. Spiritual powers do rule in this world. But the church is not called to spend time learning a lot about such powers or to speak against them, although the Lord could, of course, give a person a prophetic word to speak to that realm. Paul lists the means of spiritual warfare in Ephesians 6, and although they include prayer, they do not include direct confrontation with celestial beings. Unfortunately, in our fascination with such powers we may be tempted to speak against them (without a direct command of the Lord, but simply to try to demonstrate "our authority") or to live in fear of them. Peter expects them to be taken seriously, but the way they are taken seriously is by living a holy life free from the desires and pride to which they appear to be related (and which pastoral experience reveals to be the principal means by which they control a person). This means that the New Testament does take such celestial beings seriously, but wants Christians to focus on Christ, not on the dark powers. If Christians live in intimacy with and obedience to Christ (unlike these false teachers), then such beings can do nothing ultimate to them.[1]

Notes

[1]For further information on this area, see C. Peter Wagner and F. Douglas Pennoyer, eds., *Wrestling with Dark Angels* (Ventura, Calif.: Regal Books, 1990).

• C H A P T E R 4 5 •

Worse Off at the End Than at the Beginning

*If they have escaped the corruption of the world
by knowing our Lord and Savior Jesus Christ
and are again entangled in it and overcome,
they are worse off at the end than
they were at the beginning.*
2 PETER 2:20

Christians *recognize that before people know Christ they are in bad shape,*
for they live under the judgment of God who has commanded all
people everywhere to repent and believe the gospel. It is therefore
not hard to see how Christ enables people to escape from the corruption of the world, since this corruption is tied up with their pre-
Christian life. Nor do most of us lack for examples of people who
have again been "entangled" in the world after they knew Christ;
we may even know some who after initially turning to Christ have
later totally rejected the gospel in word as well as in action, although we recognize that most of our "backslidden" brothers and
sisters would still confess to the truth of the gospel, even if it is

playing no active role in their lives. Yet 2 Peter 2:20 does more than make these common (if sad) observations. It states that such people are "worse off" than before their initial conversion. How can this be the case? Aren't they still Christian even if they are backslidden? Will they not go to heaven despite their sinful life? And isn't this "better" than their original state? Isn't salvation by faith, not works? What 2 Peter says appears incompatible with our concept of a God of grace and mercy.

When we read this verse in context, we recognize that the people being discussed are the false teachers whom Peter opposes. They were once orthodox Christians who were "cleansed from [their] past sins" (1:9), or "washed" (2:22). They had come to know Jesus Christ, and this was a personal knowledge that released them from "the corruption of the world," or, in Pauline language, the power of sin over them had been broken. And they had come to know "the way of righteousness" (meaning a righteous lifestyle; 2:21). It is not that in some way they had been taught poorly or had not experienced the power of God freeing them from the world and its desires. They had experienced all of this. They were in every way righteous and orthodox.

But now they have done exactly what they are enticing others to do (2:18-19). They have claimed freedom, but their freedom is a freedom to live according to their desires. These desires have mastered them. They have rejected "the way of righteousness" or "the sacred command" (perhaps the teaching of Jesus or even the Old Testament standard of righteousness). They are back doing what they did before they were converted, but now they are claiming Christian justification for it.

Peter says that such people are worse off than before they were converted. Why is that? He takes his words from the story in Matthew 12:45 and Luke 11:26 about the person cleansed from a demon who ends up in a worse state because the demon returns with seven others. The implication is that the person is in more bondage than before. Yet although verbally 2 Peter is closer to the statement about the demonized person, we are reminded even more than this of Luke 12:47-48, in which Jesus says that the person who does not know his master's will is beaten with few blows, while the one knowing it and still disobeying is beaten with many blows. Applied to the people in 2 Peter this indicates that the knowingly disobedient people he refers to will get a worse punishment than they would have received had they never been converted. They had been introduced to Jesus and experienced the power and freedom of his lordship, but now they have turned their backs on his teaching and are walking in willful disobedience.

This, then, is the state of the apostate, including the moral apostate who still tries to rationalize his or her sin with Christian theology. As Hebrews 10:26-27 says (see chap. twenty-five), "If we deliberately keep on sinning after we have received the knowledge of the truth, no sacrifice for sins is left, but only a fearful expectation of judgment and of raging fire that will consume the enemies of God." These people knew the truth and had been freed from their sin, coming under the rule of Christ. Now because of their web of rationalizations Christ is no longer Lord and they "deliberately keep on sinning." Peter has already told us of their end: "Blackest darkness is reserved for them" (2 Pet 2:17). God will still forgive them if they repent, but people who have rejected truth they once knew fully and have woven a fabric of doctrine to justify their sin will be most unlikely ever to repent. This letter, then, appears to be more aimed at those people the false teachers are beginning to deceive (see 2 Pet 2:18) than at the teachers themselves, for while the teachers are not beyond grace, they are certainly not listening to the ideas of the author.

The teaching of this passage (and of the New Testament in general), then, is that people are responsible for what they know. To reject truth one has once appropriated is far more serious than never to have known it. Furthermore, only those who follow the way of righteousness, who are really following Jesus as Lord and have therefore been freed from the corruption in the world, are on the way to the kingdom. To claim to be "saved" while living in sin is self-deception of the worst type. It not only blinds one to one's own state, but it may deceive those who were getting along well in the faith, dragging them back into the quicksand in which those living in sin are themselves trapped.

This verse, then, is not implying that righteous living saves a person, but that salvation means repenting from a sinful lifestyle, turning to Christ as Lord, and living under his kingship. Where the results of this process (such as a freedom from the power of sin) are lacking—even if they once were present—we have no right to think for a moment that such people are in the kingdom, especially if they show no grief for their sin and are not attempting to forsake it. Furthermore it is dangerous to imply that such people are headed to heaven (even if without "reward"), for it cheapens the grace of God and implies to others that they too can take the "low road" to heaven and get in without truly submitting their lives to Christ. Such an implication could effect the same result that the false teachers were trying to produce in Peter's day, that is, entice a believer who is in the process of escaping the "corruption in the world" back into the entrapment.

Speeding the Coming of the Day of God

You ought to live holy and godly lives
as you look forward to the day of God and speed its coming.
2 PETER 3:11-12

Christians are familiar with the expectation that there is a coming day of judgment, even if we do not like to think about it too much. What is surprising to the reader of 2 Peter 3:12 is that it appears that the coming of that day can be speeded up. Can it be true that the behavior of Christians can speed up (or delay) the day of God? In what way can they do this? And what does this mean for the idea of the sovereignty of God? Does he not decide about the "times and seasons" without any input from us and our behavior?

The whole of 2 Peter 3 concerns the return of Christ. Two terms are used: "coming" (sometimes left untranslated as "parousia," v. 4) and "day" (v. 10). The "day" here is the "day of God" rather than the usual "day of the Lord." "Day of God" also appears in Revelation

16:14. It probably appears here because "the day of the Lord" occurs three times in the previous verses and so a change in terminology is demanded by good style.[1]

This "day of God" will be marked by the destruction of "the heavens" by fire, including the melting of the "elements." We are not told exactly what will be the mechanism of this process, but it is clear that it is caused by the "day of God" and therefore not a natural catastrophe or something touched off by human carelessness. God will remove the old heaven and earth, says Revelation 21:1, preparing the way for a new heaven and new earth (which 2 Pet 3:13 mentions). Peter refers to this event not to scare Christians, but to remind them that everything done or built on this earth is temporal. Therefore living in radical obedience to God pays the only lasting dividends, and this "day" is the time when they will receive those rewards.

Christians are to "look forward to" or "watch expectantly for" this day. This means keeping it in their awareness, and living in the light of it. For the New Testament writers eschatology determined ethics. That is, what one believed about the return of Christ would determine how one lived. If people have the lively expectation that Peter wants them to have, then they would live a holy life, whatever the immediate consequences, for they would be so expectant of ultimate reward that temporal losses would make no difference.

Yet Christians are also to "speed" the coming of that day. Jesus himself told his followers to pray for that day, for the Lord's Prayer contains the line "Your kingdom come." Furthermore, the church prayed *"Marana tha"* (1 Cor 16:22), translated in Revelation 22:20 as "Come, Lord Jesus." But Peter probably is referring to something more than prayer. There was a strong Jewish tradition based on Isaiah 60:22 (which in the Septuagint uses the same word for "speed" used here) that the coming of Messiah was held back by the sins of the people and that repentance would hasten this day. Peter appears to agree with this. He has talked throughout the letter about holiness. In the verse immediately before this one he has exhorted the people to "holy and godly lives" and two verses later he summarizes with, "Make every effort to be found spotless, blameless and at peace with him." Therefore what is said here is that the holiness of Christians both expresses their expectation of that day and hastens its coming.

If Christians have this much influence over the timing of the coming of Christ, what does that mean for God's sovereignty? Peter has already explained that. In 3:8-9 he stated that God is patient; time in our terms is not an issue to him. What is his issue is that he does not want "anyone to perish, but everyone to come to repentance." The special focus of this concern in 2 Peter is the Christian community, which is being polluted by sin. God is sovereign, and in his sovereignty he has determined to bring as many people to repentance and obedience as possible. (Peter does not explain what factors will make God call a final end to his efforts.) He has chosen to take human choices into account in setting the time of the return of Christ. What this means for Christians is that if they really desire the coming of the kingdom they had best get on with repentance and holy living so that they cooperate with God in preparing for the end.

Peter has taken our breath away. On the one hand, the vision of the earth that we know dissolving into a fireball along with all of the accomplishments and monuments of human culture shakes our security to the extent to which we are invested in this age. On the other hand, the idea that our lives, to the degree they are holy, may speed the coming of Christ and thus the whole timetable of the universe produces a sense of awesome humbling privilege. Peter hopes that together these images will prod Christians to that expectancy of Christ's return and the holy living that will in fact speed it along, for this is God's holy sovereign will.

Notes

[1]This is seen also in the use of "God" and "Lord" in 2 Peter 3: vv. 3-7 use "God," vv. 8-10 use "Lord," vv. 11-13 use "God" and vv. 14-16 use "Lord" first and then "God." There seems to be a deliberate switching back and forth between the synonymous terms.

• C H A P T E R 4 7 •

If Anyone Loves the World, They Do Not Love the Father

Do not love the world or anything
in the world. If anyone loves the world,
the love of the Father is not in him.
1 JOHN 2:15

The world is so much with us," claims the poet, and so it is. The world is all about us. How then can John say in this verse that we are not to love the world? Does this mean that Christians are to hate humankind or the environment? Doesn't that conflict with the idea that God loves the world (Jn 3:16)? And isn't John rather absolute in saying that if one loves the world, there is no love for God? This seems to be a rather black-and-white picture that does not fit with reality as we experience it.

The first question that confronts us in examining this verse more closely is what "the world" means. John uses the term six times in 1 John 2:15-17, but he also uses it seventeen more times in 1—3 John. The world in 1 John is not the planet or the creation, but the human sphere in which we live. It is, then, the sum total of human culture and institutions, the collective living human community. This community is controlled by Satan (1 Jn 5:19; compare 4:4). It is therefore at root hostile to God and those who are committed to him (3:13). In fact, "the world" is where the false teachers go when they leave the church (4:1, 3, 5). This is different from the meaning of "the world" in John 3:16, in which "the world" God loves means humanity, not the culture and institutions we have created. "The world" in 1 John focuses on this culture, which is at root hostile to God.

The Christian's relationship to such a world can hardly be a friendly one. It is true that Christians live within the world. To withdraw from the world would mean to leave human society altogether. But at the same time, Christians are not to belong to the world. We are to be of a totally different orientation (Jn 17:15-18). To maintain this orientation we must have victory over the world, not in the sense that the world is conquered and becomes Christian, but in the sense that the world does not conquer Christians and force them back into its own lifestyle and way of thinking. Rather, Christians live within the world as Christ would (1 Jn 5:4-5; 4:17).

This background, then, makes it clear why one cannot love the world. To love is to be emotionally invested in something; in Scripture this investment includes caring for or serving the object of love. Those things which characterize the world are "the cravings of sinful man" or, better, "the desires of the body," "the lust [better, desire] of his eyes" and "the boasting of what he has and does." Obviously the Christian has bodily desires and also looks at things and desires them (the English words "cravings" and "lusts" are too strongly negative to carry John's meaning accurately), but the issue is whether the Christian is emotionally invested in these desires. For most human beings in the world such desires are all that they have to live for other than "what [a person] has and does." Christians, however, have someone beyond the world to live for, namely Jesus. Thus they experience the desires and sort them out according to the principles and priorities seen in Jesus. Christians truly "march to the beat of a different drummer."

James puts the same idea differently when he speaks of friendship with the world (4:4). Friendship with the world is a life oriented around what one wants. It may include prayer, but prayer for a person who is trying to be a friend of the world is an attempt to get God to fulfill one's desires rather than an attempt to line up one's will with God's (4:2-3). James says that this friendship makes one God's enemy.

Like Jesus (Mt 6:24) and James, John makes the love of God and the love of the world mutually exclusive. We cannot be totally emotionally invested in two contradictory directions. We choose either God and his values or the world and its values. If Jesus is truly Lord (and John has written extensively in chap. 2 of obedience to Christ as being the essence of loving him), then it will be his values that will determine one's emotional investments. To pretend otherwise is to slip into exactly what James condemns, using religion to get ahead on the world's terms (in James's case, using prayer simply to obtain the material "blessings" one wants). Satan is not against religion, but against Jesus and his Father. This compromise is nothing less than spiritual adultery, for, to return to John, it fails to recognize that the world and all its values are passing away and that doing the will of God is the only path to eternal life.

This explanation has not made the passage any easier. We can see that a lot of what is called Christianity is in fact heavily colored by a love of the world. Nor will the natural human desire to be accepted and to "fit in" find these verses comfortable ones. The Christian will always live in tension with the world, suspicious of, if not rejecting, much of the product of human culture. The countercultural lifestyle of the Christian invites rejection, for living by different values suggests that the values of one's neighbors are inadequate. Yet, given that this position is based on words of Jesus himself and is a consistent one throughout the New Testament, it will not do to soften it. The tension is there. The pain is real. We cannot have it both ways. We cannot love both God and the world. At the same time God shows that he understands when John also writes, "You . . . are from God and have overcome them [those who are of the world], because the one who is in you [Jesus, through the Spirit] is greater than the one [Satan] who is in the world" (1 Jn 4:4).

• C H A P T E R 4 8 •

The Anointing
You Received
from Him

*As for you, the anointing you received from him remains in you,
and you do not need anyone to teach you. But as his anointing
teaches you about all things and as that anointing is real,
not counterfeit—just as it has taught you, remain in him.*
1 JOHN 2:27

Few of us have personal experience of anointing (even in terms of viewing ceremonies of people being anointed) other than for medicinal reasons. Of course, Scripture readers are familiar with the concept of anointing, for a number of prophets, priests and kings are anointed in the Old Testament. But what type of anointing is it that 1 John 2:27 claims the Christian receives? Is it anything like what was received in the Old Testament? Why does John then say that this means that "you do not need anyone to teach you"? How does an anointing teach us something? Does this mean that we can dispense with human teachers altogether?

This verse is a continuation of a thought first introduced in 1 John 2:20, "You have an anointing from the Holy One, and all of you know the truth." Reference to both anointing and knowing the truth appear in each of the two verses. What could this anointing be? In the Old Testament the anointing given kings and priests is with oil to consecrate them to ministry. There is clearly a consecration or initiation going on in our passage as well, but there is no mention of oil. By the time of Tertullian (A.D. 200) anointing with oil was practiced in the context of baptism, but there is no evidence that such a practice occurred as early as the New Testament period. In the New Testament oil is only connected with anointing the sick for healing (Mk 6:13; Jas 5:14-15). Yet the practice of the later church does give us a clue to the meaning here, for the oil meant the reception of the Spirit. Even in the Old Testament the anointing of kings (1 Sam 16:13) and prophets (Is 61:1) is connected with the Spirit coming upon them. Jesus at his baptism is said to be anointed with the Spirit (Acts 10:37-38; compare Acts 4:27; Heb 1:9) and in Luke 4:18 Jesus quotes, "The Spirit of the Lord is upon me, because he has anointed me" (Is 61:1), which was the theme of his ministry. Jesus was never anointed with oil (other than perhaps the perfume poured over him at the end of his ministry in Bethany), but he was anointed with the Spirit, which came upon him at his baptism. It is quite appropriate (and probably a deliberate play on words) that Christians, who are followers of the Christ (which means Messiah, or "anointed one") should bear that same anointing (the root of "Christ" and "anointing" are the same in Greek).

Paul indicates that Christians have been anointed with the Spirit when he says, "He anointed us, set his seal of ownership on us, and put his Spirit in our hearts as a deposit, guaranteeing what is to come" (2 Cor 1:21-22; the grammar indicates that this is one event, not several). The experience of the Spirit was a normative part of early Christian initiation. Paul explicitly denies the oft-repeated modern phrase that one is not supposed to experience or feel anything at conversion, when he argues that one knows if one is a Christian because of the presence of the Spirit within (Rom 8:9; see 1 Jn 3:24; 4:13). Acts also connects the reception of the Spirit to Christian initiation (2:38; 3:19; 8:15-17; 10:44-48; 19:5-6).

In the New Testament, then, baptism is normally associated with the experience of the Spirit, as are repentance from "dead works" and commitment to Christ. The four form a complex, but they are not interchangeable with each other. All need to be present for the complete initiatory experience. The data of Acts shows that at times the order of the events is different and in some cases the various parts are separated by some time. But the assumption of the New Testament writers is that all four are present. Thus in 1 John 2:27 the anointing is something that has been received at a past point in time, the point of Christian initiation. However, John is not discussing baptism here, and therefore does not identify the anointing he is talking about with baptism.

John also does not identify the anointing with the Word, although he does not place Word and Spirit over against one another. In 1 John 2:24 we read, "See that what you have heard from the beginning remains in you. If it does, you also will remain in the Son and in the Father." The "what you have heard from the beginning" is the apostolic witness to Christ (1:1-3), which in the Gospel of John became Scripture. Those anointed are not the false teachers who have rejected this apostolic witness and left the orthodox Christian community, but precisely those who have accepted the witness, in which it remains. We see a similar continuity between the Spirit and Christ in John 14:26 and 15:26. There is no conflict between the Spirit and the gospel tradition. Yet the two are not the same. The anointing is not "that which you have heard," but a complement to it, the Spirit within.

Those who have the Spirit (in whom it "remains," a continuing action), then, "do not need anyone to teach" them. This again parallels what we read in John 14:26 and 15:26, not to mention the ongoing revelation of John 16:12-15. John has at least three reasons for writing this. First, the false teachers were probably claiming to have some secret knowledge into which they had been initiated and which the orthodox Christians did not have. Nonsense, says John, you yourself have the real, not the counterfeit. Unlike them you have Truth himself within.

Second, these people already have received the apostolic witness and remain in it, the anointing of the Spirit showing them that it is indeed true. There is no need for supplementary teaching, for they already have what is true. Third, the Spirit within will guide them into truth. While teachers may be helpful and an exhortation or teaching like 1 John useful, John trusts that the Spirit himself will be the real teacher, showing them the true and exposing the false, just as Paul trusts that the Spirit will lead Christians into righteous living (Gal 5:16, 18, 22-26) and James expects the "wisdom from above" to bear the proper fruit (3:13-18). Christians who are listening to the Spirit should "smell a rat" when they see false versions of the faith or outright evil, and they should recognize the family likeness in that which is of God. Unfortunately, Christians often do not listen to the Spirit, and when they do their perceptions can be warped, so the external guidelines of Scripture are always necessary. Furthermore, in the process of conversion the human teacher also instructs students in the truth, the apostolic witness, which they must accept and remain in to receive this anointing. Again John does not separate Word from Spirit nor substitute one for the other, but he does recognize that the Spirit should be giving true discernment to the believer. Since he still has a place for the Word, John also has a place for human teachers, yet he recognizes that they may fall into error and it may be hard for Christians to sort out the true teacher from the impostor. It is the discernment taught by the Spirit that John believes will enable the believer who is committed to Christ to see correctly in this situation. The human remains important, but the divine Guide is the one in whom John places his ultimate confidence.

This passage is difficult, then, in two ways. First, it relies upon our understanding the Jewish background of anointing so that we will connect it with the Spirit and Christian initiation. Second, it expects our experience of the Spirit to be real enough that we will understand that the Spirit himself does indeed teach us and lead us into truth. The challenge of the verse is to live in this experience, not in rejecting the role of the Word, for John never does that and in fact easily slips back and forth from Spirit to Word, but in so walking in obedience to the words of Christ in Scripture and the inner voice of the Spirit that we recognize immediately when the world tries to seduce us through that which claims to be Christian, but is tainted in some way.

• C H A P T E R 4 9 •

No One Born of God Will Continue to Sin

No one who lives in him keeps on sinning.
No one who continues to sin has either seen him or known him. . .
No one who is born of God will continue to sin, because God's
seed remains in him; he cannot go on sinning,
because he has been born of God.
1 JOHN 3:6, 9

Yesterday I committed a sin. That gives me problems with 1 John. This is not the easiest epistle to read, for despite John's relatively simple vocabulary, he appears to move in circles. Verses like 1 John 3:6, 9 appear in various forms at several points, but they are not any easier to understand for that repetition. My experience is not unique. Is there any Christian who has not struggled with sin? Doesn't 1 John say, "If we claim to be without sin, we deceive ourselves" (1:8)? And what is this "seed" of God that John is talking about? The concepts in these verses appear at best overly optimistic and at worst perfectionistic enough to drive one to despair.

One answer to these questions is to point out that the verb "sin" in these verses is in the present tense and therefore continuous. The argument would be that John is talking about habitual sin, not occasional acts of sin. This is the interpretation that the NIV translation reflects. Unfortunately, however, 1 John 5:16 also uses the present tense of "sin" for what appears to be an act of sin committed by a believer. Therefore this solution by itself forces too much out of a Greek tense that John does not use with the precision claimed. Furthermore, it is hard to see how God's nature being in a person would keep them from habitual sins and not from occasional acts. Isn't sin, sin? Is God's power limited to just one type?

We begin to find the answer when we look at the people whom John opposes in his first letter. In general these people were gnosticising teachers, which means that they were not full-blown Gnostics (a type of New Age movement of that day), but were moving in that direction. Gnosticism went in two directions. One was to argue that they were sinless because they had a higher knowledge and had overcome earthly distinctions (sin being one of them), either because of their asceticism or because of their simply having transcended that level. This appears to be the type of idea opposed in 1 John 1:8—2:2. To deny sinfulness is to deceive oneself. The other direction was to argue that because they were spiritual the body did not matter (these same people denied that Jesus had a real human body). This means that their behavior did not matter. Sinful acts were not issues at all, for they were committed by or in the body. It is this type of an idea that John is combating in this passage. If one is fighting on two fronts, it is not surprising to find him turning first to the one front and then to the other, keeping the two in tension without suggesting any synthesis.

Having observed the situation of the book, we need also to observe that it is living in Christ (or remaining in him) that is the source of sinlessness. (To remain in Christ is to live in intimate relationship with him.) This freedom from sin is not a human work, but an act of grace. It comes from being born of God or intimacy with Christ. Paul would phrase this "walking in the Spirit." In fact, a person who is living in God "cannot go on sinning" because God's nature is in them and this nature does not sin. This reflects the expectation of the Jews. In Ezekiel 36:27 we read that the presence of the Spirit in God's people will cause them to "follow my decrees and be careful to keep my laws." This was underlined in many of the intertestamental works (such as 1 Enoch 5:8; 4 Esdras 9:31; Jubilees 5:12; Psalms of Solomon 17:32-33), resulting in a belief in sinlessness in the Messianic Age. John expresses this, not in terms of the Spirit, but in terms of being born of God. In fact, he speaks of God's "seed" remaining in the person, the picture being that of a father's sperm (which is what "seed" means in this case) remaining in an individual and imparting to him or her the father's nature. The rebirth imagery in John means that the Father's nature is in every Christian.

If the ability not to sin is grace, a nature given by God that one has by virtue of remaining in him (and the false teachers have not remained, but have left the church), then John is speaking of a *potential* in the Christian. Believers do not need to sin. They have the very nature of God within. All they need to do is to remain or live in Christ and they will not sin. Yet this has to be held in tension with the fact, which John has already stated in chapter 1, that believers do sin and it is deception to think otherwise. The tension is that of Christians living in this age in which we already have the life of the coming age in us but do not yet experience the fullness of that life. The potential is there, but since we do not fully remain in or live in Christ, we do not draw fully on the potential of God living within us.

In practical terms this boils down to the fact that sin and Christianity are incompatible. Those who live without this tension, who simply sin, are deceiving themselves if they believe they are Christian. They show no evidence of the nature of God within and therefore have not been born from God. If that which is born of God cannot sin, that which sins cannot have been born of God. Yet for the person who is living in this tension there is a call, "Be what you are!" Remain in intimacy with Jesus and allow the nature of God in you to work his perfection. This imperative is never fully realized—John knows that, as we see in 1 John 1:8 and 5:16—but it can be increasingly realized as Christians yield to grace and allow their real life to be revealed in all of its divine holiness.

He Came by Water and Blood

This is the one who came by water and blood—Jesus Christ.
He did not come by water only, but by water and blood.
And it is the Spirit who testifies, because the Spirit
is the truth. For there are three that testify: the Spirit,
the water and the blood; and the three are in agreement.
1 JOHN 5:6-8

Christians have rightly written and sung about the blood of Jesus, for his atonement is central to the faith. But in 1 John 5:6-8 we discover that there is water as well as blood; we do not have songs about water. What does John mean by water and blood? What does it mean to come by water and blood? Why are they placed alongside the Spirit as witnesses? And how do inanimate things bear witness? These questions must be answered if this text is to be anything more than a confused jumble.

Historically there have been three different types of answers to these questions. First, some of the church fathers linked the water and blood to the "blood and water" that came out of Jesus' side when he was pierced by a spear (Jn 19:34). Yet the essence of the cross was not that water flowed, but that blood was shed. In fact,

no other New Testament text mentions water in connection with
the cross. At the time of the spear-thrust Jesus was already dead;
it only proved that he was in fact dead. Finally, the order of words
in John 19 is different from that in our passage, which indicates that
the author was not thinking of the Gospel passage when he wrote.

Second, others have seen a sacramental emphasis here. The blood
stands for the Lord's Supper or Eucharist, the water for baptism, and
the Spirit for the reception of the Spirit in Christian initiation. In
that case part of the background would be John 3:5, being born of
water (baptism) and the Spirit, and part would be John 6:53-56, the
eating of the flesh and drinking of the blood of the Son of man. This
interpretation fits better with 1 John 5:8 than with 5:6, for the verb
in 5:6 indicates a completed act, not a repeating sacrament, while in
5:8 there is a present-time ongoing witnessing. Yet even in 5:8 the
order of the three terms is not the same as that in normal Christian
initiation in which baptism (water) precedes both Eucharist (blood)
and reception of the Spirit. Nor is the order the same as that in John
3:5. Finally, it would be unique to find the single term "blood" standing for the Eucharist. Even in John 6 both flesh and blood are mentioned. At the same time, since the Johannine writings are full of
double meanings, it is quite possible that this is a secondary meaning
implied by the author; namely that in the Christian rites we reflect
upon the historical events in the life of Christ.

Third, and probably correctly, scholars have seen the water as
standing for the baptism of Jesus and the blood for his death on the
cross. The two events mark out respectively the beginning and end
of his ministry. The context in 1 John argues that "Jesus is the Son
of God" (5:5). What John is saying is that the human Jesus is in fact
the divine, pre-existent Son. This very Son is the one who had a
real human existence marked by baptism and the cross. He is Jesus
Christ; that is, both the human man and the divine Savior. This
emphasis is reasonable in the face of the heresy John was refuting
that denied that "Jesus Christ has come in the flesh" (1 Jn 4:2). He
was really human, John states, for he was baptized, receiving the
Spirit and entering upon a ministry open to all to see, and he died
a real death marked by real blood. This whole life history of Jesus

refutes the claims of the heretics.

How, then, do these inanimate elements bear witness? It is obvious that the Spirit is the central witness of the trio and the one most emphasized by John. His ongoing witness in the heart of the believers is clear throughout 1 John. The other two are historical events, but they stand as things that happened, a silent testimony to all who will accept their witness. To deny the reality of Jesus' humanity is to fly in the face of the historical data. They function as witnesses the same way that piles of stones and other inanimate objects could function in that way in the Old Testament (see Josh 22:27). Their importance is that the Spirit witnesses to something that is real—real historical events—not to something that happened only in the suprahistorical realm.

Readers of the Authorized or King James Version will notice that in our translation 1 John 5:7 does not contain the three who "testify in heaven: the Father, the Word and the Holy Spirit." The reason for this omission is quite simple. The clause appears in late manuscripts of the Latin Vulgate, not in the early ones. And in the Greek manuscripts it does not appear before the sixteenth century. As a result, scholars universally conclude that the original text of 1 John lacked this statement, which was probably added by a pious scribe in the margin at some later time as a "Praise the Lord" and got copied into the text by a still later scribe (doubtless thinking that the first scribe was putting in the margin something that he had accidentally left out).

These verses, then, underline the importance of the real historical nature of the life and death of Jesus. Christians do not believe that salvation comes through actions that only took place in the realm of ideas or the spiritual world. Nor did Jesus come simply as a revealer of the truth, his deeds being incidental. Rather, Jesus came to do something as a real man in space and time and history. He lived a real life, accomplished a real ministry, and died a real death, bloody as it was. The markers of the water of his baptism and the blood of his cross point to this reality. To this the Spirit bears witness. And, in a secondary sense, the celebration of the Christian sacraments point to this historical foundation.

· C H A P T E R 5 1 ·

If We Ask
Anything According
to His Will

*This is the confidence we have in approaching God:
that if we ask anything according
to his will, he hears us.*
1 JOHN 5:14

All Christians believe in prayer, for the New Testament teaches us to pray; but some of the verses make us struggle with prayer. This is one of those verses. It forms part of the conclusion of 1 John and leads into a "health wish" (a standard part of the ending of Greek letters). It is not the place where we would expect radically new teaching on prayer, but a repetition of truths that the readers already know. Yet even what was a repetition for them may raise questions for us. What does it mean to ask "according to his will"? Does "he hears us" mean that he grants our request? If so, doesn't this fly in the face of the Christian experience of prayer? In other words, we are asking, What is this "confidence" that John believes we should have? Is this a misplaced confidence, or is it something that makes sense in the light of the prayer experience of the church?

John has spoken of "confidence" three times before this in this letter. Twice it has to do with the return of Christ and the final judgment (2:28; 4:17). Once it has to do with prayer (3:21-22). In all three it is a confidence that we have before God; it is this relationship with God, not our relationship with the world, that is the issue.

The confidence here is that "if we ask anything according to his will, he hears us." John makes it plain in the next verse what "hears us" means: "We know that we have what we asked of him" (5:15). Therefore the hearing is not simply that God registers our request, that there is a heavenly "Ah hum, I see; I heard that." Instead it is that God hears and answers the request, the same thing that the expression means in John's Gospel (9:31; 11:41-42).

This answered prayer is conditioned by "ask . . . according to his will." In the Johannine writings there are a series of conditions for prayer:

Passage:	Condition:
John 14:13-14	Ask "in my [Jesus'] name"
John 15:7	Remain in Jesus/His words remain in you
John 15:16	Ask "in my [Jesus'] name"
John 16:23-27	Ask "in my [Jesus'] name"
1 John 3:21-22	We obey his [God's] commands
1 John 5:14	Ask according to his [God's] will

All of these conditions boil down to being in an intimate relationship with God/Jesus. To "remain in [Jesus]" or "ask in [his] name" is to be in such a relationship with him. To "obey his commands" or for "his words to remain in [us]" are expressions of this relationship as one lives in obedience to the declared will of God/Jesus. This, then, is what asking according to God's will means; it is to ask in submission to that will.

Such a condition does not surprise us, for in Matthew 6:10 we are taught to pray, "Your will be done." Yet what John is talking about is not a general prayer, for such general prayers get general answers. In fact, if the Lord's Prayer is an outline for prayer and not a prayer itself, it too is not expressing a general wish. Instead, John is talking about knowing and praying the specific will of God in a given instance. This is not always pleasant; nor does one come to know and submit to this will easily. Jesus in Gethsemane also prays, "Yet not what I will, but what you will" (Mk 14:36). He did not come to this submission without a struggle. He appears to have begun his prayer dreading what was coming and hoping that there might be a way in the will of God for it not to happen. In his struggle in those hours he apparently saw clearly that the Father had only one way, the cross. Therefore Jesus comes to the place of submission to that will. But it was not easy; it was not without groans and cries and sweat.

John, then, is suggesting to his readers a relationship with God in which they too will pray God's will back to him. It may be no easier for them than for Jesus, who, although he wrestled with bigger issues, did not have a background of sin and disobedience to fight against and did have a more intimate relationship with the Father than believers experience. But the process is analogous. Believers live in obedience to God (having repented of sin); now they come in prayer, perhaps already knowing the divine will, but otherwise listening and praying until they know that they are in line with God. It is then that the confidence comes that this prayer will indeed be heard.

But why pray if one is only praying God's will back to him? Such a question, of course, tries to unravel the mystery of divine sovereignty and human responsibility. Yet without being able to solve that mystery, we can answer the real issue it poses. That answer is relatively straightforward. God in his sovereignty has chosen to work his will through human prayer. It appears to be his will not to do what he might like to do if human beings will not pray for it. On the one hand, this makes prayer a privilege. Christians are invited to work together with the Creator of the universe. He has chosen to make their freely willed prayers part of his plan. On the other hand, this gives prayer a security. If a believer does not correctly perceive the will of God, God is not bound to answer that prayer. We do not have to walk in fear that we will mess up the universe through ill-advised prayers.

This passage is often read as if it meant, "If we ask anything, according to his will he hears us." We do the asking, and then God decides if it is his will to hear us. This is not the relationship with God that John is presenting, for it is no confidence at all. Instead, he is presenting a relationship in which meditation on the words of Jesus (and obeying them as they are understood) and listening prayer are central.[1] Out of this struggle to hear and then, perhaps, to will that will oneself, the Christian prays. That prayer, says John, rising like incense to the Father (Rev 5:8), will certainly be heard, receiving whatever it is that is requested. This is not only the theory of John, but it is also the experience of the numerous people of prayer down the centuries who have taken the time to learn to pray in this manner.

Notes
[1]For more information on listening prayer, see Joyce Huggett, *The Joy of Listening to God* (Downers Grove, Ill.: InterVarsity Press, 1986).

A Sin
That Leads
to Death

If anyone sees his brother commit a sin that does not lead to death,
he should pray and God will give him life. I refer to those
whose sin does not lead to death. There is a sin that leads to death.
I am not saying that he should pray about that. All wrongdoing is sin,
and there is sin that does not lead to death.
1 JOHN 5:16-17

Is there a sin from which there is no recovery? When we read 1 John 5:16-17, there is certainly no problem in understanding that one should pray for a fellow Christian who sins. With John, Christians recognize that "all wrongdoing is sin" and that all of it separates individuals from God. Thus prayer and restorative counsel (Gal 6:1) appear to be in order when we observe a fellow believer who has sinned. Where John causes problems, however, is in mentioning "a sin that leads to death," for which prayer is not in order (not that it is necessarily wrong, but that it is useless). What type of sin is this? And what type of death is intended—physical or spiritual death? Since we ourselves fall into sin at times, the questions are of practical importance to each of us. This is no mere resolving an academic problem of Scripture.

In examining this passage, we note, first, that it occurs at the end of 1 John, right after an encouragement to pray (5:13-15). According to John, it is because "we know that we have what we ask from him" that one should pray for the "brother" who sins. James has a similar structure in the conclusion of his letter. After talking about prayer for healing (Jas 5:13-16), he notes the encouragement to pray that Elijah's example gives (vv. 17-18) and then talks about turning a sinner from the error of his or her way and thus saving a person from death (vv. 19-20), which is the purpose of his book. This structure of health wish plus purpose statement in the conclusion of a letter was typical of one form of Greek letters. Thus we are not surprised that in his conclusion John also has a modified health wish before reaching his final purpose statement (probably 5:20).

But what type of life and death is John talking about? This is our modern question; it was not one for John's readers, for the brevity of his reference assumes that they would know what he was talking about. We have to discover this from the rest of his letter. We note, then, that 1 John uses the term "life" thirteen times, seven of them in this chapter. Since he means spiritual life (eternal life) in every other case in which he uses the term, we would expect that this would also be the meaning here. Likewise the two other places where he uses "death" (both in 3:14) refer to spiritual death, not physical death. So even though in the New Testament sin can lead to physical death (1 Cor 11:30; compare Acts 5:1-11; 1 Cor 5:5) and physical sickness (Jas 5:15-16), it is unlikely that that is the meaning here. This is especially true in that in both his Gospel and Epistle John sees physical death as something already transcended by the believer (Jn 8:51; 11:26; 1 Jn 3:14).

What, then, is the sin (not specific acts of sin, but a quality of sin) that leads to this spiritual death? In the Old Testament some sins carried the death penalty, while others did not (Num 18:22; Deut 22:26). In particular, deliberate or willful breaking of the commandments required death, while inadvertent sin did not (Lev 4:2, 13, 22, 27; 5:15, 17-18; Num 15:27-31; Deut 17:12). Both of these distinctions were common in first-century Jewish literature as well. While all of these Old Testament references are to the physical death of the offender, it would not be surprising for John to reinterpret the concept in terms of spiritual life and death, for that is his focus. In this he had help from Jesus, who referred to a category of sin that would not be forgiven (Mk 3:28 and parallels). What type of sin is this? For Jesus it was observing the activity of the Holy Spirit and calling it the devil's work. Similarly, John has been concerned with a group of apostates, people who were part of the Christian community and have left. What is their sin? They are continuing in (and therefore condoning) sin, they are hating and separating from their fellow Christians (thus not living out the command of love), they love the world and they even deny that Jesus has come "in the flesh" (probably a denial that Christ had a real human body). These are not casual errors or lapses into this or that sin, but a knowing and deliberate turning away from the truth they experienced in the Christian community. While they would probably still consider themselves Christians, John knows that their standards and their doctrines are quite different from those of his group.

Why, then, doesn't John say that one should pray for them? The answer is because such prayer is useless. It is not that it is absolutely wrong to pray. While John clearly does not intend Christians to pray for the forgiveness of such people, he words himself carefully so as not to forbid it. The issue is that these people are not repenting nor about to repent. Like the people envisioned in Hebrews 6, they have known the truth and experienced the fullness of what God has, but have turned away. While God would surely forgive such people if they did repent, no argument will change their minds. They have left the true Christian community. They "know" *they* are right and John's group is wrong. Asking for their forgiveness is useless. Forgiveness comes to the repentant, not those willfully persisting in sin.

But that is not John's focus. His point is that Christians *should* pray for other members of the Christian community who sin. Why should they do this? First, God seems to prefer to grant forgiveness through confession to another and the other's praying (as in Jas

5:15-16). Psychologically this makes the repentance much more concrete and thus lasting. Second, sin is to be taken seriously. Today's slip, if persisted in, could turn into deception, and the brother or sister could slip farther and farther from God until they become part of the apostate group. The time to intervene is not when the person has become hardened in turning away from God, but when the first sin is observed. If one prays *then*, life will be granted and the individual will not slip further away from God.

John, then, is calling for two things that are often poorly practiced in the church today. The first is the taking of responsibility for the spiritual well-being of fellow Christians; that is, for observing errors (the point is that one "sees" the sin; it is observable), correcting the sinners (Gal 6:1-2), and praying for their forgiveness. The second is the taking of sin seriously, realizing that it can indeed lead to grave consequences if persisted in, and thus living in and calling others to live in a holy fear before God. John has no intention of our living in fear that we have sinned "the sin unto death," for the very fear is an indication of our repentance and thus that we have not sinned such a sin. John has every intention of calling us to lead lives open to each other so that we give and receive correction and thus not only keep each other from deliberate rebellion and its consequences, but also assist each other in walking in close fellowship with the God who is light (1 Jn 1:5).

· C H A P T E R 5 3 ·

The Chosen Lady

The elder, To the chosen lady and her children,
whom I love in the truth—and not I only,
but also all who know the truth.
2 JOHN 1

What would we think today if we discovered a letter from a respected church leader to a "lady" whom he does not name, but whom he says he "loves"? This verse raises such a question for us. The little books of 2 and 3 John may well have served as cover letters to personalize the general letter 1 John. Whatever their purpose, they are addressed to individual people or groups. But what or who is this "lady" to whom 2 John is addressed? Why would the elder write such a letter to a lady? What was his relationship to this lady? Was she a real lady at all? And if this is a lady, what implications does that have for church leadership?

Three different views have been held on this topic. First, some of the earliest commentators on this text read the Greek as if "chosen" or "lady" were the personal names of the woman receiving the letter. In the first case her name would be Electa (as in Rom 16:13), and in the second Kyria (which would be the Greek equivalent of the Aramaic name "Martha" and does occur in Greek literature). But unfortunately there is no definite article with this Greek term, so it is unlikely it is a proper name.

Second, another group of scholars have seen this as an honorable title for a certain woman leader in the church, although she remains anonymous (as does the author, who simply uses his title "the elder"). This would mean that a woman was serving at least as a house-church leader and possibly a city church leader at the time 2 John was written. Such a situation is certainly possible, for women such as Phoebe (Rom 16:1-2), Euodia and Syntyche (Phil 4:2) probably served in such capacities. However, the decision on the meaning of the term (as well as that of "your chosen sister" in 2 John 13) depends upon the context of this particular letter, not upon historical possibility.

Third, and most likely, is the interpretation that the "lady" is a church. It is not that the second interpretation is impossible, but that the switch in Greek to the second person *plural* in 2 John 8, 10, and 12 (before returning to the second person *singular* in 2 John 13) appears to indicate that the elder has a group in mind, not an individual. Likewise the situation in 2 John 9-11 appears to fit best in a group of house churches, not with a single individual. In fact, 2 John 9-11 would be rather strong words to address to a person whom one "loves" and who has children "walking in the truth" (although not all the "children" are). Therefore, although it is possible to explain the plurals as references to the woman and her children, the letter fits better as a message to a church, which is in turn greeted by the church in which the elder is presently residing.

The background for this interpretation is clear. Jerusalem is often seen in both testaments as a mother (see Is 54:1-8; Gal 4:25; Rev 12:17; 21:2). Furthermore, the church is viewed as the bride of Christ (see 2 Cor 11:2; Eph 5:22-32). In fact, if she is his bride, the title here is especially apt, for she is certainly chosen in that she has heard and responded to the call of God, and she is therefore a "mistress" (the more archaic translation of the Greek term translated "lady"), which is the feminine form of "lord" ("lord" in Greek is *kurios* and "lady" is *kuria*). She participates in the rule of her husband. As in the biblical passages in which a city's or a nation's citizens are her children (such as Mt 2:18 citing Jer 31:15), so the individual church members here are the children.

Our verse, then, is not easy because the interpretation is difficult. It is possible to interpret it differently than I have done. But most likely we are reading the address of the elder (who appears to supervise a number of city churches) to a particular church or house church in another city. Why would he write so crypticly? One reason would be to bring out his theology of church, making it meaningful by making it personal. Another reason would be to avoid naming names that would identify the church for Roman authorities. If this letter fell into the wrong hands it would look like a relatively innocent personal letter, while it was really a letter supporting a church. Even beyond its content, then, it gives us an example of supervisory support in the early church (when there were no offices of bishop or superintendent, which were later developments in the history of the church)[1] and of the warm mutual relationships among churches.

Notes

[1]Since none of the Johannine letters are "signed" except by the title "the elder," we do not really know who wrote them. Tradition has assigned them to the apostle John, but there are problems with this tradition and thus good reason to question whether any of the twelve apostles were associated with the Johannine literature. Thus this "elder" may well have had no formal office beyond that of "elder"—his supervision was informal, based upon his spiritual authority, not his formal position.

Deceivers Do Not Acknowledge Jesus Coming in the Flesh

*Many deceivers, who do not acknowledge Jesus Christ
as coming in the flesh, have gone out into the world.
Any such person is the deceiver and the antichrist.*

2 JOHN 7

We live in an age in which all sorts of people call themselves Christian, even if their continuity with historic Christianity is tenuous at best. This is not a new problem. All three of the Johannine letters deal with problems with schismatic groups, and in 1 and 2 John one of the characteristics of these groups is that they are heretical. But what are we to make of the heresy described in 2 John 7? In what way might a group call itself Christian and still "not acknowledge Jesus Christ as coming in the flesh"? Even the vast majority of our semi-Christian heresies acknowledge Jesus. What does it mean to "come in the flesh" anyway? This is not the language of the twentieth century, so it calls for explanation.

As we have noted, the Johannine community was struggling with heretical teaching. In 1 John 4:1 we read that "many" false prophets have left the church community for the world. In 2 John 4 we discover that "some" of the Christians are walking in the truth, while in our present verse we learn that there are "many deceivers." The impression is that the majority of the church is defecting and going "out into the world," probably to form their own groups based on their own doctrines.

The root of the heresy in both 1 John 4:2-3 and 2 John 7 is the confession of "Jesus Christ as coming in the flesh." There is a grammatical difference between the two passages that may indicate a shift in emphasis, but the root concept is the same in both. In Johannine terminology to confess something is not simply to agree that it is correct, but to acknowledge one's allegiance to it. So to confess Jesus Christ would be to state that one is committed to him as Lord. But why does John use the double title "Jesus Christ" and "in the flesh"?

This phrase in 2 John is designed to rule out Christological heresy. Two types of heresy appeared in the second century, arising out of roots already apparent in the Johannine writings in the first century. The docetic heresy, on the one hand, argued that Jesus was not a real human being (not truly "in the flesh"), but only appeared to be human. He was truly Christ; the Christ was a spirit that appeared to materialize. Being a spirit, of course, he did not die on the cross, but in one way or another only appeared to suffer and die. (The term "docetic" comes from the Greek word meaning "to seem or appear.") The Cerinthian heresy, on the other hand, argued that Jesus was really a human being, but that at his baptism the Christ spirit came upon him, forsaking him at the crucifixion. Therefore the Christ did not die, although Jesus did. Although we do not know exactly what the heretics John is fighting believed (and some of them may have believed an early form of each of these heresies), the phrase in 2 John guards against both of them. According to John, a true Christian pledges allegiance to Jesus Christ, not just the Christ. And the believer acknowledges that this whole entity, "Jesus Christ," has come from God and is really human. The form of the phraseology in 1 John 4:2-3 stresses Jesus' having come from God and becoming truly incarnate. The form here in 2 John 7 stresses that Jesus remains incarnate and did not in some way "split apart" at death or the ascension. In John's view, an incarnate, truly human, truly divine Jesus Christ presently exists.

In 1 John 4 the heretics claim to be inspired by the Holy Spirit when they teach what they do about Jesus. This does not mean that they were under direct Spirit-control at the time of their speaking, but that they were claiming that this was what the Spirit had taught them. John says that one can tell the true Spirit of God by the doctrine he teaches. The true Spirit has the right doctrine; the spirit that does not lead people to pledge their allegiance to the orthodox Christ is in fact not the Holy Spirit, but the spirit of antichrist. This statement is not grounds for calling up spirits and trying to get them to speak through people and making them affirm or deny that Jesus Christ has come in the flesh, but it is grounds for examining the doctrine of the person who claims prophetic inspiration and seeing if it corresponds with the orthodox confession.

In 2 John we do not hear of the spirit-inspiration of the heretics, but they are themselves called deceivers and antichrist. It appears that they were trying to infiltrate the orthodox house churches and were actively recruiting people to their way of thinking. That is why they are deceivers and why the people need to "watch out" that they do not lose what they have in Christ (v. 8).

The Christian church finds its unity not around this or that doctrine, but around Jesus Christ. To reject the real Jesus, either by denying his true humanity (being "in the flesh") or by denying his divinity (by denying that Jesus was really the Christ) is to break with the faith and to split from the church community. It is not that doctrine is the key issue, but that it expresses the distinguishing characteristics of the person to whom one is committed. The one not committed to the real Jesus Christ does not know either the Father or the Son, according to John. Unfortunately the church often has not kept this fact central. On the one hand, it has been willing to accept some who do deny its Lord, and, on the other hand, it has been willing to split over doctrinal differences that do not call into question real commitment to the true Jesus Christ. This letter reminds us of what is really central. It is Christ who unifies his church. Without him we have no unity. With him we have a unity that no human being dare try to destroy.

• CHAPTER 5 5 •

Do Not Take
Him into Your House
or Welcome Him

*If anyone comes to you and does not bring
this teaching, do not take him into
your house or welcome him.*
2 JOHN 10

We recognize the problem that schismatic or heretical teaching poses to any church. People begin to listen to the deceptive teaching and may soon end up slipping away to join the sectarian group. Yet 2 John 10 poses a problem for Scripture readers in that it appears to contradict an important Christian virtue, that of hospitality, not to mention the virtue of love. Is it love not to welcome a person into your house, even if you do not agree with his or her beliefs? Does not hospitality extend even to non-Christians, rather that just the Christians with whom we happen to agree? Furthermore, Christians struggle with knowing how far to take this verse. Does it mean that one may not invite inside the Jehovah's Witness (or the Mormon) who just knocked at the door? Does it mean that it was wrong to say a polite "good morning" to that person? And if it does not mean that, what does it mean?

First, as we saw in our last chapter, it is clear that 2 John is dealing with a serious problem in the church, not simply minor doctrinal differences or even significant differences over noncentral issues. A group of teachers who had left John's church did not "confess that Jesus Christ has come in the flesh." By this John probably means that these teachers argued that God was too holy to have become truly human, so Jesus only appeared to be a man. In fact, in one way or another his humanity was an illusion. This is a problem combated by the Fourth Gospel (Jn 1:14, "The Word became flesh," as well as many references to Jesus' emotions) and two of the three Johannine Epistles. In other words, these heretics were denying a central part of the gospel rather than arguing over peripheral doctrines, important as some of these doctrines may be.

Second, we noted in a previous chapter that 2 John is addressed to a church (which he calls "the elect lady"). We need to understand what this church was like. It was normal until the mid-third century for Christians to meet in houses. (It was not until the mid-fourth century that house churches were outlawed and church buildings became the only legitimate place to gather as Christians.) Given the size of rooms in even a large house in those days (due to the limitations of building materials) it is unlikely that a house church would grow beyond about sixty people. In fact, there were many reasons to keep them smaller. Since most people had only their feet for transportation, several small groups conveniently located would be more accessible than a single large group. This also tended to make the churches take on the character of the neighborhood in which they were located. Furthermore, given that the meeting involved a meal (which developed into the symbolic meal presently celebrated in the Eucharist, or Lord's Supper) one would not want to crowd the room too much, for space was needed for tables and dishes of food. Finally, smaller groups enabled the church to attract less attention and thus avoid persecution as much as possible. Most house churches, then, probably served twenty to forty people.

Therefore we need to view the early church as a series of small house churches. While Paul, for example, might write a letter to *the church* in Rome or Corinth, that single church would in fact be made up of a group of such cells. For example, in Romans 16 Paul greets several house church leaders and their groups by name.

Third, hospitality was important to the early church. Christians would travel from place to place and need safe and wholesome places to stay. Some of these travelers were apostles, prophets or teachers. When such a person came to a church, they not only brought news of the situation of the church in other places, but they also brought a fresh stream of ministry. Lacking our easy access to books and other media, this was an important way for a congregation to increase its knowledge of the faith as it received insights and graces that initially had been given to another congregation and were now shared. We see the synagogue practice, which the early church copied, in Acts 13:15: "Brothers, if you have a message of encouragement for the people, please speak." Furthermore, the house church services were relatively informal, so discussion and questions gave many people an opportunity to share their ideas.

Therefore what 2 John is referring to is the need to recognize that not every traveling Christian is to be received with such warmth. If in fact it was discovered that the visitor was carrying the serious Christological heresy that John describes, the person was not to be greeted as a brother or sister in Christ (as would have been customary, often including in those days a kiss on both cheeks). Nor should the person be received into the house church and allowed to spread false teaching there. Otherwise the whole "cell" might become infected with the distorted ideas, and they might later spread them to other house churches, making the whole city church sick (or else splitting the church into two alternative structures, both of which claimed to be the true church).

This verse, then, is not intended to apply to individual Christians greeting people at the doors of their homes, but to churches and house groups. In such contexts it is wise for leaders to be assured of the orthodoxy of visitors before giving them a platform from which they can spread their views, even the platform of an official welcome as a visiting Christian leader. Christian hospitality stops where danger to the well-being of the church begins; love does not go to the extent of endangering one's fellow Christians nor of allowing those who deny the Lord one loves to peddle their wares in that Lord's church.

• C H A P T E R 5 6 •

Receiving
No Help from
the Pagans

*It was for the sake of the Name
that they went out, receiving
no help from the pagans.*
3 JOHN 7

Christianity, like first-century Judaism, is a missionary religion. In the first century, however, there were none of the organized societies and fund-raising methods of our present age. The missionaries were assisted by voluntary giving from the people they met or else they were self-supporting, like Paul. But what does 3 John 7 mean in saying that the group of missionaries John is referring to received "no help from the pagans"? Is it that they did not accept any funds from non-Christians (the implication of the NIV translation), or is it that they did not accept any funds from gentile Christians (one interpretation of the NASB and KJV translations)? And what implications does this practice have for our evangelistic methods today?

The Johannine letters mention two types of groups that "went out" from the Christian community. The first group is the heretics, who leave the church and go out into the world (2 John 7). The second group is the one mentioned here, which went out "for the sake of the Name." The Name is Jesus (Acts 5:41; Rom 1:5; Jas 2:7). They were "going out" on his behalf, probably as evangelists since they were among "Gentiles" or "pagans." The term "pagans" (more literally "nations" or "people-groups") could indicate a Jewish-Christian mission not willing to accept funds from gentile Christians (perhaps to keep from being rejected by the Jews) and thus be translated "Gentiles" (as it often is in other contexts in the New Testament), but there is no other indication that the Johannine community was Jewish-Christian. Therefore the term is probably being used in the sense in which it is in Matthew 5:47, which distinguishes "brothers" from "pagans/Gentiles." In other words, it means "unbelievers."

Missionaries (this English term includes those called evangelists and apostles in the New Testament) had no regular means of support in the New Testament period. Paul notes that his mission was supported by the work of his own hands (Acts 18:1-4; 1 Thess 2:9). In rare cases he received funds from already established churches (Phil 4:14-19, which indicates that the Philippian church was alone in supporting him). Other missionaries (and at times perhaps Paul himself) may have had private family funds to draw on. But they held to the principle Jesus taught, "Freely you have received, freely give" (Mt 10:8). There was no fund-raising nor were collections received for the support of the missionary. While hospitality might be accepted from those who received the gospel (see Luke 10:5-7), Paul at times refused even this support (1 Cor 9:3-18).

What are the reasons for this behavior? First, of course, is the principle that the gospel is free. Even to appear to be charging for the gospel or to be making one's living by presenting it was viewed as contradicting this principle. Second, plenty of pagans were charging for their "gospels," such as Cynic and Stoic traveling philosopher-beggars (some of whom grew rich), and the devotees and priests of various cults. For example, a monument set up in Kefr-

Haunar in Syria by a self-styled "slave" of the Syrian goddess boasts that when he went begging on behalf of his goddess "each journey brought in seventy bags" of money. For this reason Jesus forbade the taking of a "bag" (Mt 10:10), for then his disciples would not be able to carry anything with them when they left a town, making it obvious that they were not profiting by their mission. It is important not only to be honest, but to appear to others to be honest.

Given this information, it is not difficult to understand what is going on in 3 John. These missionaries have left the security of their Christian community, not because they were uncomfortable there, but for the sake of their Lord. They are traveling through the area in which Gaius is located. The missionaries will need food (for they are not carrying anything with them) and a place to stay, perhaps even a short rest. To stop to earn money would detract from their travel. It is natural that Christians, especially Christian leaders, along the way should provide them the needed hospitality. John knows from experience that one of the major house church leaders, Diotrephes, will not receive them because he is rejecting John's authority (which was spiritual authority, not "official" authority). Therefore John writes to Gaius, another house church leader, requesting that he receive them, even though he may face rejection by Diotrephes because of it.

This has significant implications for Christian practice. This passage should not become an escape route for Christians who want an excuse not to support missions or their pastoral leadership. There is a clear principle that Christians should share material possessions with those giving them spiritual instruction (Rom 15:27; 1 Cor 9:11; Gal 6:6; 1 Tim 5:17-18). But, as we have seen, there is just as strong a principle that the gospel (including the healing and other ministries associated with it) should be free and that Christian workers, especially evangelistic ones, should not in any way appear to be profiting from those to whom they preach the gospel.

Given these facts and modern means of communication, it might be that the modern "Gaius" will wish to support evangelistic ministries even when they are at a distance from his home. It should *at the least* mean that the modern evangelist will want to do nothing that would make the unbeliever feel that the evangelist was trying to make his living from them. One would hope that an evangelist would rather like Paul pay his or her own way than to give such an impression. Given the present scrutiny of the church and the feeling in the world that the church is out for money, other church workers as well should avoid even the hint that they are charging for ministry. Instead, church members should see to it that church workers are supported without their having to talk about money. Following such principles would not only be the application of 3 John's teaching to the modern era, but it would also go a long way in avoiding the scandals that have accompanied the gospel in our present age.

• CHAPTER 5 7 •

Is Anyone Who Does What Is Good Really from God?

Anyone who does what is good
is from God. Anyone who does what
is evil has not seen God.
3 JOHN 11

He is a good man," we may say. Yet is this always a proper thing to say? The elder, the author of 3 John, has called upon the house-church leader Gaius to imitate good rather than evil. Now in 3 John 11 he gives him a general guideline, but this very guideline is problematic for the modern reader. Is it true that anyone who does what is good is from God? Aren't there good people who make no claim of being Christians? For example, aren't there some Hindu individuals who do good? Have not kindness and even self-sacrifice for the good of others been observed among many nations and religions? Are these people therefore from God? And what about the professing Christian who does evil? Have not Christians, for example, been convicted of crimes? Are they therefore not from God? These are the types of issues that trouble us with this verse.

This particular verse is part of a whole series of Johannine statements, including 1 John 2:29 ("If you know that he is righteous, you know that everyone who does what is right has been born of him.") and 1 John 4:7-8 ("Everyone who loves has been born of God and knows God. Whoever does not love does not know God, because God is love."). Each of these statements connects righteous living in some form (for example, love, doing good) to being a Christian (being born of God, being from God). Taken out of context any one of them would seem to imply that a person could deny Christ and yet qualify as being "from God." In fact, a guru who turned out to be genuinely caring and loving, but embraced Hindu theology, might on that basis find John endorsing his claim to be an incarnation of divinity! The key to this interpretive dilemma, however, is precisely the phrase "taken out of context," for within the context such a meaning is impossible.

In our present context, for example, the wider issue is the behavior of Diotrephes. Diotrephes is a powerful church leader who may have the power to exclude Gaius and his house church from the wider Christian community if Gaius follows the elder's instructions and receives the traveling missionaries. The author is telling Gaius not to follow evil, but good. The verse in question, then, suggests that Diotrephes is not from God or has not seen God, for he is doing evil, not good. This is no more than an application of the principle that Jesus spoke concerning false prophets, "By their fruit you will recognize them" (Mt 7:16). If a person is truly a Christian, the proper lifestyle should be evident. If it is not, then, far from copying their behavior, one should doubt the reality of their new birth.

The same issue occurs in each of the other contexts. First John 2:29 begins a series of statements on righteousness (3:3, 6, 7, 9) that culminates in, "This is how we know who the children of God are and who the children of the devil are: Anyone who does not do what is right is not a child of God; nor is anyone who does not love his brother" (v. 10). The issue, then, is not whether those *outside* the church are or are not Christian (their status is known), but whether those *within* the church are truly born again. If people claim to believe orthodox theology and do not live righteously, John states, the regeneration of those people should be doubted, for their life shows that they are still a child of the devil.

The saying in 1 John 4:7-8 is in a similar context. This verse begins a series of sayings that culminates in 1 John 4:21, "Whoever loves God must also love his brother." The upshot of the discussion is that those claiming to love God and not loving their brothers are liars. They do not really love God. In other words, in each of these three cases the point of the saying is to distinguish genuine professing Christians from those who are not genuine. One way to do this is through looking at their behavior.

The author of the Johannine literature is quite clear. No one is born of God if that person is not committed to Jesus as Lord. That this commitment includes orthodox belief is clear in 2 John 9 and 1 John 2:22-23, 3:23 and 4:3. But that the commitment also includes living in obedience to Jesus is clear in the passages we have been studying. In fact, there are three tests of Christian faith in 1 John (and if 2 and 3 John are cover letters for 1 John, also implied in them). One is the experience of the Spirit. But how does one know it is the right Spirit a person is experiencing? The answer is, It must be the Spirit that leads one into commitment to Jesus as being the Christ and truly incarnate; in other words, right doctrine. But can one have right doctrine without being born again? Yes, one can. This is true. Therefore the third element comes in, which is a right character or a life that shows obedience to the Father and the Son. This fruit of the Spirit shows that the life of God is really within a person. To the extent to which any one of these three is missing, one should be uncertain about the reality of the new birth. Where all three are present, there should be no doubt but that one is truly a child of God. Therefore to isolate one of these elements and make it absolute (in our example, to isolate right character) is to violate the whole fabric of John's argument. It is not one element alone that proves that one is born of God, but three of them together.

Our verse, then, does not in any way argue that a non-Christian who shows the characteristics of Christian living is therefore born of God—such a person still lacks two of the three marks of a true child of God. What it does say is that those who claim to be Christian should be doubted, despite their orthodox theology, if they fail to live righteously. At the best, such people need to come to repentance before they themselves should be certain of their salvation. At the worst, they are a wolf in sheep's clothing or a "still-birth" in terms of faith, and need to be recognized as such and made subjects of evangelism, not accepted as true members of the body of Christ.

• CHAPTER 58 •

Are the Pseudepigrapha Canonical?

*But even the archangel Michael, when he was disputing
with the devil about the body of Moses, did not dare to bring
a slanderous accusation against him. . . . Enoch, the seventh
from Adam, prophesied about these men.*
JUDE 9, 14-15

One can search the Old Testament from one end to the other and no-where find a prophecy of Enoch. Likewise, the archangel Michael is mentioned in the Old Testament (Dan 10:13), but not in connection with Moses. Nor do we ever hear of a dispute with anybody about Moses' body. When we know this and read Jude 9 and Jude 14-15, it becomes obvious that Jude has sources outside of the canonical Old Testament. What are these sources? Are they canonical? Did Jude think of them as canonical? And what does Jude's use of them mean for our concept of Scripture or canon?

The first question is easier to answer than the others. First, the reference to Michael is probably from a pseudepigraphal work known as the Assumption of Moses or the Testament of Moses, also used by Jude in verse 16. This first-century work is extant today, but the problem is that the ending, which should contain this passage, is missing. However, the church fathers agree that this was Jude's source and a number of Jewish traditions that parallel it enable us to reconstruct the essence of this ending as follows: After the death of Moses the archangel Michael was sent to bury the body. Satan came and argued that Moses was not worthy of a decent burial, for he was a murderer, having killed an Egyptian and hidden him in the sand. Michael's response, "The LORD rebuke you" (a phrase from Zech 3:2), was here, as in Zechariah, a call for God's commanding word, which would assert his authority over Satan.

Second, the prophecy of Enoch is more easily identified, for it comes from 1 Enoch 1:9. While 1 Enoch was probably not in its final form when Jude wrote his letter, it is clear from his citation that at least the first part of the book was finished. This first section also contains the tradition of the imprisonment of the "sons of God" (called "Watchers" in 1 Enoch) from Genesis 6:1-4, which is referred to in Jude 6; 2 Peter 2:4, 9; and 1 Peter 3:19-20. It appears that these stories were favorites in the churches that 1 and 2 Peter and Jude represent.

The other questions are difficult because we find these few references to pseudepigraphal works in such short biblical books. Clearly Jude parallels the prophecy of Enoch with the words of the apostles (v. 17); likewise the story of Michael and Satan is not differentiated from the biblical stories he cites in verse 11. Jude (and probably 2 Peter, which refers to both of these topics but does not use direct references) obviously considers these stories true and authoritative. In fact, in labeling the 1 Enoch reference "prophecy," Jude appears to recognize it as divinely inspired, for he certainly would not cite a prophecy that he believed was not from God. This much is clear.

But did Jude recognize the *books* these stories come from as canonical, or did he just cite the stories themselves as authoritative? That question is impossible to answer. We have no evidence that anyone in the New Testament period, Jew or Christian, wanted to include these works within the Old Testament collection used in the synagogue (or church), although the Apocrypha was bound into biblical codices as early as the fourth century.[1] But the issue of what should or should not be in the canon of Scripture was not being asked in the church at the time Jude was writing. Even the Jewish debates about canon between A.D. 70 and 90 were not over issues that we would consider central to the canonical debate. This, of course, is the reason that Jude can make these citations so casually. He did not have to deal with our post-Reformation questions of canon.

What we can say is that Jude did consider the Old Testament authoritative. He also considered authoritative at least two pseudepigraphal writings and the tradition of the apostles (in whatever form he had it, written or oral). Even though he only uses two brief citations from these works, his failure to differentiate them from the Scripture he does cite indicates that in his mind there was probably no distinction to be made. Nor does he inform us that only these two passages are to be trusted, and the rest of the books rejected. However, all of this information we gain by "reading between the lines" in Jude. He does not say anything directly about our issue. While the later church did not believe that any of the pseudepigrapha were inspired Scripture, it did accept Jude with its use of them. In other words, it did not endorse whatever views Jude may have had about the works from which he took these citations, but it did endorse the explicit teaching in his letter.

This is not a clean and neat answer to our question, but no such answer is possible. First-century Jews used the Old Testament, but alongside it various Jewish groups read and valued a number of types of supplementary literature, ranging from the Apocrypha to the Dead Sea Scrolls to the pseudepigrapha. Early Christians likewise valued the Old Testament and gradually acquired collections of gospels and letters as they were produced and gathered. But they also read many of the works in the Apocrypha and other Christian literature such as the Epistle of Barnabas and the Shepherd of Hermas, binding many of these works into their Bibles as such codices began to replace scrolls. The situation was relatively fluid and imprecise. Only as the challenge of heresy forced the church to decide which books should be read in church and which should not were the lines begun to be drawn more clearly. Jude was written long before this time. It is therefore wrong to expect in him the precision of the later distinctions. It is also wrong to look at his casual use of what was being read in his church and assume that he meant to equate these works with Scripture in the sense that we use the term. Rather, we need to accept him on his own terms, but also to accept that the Holy Spirit through the church has given God's people increasing clear direction about what bears his full imprimatur and what does not.

Finally, this brings us to an issue in biblical interpretation. What is considered authoritative or inspired in a biblical author is what they intended to communicate or teach, as that can be determined from the text. Often we can discover information that the author accidentally gives us about what he believed, the social class he came from, or the way his church assembled. While this is interesting information and may give us background that helps us understand what the author means by what he does intend to communicate, it is not in itself inspired. It may form a historical precedent for how a church or person might live or might believe, but it is not normative. If Jude accidentally reveals that he saw 1 Enoch on a par with Scripture, that is interesting, but since it is certainly not in the least his intention to give us that information (in fact, he was totally unaware it would even interest us) it does not form part of the teaching of Scripture. The same can be said about the meeting of churches in houses in Acts or the indication in 1 Corinthians 15:52 that Paul at that time believed he would be alive when Christ returned. As interesting as this is, it should not form the topic for a sermon or the basis for a doctrine. It does provide information about the history of the early church and examples of what might be legitimate today, but it is not normative. Once we master this distinction, we will realize that the incredible wealth of information that can be gathered from Scripture (which makes it come to life as we see the writers as real people in a real culture) must not obscure the message from God that these men wished to communicate to their generation and that we believe is still a message for us today.[2]

Notes

[1]The Apocrypha are the books and additions to books written during the intertestamental period that are found in the Roman Catholic canon, but considered at best semicanonical in Protestant traditions. The pseudepigrapha are Jewish works, mostly from the period of 100 B.C. to A.D. 100, which no modern Christian group has included in their canon. Examples of Apocrypha include 1 and 2 Maccabees, Tobit, Judith, Wisdom of Solomon, and Sirach, while 1 Enoch, Assumption of Moses, Testaments of the Twelve Patriarchs, and Jubilees are examples of pseudepigrapha.

[2]For more information on this distinction, see Gordon D. Fee and Douglas Stuart, *How to Read the Bible for All Its Worth* (Grand Rapids, Mich.: Zondervan, 1982), especially chapter six.

· C H A P T E R 5 9 ·

Where
Does Satan
Live?

I know where you live—where Satan has his throne.
Yet you remain true to my name. You did not renounce your faith in me,
even in the days of Antipas, my faithful witness, who was put
to death in your city—where Satan lives.
REVELATION 2:13

I once lived next to a man who was reputed to have been quite a street fighter and a member of the Mafia. I had no problems (in fact, for his own reasons he was quite protective toward my family), but other folk might not have wanted to live on his street. Yet how would I have felt had the house been occupied by Satan? I am not sure I would have wanted to live in the same city! Revelation 2:13 raises this issue, although it was written to the church in the city of Pergamum in Asia Minor. To us it seems a little strange, for it mentions that Satan had his "throne" in that very city. Since we are accustomed to thinking about Satan as traveling everywhere in the world (Job 1:7; 2:2), we wonder, is there really a locality in which Satan himself lives? Does Satan have an actual throne? And is it visible?

Should this affect our own decisions on our place of residence? How did this church experience what John is writing about? What should this mean for us?

On the one hand, it is clear that Satan, as a finite being, must have a localized existence. Unlike God, he is not omnipresent, so he must be somewhere (and not be everywhere) at any given point in time. But Satan is also a spiritual being, probably the one identified in Ephesians 2:2 as the "ruler of the kingdom of the air." This means that he does not appear to be physically localized in our material sense, but rather lives in the spiritual world (or heavenlies) through which he has access to the physical world. Although we do not fully understand the relationship of the spiritual to the physical, we would be surprised to discover that Satan had limited himself to a specific physical locality by setting up his throne in a given city. Indeed, what we find elsewhere in Revelation is that when he rules on earth he does so through a human being whom he controls (see Rev 13:2).

On the other hand, Pergamum is a place known to us from history. It was an independent city until 133 B.C., when its last king willed it to Rome. It thereafter became the capital city of Roman Asia, the seat of the proconsul who as the senatorial governor of the province had an almost unlimited power for the period of his office. By 29 B.C. the city had become the center of the imperial cult with a temple erected to "the divine Augustus and the goddess Roma." The city also had a great temple to Zeus Soter (Savior Zeus), and its citizens worshiped the serpent god Asclepius, who was the god of healing. This history gives a rich background for identifying the city with Satan.

Any of the images we have mentioned would have served Satan well. Asclepius as a serpent (found on the coat of arms of the city and used as a symbol of medicine today) would remind one of Satan as the serpent and dragon in Revelation. The altar of Zeus was said to have been thronelike, the temple dominating the city. He was, after all, the king of the Greek gods. But the central image in our passage appears to have been that of Roman rule.

The key to this identification is the reference to Antipas, a Christian martyr. Given that the proconsul did have the power to put people to death, this probably indicates official persecution (although it may have been localized). Where else but at the center of imperial rule would the church be more likely to come into direct conflict with Rome? Imperial rule was not separated from imperial cult. While educated people did not take the cult seriously—they looked upon it as a patriotic ceremony, much as pledging allegiance to the flag is seen in the USA today—the church saw in it a clash between the call of Christians to worship God alone and the demand of the state to have one's ultimate allegiance. What is more, the state always kept a watchful eye on unsanctioned societies. The growth of the Christian community and its influence in the lower classes, especially among slaves (who had been known to revolt in Rome itself), was threatening. Here was a group who called Jesus, not Caesar, Lord, a group that could not be controlled. The clash was inevitable. Antipas had been martyred. And in the aftermath of his martyrdom the church must have lived in fear, for they were located in the very seat of Roman power and could hardly escape the notice of Rome.

This throne of Caesar, then, is the throne of Satan. Satan is not identified with Rome totally; he is independent of all of his tools. But in Revelation 13 it is Roman rulers through whom Satan works. The Roman state was the most powerful state of that day. Like all of the kingdoms of human beings, it was under the control of Satan (see Lk 4:5-6, in which Jesus does not dispute this claim on the part of Satan). The seat of Roman power, then, is in this sense the throne of Satan. It is the means through which Satan rules and controls that area, in this case Asia Minor. It is therefore also the means through which he persecutes the church of God.

The relevance of this passage to Christians today is obvious. While there may not be any recent martyrs in some Christian localities, many, if not most, Christians live under governments that claim absolute allegiance ("My country, right or wrong."). John reminds us that all such claims fly in the face of absolute obedience to Christ. They are satanic in origin. To the extent that the country decides to enforce its claim, either ceremonially or in action, a clash with a faithful church is inevitable. The closer one is to the center of government, the more certain the clash and the more inescapable the consequences. As Satan's throne appears behind whatever the architectural façade of our capital may be, the Christian will be forced to decide whom he or she serves. John lets us know that the decision is difficult, but he is encouraging us to be faithful, even if it means following in the footsteps of Antipas.[2]

A secondary application is also probable. Paul speaks eight times of "principalities and powers," which are part of the demonic hierarchy of Satan's kingdom (see Eph 6:12). Some such forces are on occasion identified with a particular people or land (see Dan 10:13). Thus, some demonic spirits appear to be localized, an idea that is confirmed by the experience of many Christian workers.[3] This means that some areas may be more directly under the control of such powerful beings than are others, or that the being that controls a given area may himself be more powerful than the one controlling another area. Paul lists various articles of armor with which Christians are armed for battle with such beings (Eph 6:13-18). He does not mention direct prayer against them (such as "binding them" or "casting them out"), but rather exemplary Christian faith and conduct, such as the conduct that probably got Antipas in trouble and the faith that sustained him through his martyrdom.[4]

If this analysis is accurate, then some Christians should recognize that they live in very difficult territory. Such a recognition is not a call to move, but an acknowledgment that the situation they face is tougher than normal and therefore the virtues they must arm themselves with are more than normal. At the same time, this verse reminds us that Christ is in total control of these powers. Even our martyrdom is under his control. Although our area of the battle may be tough, there is no danger of losing. The important thing is that we, like the believers in Pergamum, hold out and remain faithful, even in the face of death itself.

Notes

[1]A. Deissmann, *Light from the Ancient East* (Grand Rapids, Mich.: Baker Book House, 1978), p. 109.

[2]An encouragement in this direction is found in John White's excellent

Magnificent Obsession (Downers Grove, Ill.: InterVarsity Press, 1990).

[3]See C. Peter Wagner, "Territorial Spirits," in C. Peter Wagner and F. Douglas Pennoyer, eds., *Wrestling with Dark Angels* (Ventura, Calif.: Regal Books, 1990), pp. 73-100, for one description of this phenomena.

[4]This does not imply that Christians are never called upon to pray directly against such beings, but that such activity is not their normal occupation; it should be engaged in only at the direct command of God.

• CHAPTER 60 •

Who Were the Nicolaitans?

But you have this in your favor:
You hate the practices of the Nicolaitans,
which I also hate. . . . Likewise you also have those
who hold to the teaching of the Nicolaitans.
REVELATION 2:6, 15

Revelation has many strange symbols and images, but there are also unusual names. In Revelation 2:6, 15, the unfamiliar name blocks understanding. Here in two verses in letters written to two different churches (Ephesus and Pergamum) we discover the Nicolaitans. Who in the world were they? Presumably the author believed that the readers of the letters would know, but we are not in their same position. What were their practices? Why would God hate those deeds? Until we understand this, the criticism of these people will remain a total mystery to us. We might even be doing the very same things without knowing it.

The earliest identification of the Nicolaitans, found in the church fathers, was as followers of Nicolas of Antioch, a proselyte to Judaism, who was one of the Seven (Acts 6:5). Unfortunately, none of the writers seems to know much about the heresy, and one, in fact, argues that Nicolas himself was orthodox but had been misunderstood. While it is possible that some of this information is accurate (there have been Spirit-filled church leaders who have lapsed into heresy), this looks like an attempt to find some name in Scripture to use to identify this sect. Nicolas may have simply had the misfortune of bearing the wrong name. Still, even if the Nicolas of Acts had nothing to do with the movement, it is probable that some Nicolas was the leader of the group (after all, Nicolas was a reasonably common name).

A second identification common in some theological circles is to look at the Greek etymology of "Nicolaitan" (nikan and laos meaning respectively "conquer" and "people") and argue that this was a group that suppressed the laity in favor of the developing clergy. However, this explanation is determined more by modern concepts of clergy and laity than by any first-century information, for such terminology (such as the use of laos for only a section of the church) was unknown this early. Etymology is a notoriously dangerous way to discover the meaning of a term. We need only observe English terms such as "awful" (which does not mean "full of awe") to learn this lesson. Furthermore, there is nothing in the text to support this meaning.

The clue to the real meaning of this term is found in the identification of the Nicolaitans with "the teaching of Balaam" in Revelation 2:14-15. Not only is it possible that "Nikolaitan" is a Greek form of "Balaam" (as understood by the rabbis) but, more important, this interpretation fits both the text and the first-century situation.

John identifies the teaching of Balaam with two problems: "eating food sacrificed to idols" and "sexual immorality." The early church constantly struggled with compromises with paganism, as we see in Paul's long discussion in 1 Corinthians 8—10, as well as in the conclusions reached in Acts 15:20, 29. Both of these center on food offered to idols, Paul's conclusion being that one could eat such food if purchased in the marketplace, but one should not go to a meal in a pagan temple. Following this Pauline rule, however, would cut one off from membership in trade guilds, patriotic celebrations (including ceremonies honoring the emperor, considered essential to good citizenship, although not taken seriously by the upper classes as religious events) and many family celebrations. We can easily see the pressure to rationalize and thereby develop a compromise.

The issue of sexual immorality is more difficult, for it is also mentioned in Revelation 2:20, 22, in the case of Jezebel (an Old Testament code word for a New Testament woman leader of the church in Thyatira, indicating her spirit and God's evaluation, rather than the woman's actual name). On the one hand, sexual immorality was a problem in the early church, as Paul's discussions show (1 Cor 5:1; 6:12-20; compare Heb 13:4). In the middle of a pagan society that accepted the use of prostitutes (although wives were expected to remain faithful), it was difficult to remain obedient on this point and relatively easy to compromise. On the other hand, "sexual immorality" was used in the Old Testament for involvement with pagan deities. For example, the Old Testament Jezebel was not to our knowledge physically immoral—she was likely faithful to Ahab all her life—but she did lead Israel into Baal worship. Since Israel was God's "bride," such involvement with other gods was called "adultery" or "sexual immorality."

Furthermore, the line between the two meanings of "immorality" was difficult to draw. Sexual immorality was involved in the Peor incident (connected to Balaam, Num 25:1-18), but the act of sexual intercourse itself with the women broke no known Old Testament law. Old Testament law did not prohibit a man from intercourse with a prostitute, only from intercourse with a married woman who was not his wife. The issue at Peor was that the women were Moabite or Middianite, pagan women, and the women in turn led the men to eat feasts associated with their gods and then to worship the gods themselves. In other words, the sexual immorality was wrong because it was associated with the worship of other gods, a commonplace in the pagan world in which many temples had prostitutes in them through whom a man could become "joined" to the god.

If, then, John is taking the Old Testament examples as the basis for his discussion, the sexual immorality is figurative, standing for their worship of other deities, which was implied in their attending feasts in idol temples. If, on the other hand, he is using the Old Testament examples loosely, he may be indicating two related problems, attending feasts in idol temples and engaging in extramarital sexual intercourse, probably with prostitutes. The difference between the two explanations is narrow. Both types of problems are condemned elsewhere in the New Testament, however one may interpret this particular passage.

The Nicolaitans, then, appear to be a group that corrupted God's people by suggesting compromise with the culture of the day. Rather than worship God and him alone, they suggested that it was appropriate to engage in patriotic ceremonies (such as feasts associated with the worship of the emperor) and other cultural institutions (for example, trade guilds, something like our modern unions or professional associations, and their worship). It is possible that either as part of these ceremonies or as a separate area of compromise they also permitted the use of prostitutes (perhaps as an accepted part of the "business ethic" of their day). Jesus (who is speaking through John) was not impressed. In fact, he threatened judgment on the church.

While the exact issues are different, similar compromises face the church today. Each society has its own "idols" that it expects all its citizens to worship, whether those idols be the government itself or some values or practices of the society, whether concretized as physical idols or not. These "idols" are the places at which the values of the society conflict with total allegiance to Christ. Furthermore, the Nicolaitans are still with us under a variety of names, for there are always people who in the name of being "realistic" or under any number of other theological justifications counsel compromise with the dominant culture. This passage warns us that Jesus will not "buy" these justifications. He demands nothing less than total loyalty to his own person and directions. Anything less than this will put those who compromise in danger of his judgment.

Who Are the 144,000?

*I heard the number of those
who were sealed: 144,000 from
all the tribes of Israel.*
REVELATION 7:4

T*he doorbell rings on a Saturday morning and two people stand on our* porch offering literature about the return of Christ. If questioned, they might reveal that they are Jehovah's Witnesses. Their motives for their door-to-door activity are not simply to gain converts for the movement, but rather to gain merit for themselves through their exemplary zeal. Their hope (faint though it may be, given the number of Witnesses worldwide) might be to become one of the 144,000 of Revelation, who will reign with Christ. While there are certainly a number of more important places at which orthodox Christians would take issue with these Witnesses in terms of doctrine, what they say about the 144,000 remains troubling, not because it is believed, but because we ourselves do not know what this number means. Who in the world are these people? What relevancy does this number have to the church today? Is there any legitimacy to the Witness claim?

The problem with this number is that it is clearly symbolic, but saying that does not thereby solve the issue. The question remains, Symbolic for what? Three major scholarly options have been given. The first is that this figure is symbolic for a group of Jews whom God will redeem at the end of the age. The second is that this is symbolic for a group of martyrs whom God preserves for martyrdom. The third is that this number is symbolic for the whole of the church, which God will protect through the tribulation at the end of the age. Only an examination of the data will show which of these is most likely to be correct.

John's picture draws on two Old Testament images. The first is that of Passover (Ex 12:12-13), during which the blood on the doorposts of the Hebrews' homes was a sign protecting them from the judgment that the Egyptians were receiving. The significant elements in Exodus are that the world around the Hebrews was experiencing judgment and a God-given sign protected the people of God from this judgment. The second Old Testament image is that of Ezekiel's man with an ink horn (Ezek 9). Again, the context is one of judgment. Again the people true to God are marked to be spared. In this case "a man clothed with linen who had a writing kit at his side" goes through the city and marks a Hebrew *tāw*, which in those days was an X or a +, on the forehead of each person faithful to God.

There may also be a New Testament background for John's picture. In 2 Corinthians 1:22; Ephesians 1:13 and 4:30, Paul writes that Christians are sealed with the Holy Spirit. While the Spirit is not said to protect believers from anything, the image is one of security. Likewise, "the Lord knows those who are his" stands as a seal in 2 Timothy 2:19. While there is no evidence that John had read any of these books, the fact that Paul used sealing language implies that it was used around the church before John wrote.

In the picture in Revelation 7 the judgment of God announced in Revelation 6 is held back until the sealing is complete. The sealed are identified as "the servants of our God." The image is that of Ezekiel, both in the placement of the seal on the forehead and in the idea of only a remnant (in Ezekiel a remnant of Israel) being sealed from the judgment. This theme is picked up again in Revelation 9:4 in the fifth of the trumpet judgments, in which the "locusts" are to hurt only those "who did not have the seal of God on their foreheads." The sealed are protected in the midst of judgment all around them.

In Revelation 14 the 144,000 are "the 144,000 who had been redeemed from the earth." They are described as celibate virgins, which in Revelation means that they have not been seduced by the forces of evil nor made a compromise with idolatry. They are also totally truthful. "They were purchased from among men and offered as firstfruits to God and the Lamb" (v. 4). The firstfruit picture appears in James 1:18 for all Christians in relation to the world and in Romans 11:16 for gentile believers in relation to the full repentance of Israel.

Who are these 144,000, then? The theory that they are the martyrs of the last days is attractive, but in the end unconvincing because nothing is said in these passages of their being martyrs. Instead it appears that *all* of the "servants of God" are sealed. These "servants" are part of a larger group that is not serving God. That many of these folk might become martyrs is reasonable, given the persecution described in Revelation 13, but John says nothing to make us think that they are exclusively martyrs.

The theory that they are the Jewish believers of the end time is also attractive since the tribes of Israel are named. However, there are also problems here. Both the order of the tribal list and the names included are unusual. For example, both Manasseh and his father, Joseph, are included (Joseph apparently standing for Ephraim). Dan is missing, although he is present in Ezekiel's end time list (chap. 48). Thus John appears to indicate that the list stands for something other than any known form of Israel. Yet another problem is that most of "Israel" is not saved (that is, is not in the 144,000), while Paul's expectation (Rom 11:26) is that "all Israel will be saved." If both John and Paul have versions of Christian expectation about the Jews, there must have been two competing expectations in the early church. Finally, in Revelation 7 these folk are called simply the "servants of God," which is not a term unique to Jewish believers. Likewise the description of them in Revelation 14 could fit any believer who is faithful to God and does not compromise with the "beast" and the "false prophet." In Revelation 9 all who are not sealed are tormented. Does this mean that Gentile believers are tormented while Jewish ones are not? And doesn't a Jew-Gentile distinction *within the church* run counter to all of Paul's arguments about God's breaking down the walls between the races? These reasons persuade me that this cannot be the correct explanation.

The 144,000, then, stand for God's faithful people, Jew or Gentile. They are, just as the text says, "the servants of our God." The image of Israel is probably drawn from the picture in Ezekiel 9. Just as all of the tribes of Israel present in Jerusalem (the last stand of Judaism before the Exile) were included then, so all of the tribes of humanity will be included in the end. The 12 × 12 × 1000 stresses the completeness of this number; all of God's servants from all of humanity are sealed. The purpose of their sealing is not to protect them from temptation or martyrdom, but from the judgment of God. This is God's church of the end times, when God's judgment is coming to a peak. Since they are faithful, there is no reason for judgment to fall upon them. In Revelation 7 the image of the 144,000 protected on earth is coupled with a parallel image of the church in heaven, an encouragement to persevere. In Revelation 14 the 144,000 are in heaven, for in the same chapter is the harvest of the earth. The final judgments, which will destroy everything and everyone in their path, are about to begin. No wonder that the church is withdrawn before that final curtain comes down.

What does this image say to the church today? On the assumption that we live in the last days (which in New Testament thought runs from the time of Christ to the end), our Jehovah's Witness friends are right to wish to be numbered in the 144,000. The sad thing is that they are going about it the wrong way. It is not a limited number to which one gains entrance by merit, but the complete number of God's faithful servants. One is counted in that number if he or she does not compromise the faith by going after the idols of the world and does not live in falsehood, but speaks and lives in truth. Another way of putting it is that "they follow the Lamb wherever he goes" (Rev 14:4). In the context of Revelation this means that they follow him in heaven (and perhaps in his conquest of earth in Rev 19), but they do so in heaven because they have already been his followers on earth, whatever the cost. Our Witness friends want to be followers of Jehovah without becoming equally followers of the Lamb and seeing his death as the only means of removing sin. While their zeal and commitment is commendable, without following the Lamb they will never become part of his "144,000" protected followers.

· C H A P T E R   6 2 ·

What
Is the
Abyss?

The fifth angel sounded his trumpet,
and I saw a star that had fallen from the sky
to the earth. The star was given the key
to the shaft of the Abyss.
REVELATION 9:1

Modern fantasy, whether in book, movie, or game form, is full of great
pits and bottomless places; we wonder at times if this has invaded
the Bible. A basis for such a claim is one of the places referred to
in Revelation as "the Abyss." It does not seem to correspond to
anything, such as heaven and hell, in standard church vocabulary.
What does this term mean? How can the modern Scripture reader
relate to a concept that seems more like the stuff of a horror movie
than of reality? From where did John get this term?

The term "Abyss" occurs nine times in five different passages in
the New Testament. In Luke 8:31 it is the place to which demons
do not wish to be sent. In Romans 10:7 it is translated "the deep"
and is the opposite of heaven, the one being above the earth and

the other below. In Revelation 9:1-2 the "shaft [or well or pit] of the Abyss" is opened. In Revelation 11:7 there is a "beast that comes up from the Abyss." And finally in Revelation 20:1-3 Satan is chained and thrown into the Abyss for 1000 years, the shaft being locked and sealed over him. This is the New Testament data that we have to work with.

The Greek translation of the Old Testament uses "Abyss" to translate "the deep" (Gen 1:2; Pss 42:7; 107:26) and "the depths of the earth" (Ps 71:20). In the first group of passages it refers to the deep seas or primeval deep from which solid ground is separated and which in some Hebrew cosmologies lie under the earth. In the second passage it refers to the place of the dead. These probably give us the background of Romans 10:7 (either the place of the dead into which no living person can go or the deep as opposed to the heights of heaven), but they do not help us with Revelation.

In the intertestamental literature we discover what a first-century Jew like the author of Revelation thought of when he wrote "the Abyss." In 1 Enoch 10:4 a rebellious angel is bound and cast into darkness in a hole. This hole seems to be distinguished from the final place of judgment, a place of fire mentioned in 1 Enoch 18:11 and 21:7, although this is also a pit. Likewise in Jubilees 5:6-11 the fallen angels are bound in a pit. With this background we can now understand John's image.

The Abyss is apparently the prison of demons and fallen angelic beings (some Jews believed demons were fallen angels, while others distinguished them as being their offspring). This explains the fear of the demons in Luke 8:31. They wanted to remain free, not be placed in prison. Jesus apparently allows them freedom because the time of judgment has not yet arrived. Likewise it explains why Satan is imprisoned in the Abyss, for it is the standard place to imprison such beings.

Yet the Abyss can be opened. In Revelation 9 it is opened to let out what are apparently demonic beings to torment people. These beings are not unorganized, but have "as king over them the angel of the Abyss, whose name in Hebrew is Abaddon, and in Greek, Apollyon" (Rev 9:11). The name means "destroyer" in either language. The identity of this ruler is unclear. Is he an angel, perhaps the one who opens the pit and then is sent to control the host he allows out? John normally uses "angel" for one of those loyal to God; there is also plenty of evidence in Scripture to accept the idea of a destroying angel. Or is he one of the host allowed out, himself a fallen angel or demon? The evidence is fairly well balanced, but given John's use of the term "angel," we suspect that the first suggestion is correct.[1]

Not only do these demonic beings come up out of the Abyss, but "the beast" does as well. Revelation 11 does not explain this being, but given the connection of "the deep" with the sea, John identifies him as the beast "coming out of the sea" in Revelation 13:1, a world ruler who is inspired by Satan himself. This identification is repeated in Revelation 17:8, which combines elements of both the previous passages. In Revelation 11 he fights against God's witnesses, although they are protected by God until the time of their martyrdom.

The Abyss does not appear in the final two chapters of Revelation because it is no longer needed. After Revelation 20 there is no need for a prison. The time of the final judgment has arrived, and both the devil and those belonging to him are cast into their final place of torment, the lake of fire (Rev 20:10).

How should Christians relate to this information? Certainly the images in these passages are fearful. But other elements are at work as well. As previously noted, the witnesses in Revelation 11 are protected until such a time as God allows them to be injured. In all of the passages it is God and his angels who have the keys to the Abyss. Nothing comes out that God does not allow out. The beings that get out are not released to do their own will (although they may think that that is what they are doing), but to serve God's purposes. Finally, in Revelation 9:4 we read that the demonic beings from the Abyss are not allowed to touch those who have "the seal of God on their foreheads." Who are these? They are "the servants of our God" (7:3), who remain faithful to God and the Lamb (14:4-5). These people are not necessarily protected from martyrdom, but they are not able to be tormented or truly injured by the creatures of the pit. God remains in control even of the devil and his hosts. Thus, those who serve God should have no fear of the creatures of the Abyss, but instead should have a concern for others who do not walk under the protection of their Lord. This is an implied call to evangelism and to total faithfulness, even in the face of martyrdom.

Notes

[1]John uses "angel" in Revelation almost as many times as it appears in the whole rest of the New Testament put together. While there is one time when it does refer to fallen angels (Rev. 12:7, 9, the dragon's angels) and one time when it might do so (Rev 9:14-15), the vast majority of the time it refers to God's angels.

· C H A P T E R 6 3 ·

They Will Trample the Holy City for 42 Months

But exclude the outer court; do not measure it,
because it has been given to the Gentiles. They will trample
on the holy city for 42 months. And I will give power to
my two witnesses, and they will prophesy
for 1,260 days, clothed in sackcloth.
REVELATION 11:2-3

Most of us have had to convert between various measuring systems, such as English feet to metric meters. While the numbers may baffle us briefly, conversion charts and formulas help us determine the right values. When this type of problem confronts us in the Bible, we are lost without a way to understand the numbers. In addition to its unusual personages and symbols, Revelation has some numbers that are difficult to decipher. Those in Revelation 11:2-3 are as confusing as anywhere. In fact, they are so confusing that commentators from all positions approach this particular passage with caution, admitting that in the end they are not certain of their identifications. What does it mean for the holy city to be trampled for 42 months? And who are these witnesses who proph-

esy for 1,260 days? How do these periods of time relate? We can
only give tentative answers to these questions.

The context of our passage is the sixth of the series of trumpet
judgments, the penultimate judgments of Revelation. This second
"woe" (the last three of the seven trumpet judgments are called
"woes") blew in Revelation 9:13; its judgment is finished in 11:14.
This last part of the judgment contains both the numbers we mentioned above and the 3.5 days that the witnesses (the main subjects
of this last judgment scene) are to lie dead before their resurrection.
Although the 3.5 days are a separate issue, the other two numbers
are the same, for it does not take much math skill to discover that
42 months equals 3.5 years. Likewise the 1,260 days equals 42
months of 30 days each or 3.5 years of 360 days each. Furthermore,
in Revelation 12:14, which is the end of the next chapter, we discover that "the woman" will be protected for "a time, times, and half
a time," or 3.5 years. Therefore Revelation has three different ways
of referring to the same length of time.

It is clear that this time period is symbolic. In Daniel 7:25 the
fourth beast will oppress the saints of the Most High for "a time,
times, and half a time." The same timing is mentioned in 12:7,
although two other periods of 1,290 (43 months) and 1,335 days
(44.5 months) respectively are mentioned in Daniel 12:11-12. Daniel 8:14 notes a period of 2,300 days (76.7 months or 6 years and
4.7 months) when the "little horn," Antiochus IV Epiphanes, would
suppress Judaism. (This ruler, who deposed the last Zadokite high
priest in 170 B.C. and suppressed sacrifice in Jerusalem from 167
to 164 B.C., is the model for much that happens in Revelation.) John
does not use all of these numbers from Daniel. What he does use
is the 3.5-year period, a period during which there will be oppression and the rule of "the beast," but also the protection of "the
woman" and the activity of "the two witnesses."

When it comes to identifying this period and these individuals
there are three basic schools of thought. One group sees the temple
as a literal rebuilt temple in Jerusalem and the witnesses as two
specific individuals. Given the nature of their miracles, they appear
to be most like Moses and Elijah, the greatest of the Old Testament

prophetic figures. The 3.5 years, then, is also a literal period at the end of the age during what John calls "the great tribulation," when the Antichrist, who will be a world ruler, will oppress the temple worship. The problem with this view is that the oppression excludes the altar and inner court of the temple, which makes it appear to be more a symbolic temple than a literal one. Who would control the outer court of the temple and ignore the inner one?

A second interpretation sees the temple and Jerusalem (where the two witnesses are active) as symbols for the Jewish people. The Antichrist oppresses the Jewish people as a whole in the end of the age for 3.5 years, but the faithful remnant (the worshipers in the inner court) will be protected (perhaps meaning the same thing as the protection of "the woman" in the next chapter). During this period of protection in the middle of the reign of evil, two eschatological personages will witness to the Jewish people (symbolized by Jerusalem), calling them to Christ. This interpretation has the advantage of retaining the sense of literality in the first interpretation, while avoiding the problems it faced in viewing the temple as a literal temple.

A third interpretation sees the temple and Jerusalem as symbols for the church and the world. The inner court is the true worshipers. The outer court is those members of the church who are corrupted by the world (the Nicolaitans and followers of Jezebel; see Rev 2). The holy city (Jerusalem) is the world outside the church. The church is oppressed by evil for a definite period (the 3.5 years normally are interpreted symbolically). Yet during this period witness will go on (the two witnesses being symbols for the witness of the church), although the witness will entail martyrdom. The strength of this position is that it takes seriously John's calling Judaism "the synagogue of Satan" (Rev 2:9; 3:9) and Jerusalem "Sodom and Egypt" (11:8), therefore assuming that John would not be interested in preserving either Judaism or Jewish institutions such as the temple. Furthermore, each of the pictures receives an interpretation from within Revelation. The problem is that in most apocalyptic scenarios (including intertestamental apocalyptic) there are real people and places with which the author is concerned, not simply symbolic groups. This interpretation appears to loose itself from history in any form.

Obviously, we cannot be sure of the interpretation of this passage. Too many good Christian scholars have taken too divergent positions to speak with any dogmatism. But from my point of view the second interpretation appears to fit John's perspective best. In his day the temple was gone and Judaism was oppressed. This, he says, will continue. There will be a period of intense persecution in the end of the age, when the embodiment of evil himself, the Antichrist, will rule (at least in the Roman world). The Jews, symbolized by Jerusalem in chapter 11, will be "trampled down" by this ruler, but a remnant that is faithful to God (the inner court of chap. 11 and perhaps the woman of chap. 12) will be protected. Just as there will be an embodiment of evil, so witness will be embodied in two individuals who will come in the spirit of Moses and Elijah. After 3.5 years they will be martyred, then raised to life. Yet this will lead to a turning of the Jews as a whole to Christ (11:13). It will also happen just before the final end of the age (which, if John is using Daniel's chronology, should happen within two or three months). This interpretation fits with Jesus' predictions about Judaism (Lk 21:24) and the temple (Mk 13:2 and parallels—there is no mention of its rebuilding) and takes the symbols as meaning something concrete.

This, then, is our understanding of what John anticipated in the end of the age. He appears to believe that it would happen within a short time. It did not happen that way during his lifetime, but perhaps we should look at the rapid spread of Christianity within the Roman Empire as a parallel to the repentance of Nineveh in Jonah. It led to the eventual repentance of Rome and perhaps, like in the case of Nineveh, to a putting of the judgment on hold. That is certainly in tune with the desire of God for repentance (rather than judgment) within Revelation. This may move the judgment picture to the end of the age, whenever this may happen to be. Yet will the judgment happen any less concretely or even any differently than John envisioned it 1900 years ago? Only our hindsight from heaven will reveal the truth—and the fully correct interpretation of this verse—which God alone knows.

• C H A P T E R 6 4 •

The Woman and the Dragon

A great and wondrous sign appeared in heaven:
a woman clothed with the sun, with the moon under her
feet and a crown of twelve stars on her head. . . . Then another
sign appeared in heaven: an enormous red dragon with seven
heads and ten horns and seven crowns on his heads.
REVELATION 12:1-3

Dragons are getting popular again in fantasy books and fantasy games. Since the Bible does not belong to the realm of fantasy, it disturbs us to discover them roaming its pages. The pictures presented in Revelation are vivid. The one in Revelation 12:1-3 is part of a set of pictures that serve as a prelude to the final end of the age, since the seventh trumpet, the penultimate judgment, has already blown. Yet what are we to make of this picture? Who is this woman? What is this dragon? How do we interpret such images, which remind us more of Greek mythology than of most Scripture?

John's images are intended to be meaningful, but at the same time he uses images because they can also be fluid. Both the woman and the dragon have a fluidity about them that allows them to be useful to our author.

First, we look at the woman. There are two women in this section of Revelation. The first is this woman, God's woman. The second is the woman of chapter 17, a prostitute. The opposition reminds us of the two women of Proverbs 1—10, the one lady wisdom and the other the loose woman. Here the first woman is clothed with heavenly glory, the sun, with the moon being under her feet. The second woman is clothed in "purple and scarlet," colors of earthly emperors. The first woman has twelve stars for a crown. The second woman has gold and jewels. The first woman gives birth, but the second woman appears sterile. There is a contrast in every way.

We recognize that the second woman is Rome; is the first woman Jerusalem? There have been several answers to that question. Some scholars point to the twelve stars and argue the parallel to twelve patriarchs. Indeed, the whole picture, including the sun and the moon, reminds us of Joseph's dream (Gen 37:9). Other scholars look at the incident of the birth of the child and claim that the woman is Mary. Still others point out that the sign appears in heaven, so this must be some idealization of the people of God, God's true bride. I do not see that one must choose among these interpretations. Jewish thought often oscillates between the one and the many. For example, in the servant songs of the second part of Isaiah the servant is sometimes Israel (Is 49:3) and sometimes an individual (49:5), and in Daniel the Son of man (7:13-14) and "the saints of the Most High" (7:18) also alternate. So in our image the woman is God's people, the faithful of Israel. The woman is also Mary, who individualized that faithful group in giving birth to the Messiah.

In the second part of the chapter the image of the woman shifts, for she is persecuted. Is she still the faithful in Israel? Or is she now the wider people of God, Jew as well as Gentile? Certainly in her flight to the wilderness we are reminded of Jesus' words (Mk 13:14; Lk 21:21), which the Jewish-Christian church acted upon just before A.D. 70. Does it then mean that God will protect a Jewish-Christian group? Or should we remember his words in Matthew 16:18 that "the gates of Hades" would not overcome his church, therefore interpreting this as a reference to his whole church? Perhaps the correct answer is Both. The image is that of the flight of Israel from Pharaoh into the wilderness and the flight of the church from Jerusalem in the A.D. 66-70 war. This shows that God will care for and protect his church, specifically during the time when the forces of evil reign apparently triumphant, the 1,260 days. All of the lies and demonic forces that the dragon can spit out cannot destroy this church. But at the same time the dragon makes war with the woman's children, the Christians. So while the church as a whole is protected and cannot be stamped out, Christians as individuals will experience the anger of Satan, even martyrdom.

Second, then, we have the dragon. This image is drawn from Old Testament pictures of Leviathan, the many-headed sea monster (Ps 74:13-14). The monster is sometimes mythological in the sense that he is not identified with any historical embodiment, and sometimes a specific enemy of God's people, such as Egypt (Ps 74:14; Ezek 29:3) or Assyria (Is 27:1). This picture was mediated to John via Daniel, who describes a fourth beast with ten horns (7:7). John, of course, makes very clear about whom he believes Daniel is talking (or in terms of whom he is reinterpreting Daniel), for he writes in Revelation 12:9, "The great dragon was hurled down—that ancient serpent called the devil, or Satan, who leads the whole world astray." Yet this dragon also has an earthly embodiment. The "beast coming out of the sea" (Rev 13:1) has seven heads and ten horns like the dragon, as does the beast the great prostitute rides (17:3). And as the prostitute parodied the woman clothed in the sun, so the dragon parodies someone else. Revelation 12:3 notes that he has seven crowns, while in Revelation 19:12 the "King of kings and Lord of lords" has many crowns on his head.

The dragon naturally tried to destroy Christ, the child in our story. John is not interested at this point in the life and death of Christ, but moves from his birth to his ascension. However, we must remember than in his Gospel the "lifting up" of the Son of man is both cross and ascension, so this does not mean that the cross is absent from his thought.

John's concern is with the war of the dragon against God's people.

The war has two phases, a heavenly and an earthly. The heavenly phase is fought by Michael, "the great prince who protects your [that is, Daniel's] people" (Dan 12:1), and his angels. The dragon has swept one-third of the angels with him in his fall, so he also has angels to fight with. But he is the loser. Even though God never appears on the scene but fights through his angels, the victory is secured. Satan loses his access to heaven. When does John see this as happening? Although some scholars refer this to the original fall of Satan, it probably happens at the end of the age, for it happens after the child is caught up to heaven. Furthermore, there is plenty of Jewish testimony to the idea of Satan's having access to heaven during world history.

There is also a battle on earth. The human beings apparently do not see their foe. Yet they defeat the devil. In fact, the outcome of the war in heaven appears to be parallel to that on earth, just as Daniel's prayers in chapter 10 appear to be parallel to a battle going on in the spiritual realm, a battle Daniel knows nothing about until he is informed. In Revelation the human beings win, not because of their strength and wisdom, but because of their trust in "the blood of the Lamb" and their open confession of their faith in him. They were so firm in this trust and confession that "they did not love their lives so much as to shrink from death" (12:11). The devil could make martyrs, but each martyr was the devil's own defeat. The martyr was safe with God in heaven; the devil's power over the person had crumbled. In other words, the primary means of spiritual warfare is commitment to God and his redemption in Christ, a commitment so openly confessed and so radical that even death will not shake one from it.

This battle is fought throughout the Christian age, but it is most intense at the end of the age. In this period of 42 months the devil is fully aware that he has lost, both in heaven and on earth. Now he just wishes to destroy, to "make war" against "those who obey God's commandments and hold to the testimony of Jesus." The reason John is writing this picture is so that such people will hold on until martyrdom or the end of the age.

Like all of his apocalyptic pictures, this one is not intended to

scare Christians. It does portray them as characters in an eschatological battle of gigantic proportions, but at the same time it portrays the limitations of the devil himself, not to mention his angels,
and his final end. Furthermore, it portrays the protection of God
over his saints, as well as his eventual victory. This is designed to
encourage the Christian to stand fast, whether he or she is living
in the ongoing struggle of the Christian age or in the intense struggle of the final phase of that time. Dragons may be the stuff of
fantasy, but in this case the fantasy is real, even if hidden in the
spiritual realm, and the stakes are high. Yet the outcome is sure for
those who remain firm in their commitment to Christ.

• C H A P T E R 6 5 •

They Overcame
Him by the Blood
of the Lamb

*They overcame him by the blood of the Lamb and by the
word of their testimony; they did not love their
lives so much as to shrink from death.*
REVELATION 12:11

Our acquaintance with video games and fantasy may prepare us for the use of some strange weapons in warfare, but Revelation 12:11 has some of the strangest ones, even given the context of fantasy. In our previous chapter we more or less assumed the discussion in this chapter, but it is important that we take a careful look at what is going on here. When we read about overcoming Satan by "the blood of the Lamb," don't we wonder how this is done? Blood is an exceedingly strange weapon. The blood is not a physical entity that can be used in a battle, is it? Furthermore, is the testimony given to Satan? Who does receive it? And how does testimony function as a weapon? It isn't a type of curse or magic, is it? And while we may understand the usefulness of the courage implied in not loving one's life, how can these other things be weapons in a spiritual battle?

In the previous chapter we observed the context for this verse. There has been a war in heaven between the devil and his angels and the archangel Michael and his angels. Michael, fighting in the name of God, has won. However, as the scene shifts to earth with the fall of the dragon, John inserts a hymn into the passage, which comments on the battle that has just taken place. First, the devil is called "the accuser of our brothers," and apparently had access to the presence of God to accuse Christians up until this point. Second, the battle itself is described, but we no longer hear of Michael and his angels. Instead we hear of the deeds of human beings.

It is clear from the setting that John is painting a picture of parallel scenes. One is a heavenly battle with angelic participants. The other is an earthly battle, with the devil on one side and the Christians on the other. Yet the two appear to be parallel. The casting down of Satan from heaven is attributed to the faithfulness of Christians on earth. The heavenly battle is apparently influenced by the earthly. It is analogous to Daniel 10, in which Daniel prays for twenty-one days. He is eventually told that his prayer had been answered the first day, but that there had been a heavenly battle preventing the answering angel from getting through to him until Michael came to take over the fight. All of this time Daniel is praying on earth, oblivious to the battle in the spiritual world. Is the author there implying that Daniel's struggles in prayer are part of what is affecting the outcome of the heavenly battle?

What, then, are the weapons of this earthly battle? The first is "the blood of the Lamb." John has already referred to the death of Christ, saying that the Lamb (Christ) appears "looking as if it had been slain" (Rev. 5:6). Furthermore, John has confessed "to him who loves us and has freed us from our sins by his blood" (Rev 1:5). So this image of blood indicates what Christ has done for the Christian on the cross. It is a weapon, not in that it is flung in the teeth of Satan as a talisman, but in that the Christian is committed to it. It is this sacrifice in which the Christian trusts, and it does not fail him when the accuser roars out his accusations.

The second weapon is "the word of their testimony." Revelation 1:5 presents Jesus Christ as "the faithful witness." In Revelation 2:13 Antipas, "my faithful witness," has been put to death. The theme of witness or testimony (the same Greek word can be translated by either English word) flows from one end of the book to the other. This testimony, then, is the confession of obedience to Christ. It is not the story about what Christ has done for us (which is the common modern evangelical meaning of the term), but the statement that one is loyal to Christ and therefore will not compromise. Because it is something spoken, probably in the context of a demand for the explanation of one's behavior, it is a word.

The third item really is not a weapon, although it is in a parallel clause. Rather, it is an attitude of mind that underlies the other two: "they did not love their lives so much as to shrink from death." As Jesus said, "He who stands firm to the end will be saved" (Mk 13:13). If death remains a threat to a person, then there is a point at which they will compromise their commitment to the blood of Christ and certainly a point at which they will mute their word of testimony. The genuineness of commitment is seen when the heat is on. Those who pass the test are those who will not cling to life even under the threat of death, if it would mean compromising on their commitment to Christ.

In this context the devil has been presented as "the accuser of our brothers." This is the war that he wages against the people of God, for his weapons are lies and accusations. But these people have not believed the lie, for they have seen through Satan's deception to the reality of Christ. They know that life is not more precious than obedience to Jesus. And the accusations of Satan have no hold on them. Accuse as he will, he will only receive the response "I am trusting in the blood of Christ." And should he accuse them of being hypocrites, their faithful word of testimony even in the face of threatened death shows such an accusation to be the hot air that it is.

In other words, John is not saying that Christians win the battle against Satan by talking about the blood of Christ, telling Satan about that blood (he already knows about it all too well), or using it as a magic word in prayer ("by the power of the blood of Jesus"). Instead, Christians trust in the power of the death of Christ with a quiet confidence that is inwardly lived and outwardly confessed in word and deed (life matching speech), no matter what the threat. This radical commitment, John claims, is what defeats Satan.

John does not present this as super-Christianity, for martyrs only. Rather, it is normal Christianity. It is a Christianity that does not love Babylon (his image for the world and all it has to offer in power, wealth and advancement, as Rev 18 shows). It is a Christianity that is dedication to Christ, or, as he puts it, a faithful witness. This for him is spiritual warfare. No demons are necessarily seen,[1] just as Daniel saw no spiritual battle, but despite the lack of visible pyrotechnics, the devil is cast down. In such faithfulness the devil discovers that his time is short.

Notes

[1]This does not imply that John in any way rejects the expulsion of demons from the demonized, for this activity was universally part of the essence of spiritual warfare. Demon expulsion, evangelistic proclamation, healing the sick and caring for the poor are all part of the lifestyle of the gospel, but they flow out of the more basic trust in the blood of Christ and concomitant personal commitment to him, rather than replace it.

A Beast Coming out of the Sea

And I saw a beast coming out of the sea.
He had ten horns and seven heads, with ten crowns on
his horns, and on each head a blasphemous name.

REVELATION 13:1

Once in my early teens I saw a movie in which a huge monster rose out of the sea to terrify the inhabitants of a large human city. When we read Revelation 13:1, we might think that we are in the same Hollywood world. We have already seen that there are symbolic animals in Revelation; the dragon in the preceding chapter (Rev 12) is a case in point. But what is this animal, this beast? It is certainly unlike any other animal in existence. Is it a mythical animal? Is it a creation of an early Hollywood imagination? What does it mean?

John may well have drawn his basis for such a picture from Daniel 7, which lists a series of four beasts. The first three are similar to recognizable animals, although with additions or modifications. The fourth is compared to no known animal, but is simply "terrifying and frightening and very powerful." The only physical description is that it has iron teeth and ten horns. Our beast in Revelation appears related to that one.

This beast is an embodiment of Satan. The seven heads and ten horns on the beast are copied from the picture of Satan in Revelation 12:3. And this is no wonder, for "the dragon [Satan] gave the beast his power and his throne and great authority." He represents the power of Satan on earth and is to Satan what Christ is to the Father. He is even more a pseudo-Christ in that he receives a mortal wound from which he is healed, a mimicked death and resurrection. Because of this event he is worshiped on earth.

The second place where this beast appears is in Revelation 17:3. This chapter explains (vv. 8-13) that the symbolism has more than one meaning. The ten horns are ten kings who rule along with a great ruler and support that ruler. The seven heads are both seven hills (a transparent symbol for Rome) and seven kings. Unlike the ten who rule simultaneously, these seven come one after another. John is living in the time when the sixth of them is ruling. The beast himself is an eighth. Yet, inspired by Satan as he is, his real origin is in "the Abyss," the place where Satanic spirits are imprisoned.

Because of the transparency of the symbolism in Revelation 17:9, it would seem that if we knew how John counted the rulers of Rome, it would be fairly easy to discover who the beast was. He should be the eighth emperor of Rome, John living in the age of the sixth. The fact that the Roman Senate declared several emperors to be divine and that some, especially Domitian, claimed divinity during their lifetimes, and one, Caligula, tried to have his statue erected in the temple in Jerusalem, adds to this impression (compare Rev 13:8, 14). Unfortunately we do not know either with whom John would start such a count or whether he would skip some of the emperors who reigned only a short time. Nor are we sure exactly when he lived, for a good case has been made for the time of Domitian (A.D. 91-96, the traditional date) as well as that of Galba (A.D. 68). Neither of these dates would meet the requirement of having an eighth emperor fitting the description of the beast.

Yet there is a further problem with the identification of this beast. As we have seen, the seven heads have two meanings, one of which is Rome (the seven hills) and the other seven kings. Some see these kings as literal rulers of Rome (as in the scheme above) and others see them as kingdoms or empires. In Daniel 7:17 the term translated "kingdoms" in the NIV is literally "kings" in Aramaic. That means that John could be shifting from a vision of literal Rome and its emperors to one of a succession of empires.

Finally, in apocalyptic scenarios there is often a place in which the writer "fades out" from the present historical circumstances and sees beyond them to future events. A good example of this is Daniel 12:1. Chapter 11 gives us a picture of the conflict between the Seleucid and Ptolemaic empires, culminating in the Seleucid ruler Antiochus IV Epiphanes (175—163 B.C.). If one reads 1 Maccabees or Josephus's histories, it is easy to identify everyone. But in Daniel 12 we are no longer in the realm of history. We are seeing beyond the period of Daniel 11 to the end of history. Since the beast "once was, now is not, and will come up out of the Abyss" (Rev 17:8), John appears to be suggesting that an evil force that had once been destroyed (or perhaps consigned to the Abyss) would reappear, not that a new emperor would appear. This would go beyond anything present in the Roman Empire.

What, then, can we say about the beast? John saw in his vision a personage coming at the end of time who would be the devil incarnate and demand worship. This personage would be accompanied by a second who would seem to be harmless enough ("two horns like a lamb," perhaps suggesting a likeness to Christ, the Lamb), but would speak for the devil ("he spoke like a dragon," Rev 13:11). The second personage will direct worship toward the first. The appearance of these two will be associated with the 3.5-year period of intense persecution at the end of the age. John saw this in terms of the Rome that he knew, perhaps expecting in his own heart that it would happen in his lifetime. We have previously suggested that the vision of Revelation may have been delayed, like Jonah's, due to the widespread conversion to Christianity in the Roman Empire. Whether or not this is the case, all scenarios of the end (such as Paul's in 2 Thess 2) agree in seeing an embodiment of

evil, like Antiochus IV Epiphanes was in his day, before the incarnation of good, Jesus Christ, appears.

What this means for the church is that its expectation of the end
is not one of gradual improvement or Christianizing of the world
until Christ appears, but one of evangelization in the face of persecution, a persecution that will become most severe just before the
end. Certainly many Christians have felt they have lived in the
times of the beast, such as those living under Napoleon or Hitler
or Stalin. Yet they have been wrong in that the end has not come.
But will those who live in the age of the real beast have any better
insight? None of us evaluate our own times well. The important
thing is that Christians respond appropriately to persecutors,
whether a beastlike person (such as Hitler) or the genuine beast.
John's picture shows that the beast is under the ultimate control of
God. His time is limited. His coming and destruction are under the
power of God. His persecution will be used by God for the perfection of God's church. The response expected, then, is firm commitment to God. That response will not be wrong in the face of *any*
persecution, even if we are not sure whether or not it is the genuine
beast.

His
Number
Is 666

This calls for wisdom. If anyone has insight,
let him calculate the number of the beast,
for it is man's number. His number is 666.
REVELATION 13:18

I can be described by a number of numbers. I have a *Social Security number* and a Canadian social insurance number. I am one number to the Society of Biblical Literature's computer and another to CompuServ Information Service. We expect this in our computer age, but are surprised to find people in the Bible described in terms of a number. Therefore we correctly suspect that the numbers are something more than mere identification for filing purposes. In the previous chapter I introduced the concept of the "beast coming out of the sea." His description was problematic, but the one thing about him that has caused more difficulty and speculation than any of the others is his enigmatic number noted in Revelation 13:18. What does it mean to say that a person's number is something? If numbers are not for filing or identification, how does a person get one? How does one "calculate" such a number? Don't numbers just exist? What does it mean?

It is not surprising that numbers had meaning in the symbolic world of John's vision, for they had more than numerical meaning in his outer world as well. Numbers and letters were interchangeable. For example, many rabbinic scriptures to this day do not use Arabic numerals, but instead use Hebrew letters to stand for the various verse and chapter numbers. This led some rabbis to interpret Scripture via gematria, the turning of names into numbers and vice versa. For this reason many scholars believe that the fourteen generations counted three times in Matthew 1 are related to the name David, for DVD in Hebrew (the vowels were not written) would be 4 + 6 + 4 or 14.[1] The Greeks did a similar thing with their own alphabet. In the early Christian *Sibylline Oracles* Jesus is enumerated as 888. It was only with the spread first of Roman and then of Arabic numerals that this practice died out for most of the Western world.

We would expect, then, that the number 666 would stand for something, especially that it would stand for a name. One theory is that it stands for Nero Caesar. Nero is selected because he persecuted Christians and a legend arose after his suicide that he had not died, but had fled to the east and would return in triumph. Two false Neros tried to fulfill this legend and failed. Still, Nero Caesar in Greek totals 1,005, so one has to transliterate the Greek name into Hebrew to get the required 666. Did John, who wrote in Greek, expect his readers to know Hebrew or Hebrew letter values?

Two other methods to obtain the name of an emperor have been attempted. One added the values of the initial letters of the names of all of the Roman emperors up until a certain point (something that the *Sibylline Oracles* also does). Another used the abbreviation for the title of Domitian, another persecuting emperor. Unfortunately, for the first theory at least one of the emperors must be left out of the list to get an even 666 from the emperors' initials, and while we know of the abbreviations of Domitian's title, they do not appear together anywhere, which weakens the second theory.

Another solution has been via the observation that 666 is the triangular number of 36 (1 + 2 + 3 + 4 and on up to 36). The number 36 is the triangular number of 8 (1 + 2 + 3 + 4 + 5 + 6 + 7 + 8 = 36). The beast, of course, is the eighth king (Rev 17:11). Triangular numbers were seen as sinister in contrast to the square numbers, which are assigned to the martyrs (7:4) and the heavenly city (21:16). While this math is interesting and fits the Greek concern with geometry (because they did not have a mathematically useful system of numerals), it not come up with a name. Nor can we be sure that such a complicated system was in John's mind. After all, there are other triangular numbers in Scripture that are not sinister at all, such as the 153 fish in John 21:11.

None of the solutions above has been found completely satisfactory. Perhaps the best observation is that 666 consistently (three times) falls short of the number of perfection, 7, and the number of Christ, 888. Rather than refer to a specific name, 666 may indicate that the person will be a parody of Christ. He will not come up to perfection, but as the prostitute of Revelation 17 mimics the faithful woman of Revelation 12 and the dragon in Revelation 12 mimics Christ in Revelation 19, so the beast mimics the incarnate Christ, being the embodiment of evil (the devil not being capable of true incarnation). Beyond this we can only observe that when such a personage appears, those who are wise in John's terms (which means first of all that they have divine insight) will recognize him and see that 666 does indeed fit.

Notes
[1]In transliteration the Hebrew alphabet runs ' B G D H V for the numbers 1-6.

• C H A P T E R 6 8 •

Blessed Is He Who Stays Awake and Keeps His Clothes with Him

Behold, I come like a thief! Blessed is he who stays
awake and keeps his clothes with him, so that he
may not go naked and be shamefully exposed.
REVELATION 16:15

Various people in Scripture were "caught with their pants down" in both the literal and figurative sense of that expression. We may not be surprised at the strange images and characters in Revelation, but this verse appears to reflect some sense of the modern idiom more than an idea we would expect in Scripture. Furthermore, it occurs quite suddenly in the flow of the book and is apparently addressed to Christians. But what does it mean to stay awake? Does it mean that the blessed Christian will not be asleep in bed when Christ returns? How might a Christian be naked at such a time? Are we to fear this coming happening when we are in the bath? Particularly because the verse is an exhortation from Christ himself, we readers of Revelation will want to be sure of what this means.

The context of this verse is the pouring out of the first six bowls of the final judgment of God. The previous verse mentioned that the way has now been prepared for the final battle of "the great day of God Almighty." The next verse describes the gathering of the nations for that battle, which will not take place until Revelation 19:11-21. Yet when that battle does take place the people of God are with their king, so they obviously have been gathered together, an event often referred to as "the rapture" (Mk 13:27; 1 Cor 15:51-52; 1 Thess 4:16-17).

The wider context of this verse is the sayings of Jesus that he would come "like a thief" (Mt 24:43; Lk 12:39; compare Mk 13:32-37). This image is picked up by Paul (1 Thess 5:2, 4; compare 2 Pet 3:10) and has already been mentioned once by John (Rev 3:3). The point of all of these sayings is that a thief does not announce his coming, but surprises the inhabitants of the house by coming when they are out or least likely to suspect his or her presence. Stealth and surprise are the chief weapon. To say that the day of the Lord is like this is to say that it too will come when least expected. As Jesus noted, no one knows the day or the hour (Mk 13:32); those who have claimed to have calculated it repeatedly have been proved wrong. But this does not mean that one cannot be prepared; instead it means that one must always be prepared, like servants waiting up through the night for their master to return from a party (Lk 12:35-40).

John has been writing about the gathering of the world's armies and the final battle between the beast and Christ. The alarming events in the world or even the expectation that this gathering must take place before Christ could return could distract his readers from their central focus, namely faithfulness to and expectation of Christ. He, not the armies of the Antichrist, is to be their central concern. Therefore it is quite appropriate that the voice of Jesus himself interject a warning in the middle of the gathering storm, just as he previously interjected a blessing about the death of Christians to contrast with that of the destruction of "Babylon" (Rev 14:13).

The warning is to "stay awake" or "watch." The image is that of the watchmen at their posts, alert for any sign of their lord and expectant of his coming. As we saw above, this picture is drawn from the sayings of Jesus. This alertness, of course, implies that the Christian will be found doing what the master has commanded him or her to do, which includes sleep at appropriate times.[1] The wakefulness, then, is not the avoidance of physical sleep, but a moral wakefulness that does not allow the world to lull one into a laxity about the directions that Christ has given and the standards he has set.

The picture of the watching servant is connected to that for nakedness. When lying down to sleep, a person would take off the outer garment and use it as a blanket, or perhaps lay it aside altogether and sleep under a blanket or covered in straw (as rabbi Akiba and his wife were forced to do since they had only one outer garment for the two of them). A poor person's clothing was his or her most valuable possession; a thief would not miss the chance to steal it upon breaking into a house during the night (see Lk 10:30). Likewise if a person were asleep but would have to rush out in an emergency without taking the time to get clothed, he or she could lose the outer garment (see Mk 13:15-16). To be without that outer garment in public would be to be "naked" in terms of that culture (something like being in a shopping mall clothed only in underwear in our day). Jesus thus counsels keeping one's "clothes with him" or "guarding their clothing" to prevent the surprise of the moment finding them "shamefully exposed." The *Mishnah* reports that the captain of the temple would go around at night and, if he found temple police asleep at their posts, take their clothing and burn it, forcing them to leave the temple naked.[2] In our text the surprise of the moment finds the believer similarly "undressed."

The clothing of the Christian is mentioned several times in Revelation. Those in the church of Sardis whose deeds are not right have soiled clothes, while the worthy ones will be dressed in white (3:4). The church of Laodicea is naked, and needs to purchase white clothing to wear (3:17-18). The martyrs under the altar are clothed in white (6:11), as is the multitude before the throne (7:9). The key to the image of clothing is found in Revelation 19:8, in which the bride of Christ is given "fine linen, bright and clean," to wear. Then comes the comment, "Fine linen stands for the righteous acts of the saints." If one is not acting righteously, which means following the commands of Christ, he or she is naked before him, and his coming will leave such a person "shamefully exposed."

The two parts of the warning, then, fit together. The coming of Christ cannot be calculated. Certainly the last thing that John wishes is that his readers would try to calculate the time of that coming using the images in his book. That would be to put their focus on the world and the evil personages rather than on Christ. The goal of the whole of this book is that, given the ultimate end of all of the principalities and powers of this world and the final triumph of Christ, Christians will remain faithful whatever the cost. They are to be prepared for the coming of Christ at all times. This means not only expecting this coming verbally or doctrinally, but also living a life appropriate to that expectation. This means living in obedience to Jesus, however crazy such a lifestyle might appear in the light of the values of this world, and "clothing oneself" with righteous deeds. It is for such people that the coming of Christ will not be something for which they are unprepared. Instead, they will joyfully welcome it and, fully "clothed," join their Lord's throng as he completes his conquest of the world and ends this age.

Notes

[1]As one Christian teacher pointed out, so long as one is obeying Christ, whether sleeping or raising the dead, "the pay is the same"—both are simply obedient servants.

[2]So F. F. Bruce, "The Revelation to John," in G. C. D. Howley et al., eds., *The New Layman's Bible Commentary* (Grand Rapids, Mich.: Zondervan, 1979), p. 1703.

• C H A P T E R 6 9 •

The Testimony
of Jesus Is the
Spirit of Prophecy

*At this I fell at his feet to worship him. But he said to me,
"Do not do it! I am a fellow servant with you and with your
brothers who hold to the testimony of Jesus. Worship God!
For the testimony of Jesus is the spirit of prophecy."*
REVELATION 19:10

For a long period of time the church has relegated prophecy either to the
classical prophets of the biblical period or to preaching (which is
normally the gift of teaching, not prophecy). While the revival of
interest in prophecy in the church began close to 200 years ago,
there has been a recent upsurge in interest in prophecy, both in
scholarly circles and in church ministry. Revelation 19:10 appears
to have something to say to this trend, especially since it comes
from a Christian prophet. In the middle of a picture of "the wedding
supper of the Lamb," when the hopes of the church will be consummated in union with her Lord, John is overwhelmed. He falls at the
feet of the angel who is explaining everything to him, bowing his
head to the pavement in oriental-fashion worship. We are not sur-

prised that the angel stops him (and will do so again in Rev 22:8-9), but the statement that "the testimony of Jesus is the spirit of prophecy" needs explanation. What does it mean? What is "the testimony of Jesus"? Just what is the "spirit of prophecy"? What might either of these have to do with prophecy today?

The New Testament mentions the gift of prophecy several times, most significantly in 1 Corinthians 12—14, although Acts mentions prophets several times as well. Yet we know very little concerning what New Testament prophets spoke about, other than the words of Agabus (Acts 11:27; 21:1), with the exception of Revelation.[1] This whole book is designated as prophecy (1:3; 22:7, 18-19) and is therefore our most extensive example of Christian prophecy. Within this context John says that "the testimony of Jesus" is "the spirit" of this prophecy.

Prophecy was not, of course, to be accepted without any criteria for testing it to see if it were genuine or distorted in some way. Several New Testament passages address this issue. Colossians 2:18 suggests that some Christians had been led into the worship of angels, probably through prophetic speculation. The church is called to weigh prophecy (1 Cor 14:29) for, given our fallenness, prophetic words are normally more or less words from God, not the pure word. According to 1 John 4:1, Christians are not to trust every spirit, as not all are the Holy Spirit. Finally, in Revelation, "Jezebel" "calls herself a prophetess," functioning within the church (2:20), and the beast "out of the earth" (13:11), who persecutes the church, is called a false prophet (19:20). All of this shows the need for knowing the criteria for testing prophecy.

The angel in this verse notes that he and the Christians "hold to the testimony of Jesus" and that this same "testimony" is "the spirit of prophecy." That is, it is by this testimony or witness that one can discern the genuine prophetic Spirit. But what is "the testimony [or witness] of Jesus"? The phrase itself occurs several times in Revelation (1:2, 9; 12:17; 19:10; 20:4), while a related phrase occurs in 17:6. There are two interpretations of it. In the first, it is the testimony or witness that Jesus bore to God in his life and teaching, carrying that witness to the point of death and still bearing it from his exalted place in heaven. In support of this interpretation we see that Jesus is called the "faithful witness" (1:5; 3:14) and the whole book of Revelation is referred to as his testimony through his angel (22:16). The second interpretation is that this is a testimony about Jesus that one makes by conforming to his commands and confessing one's allegiance and his truth with one's mouth. In support of this we note those who are called witnesses or who give testimony, such as Antipas (2:13), the martyrs (6:9), the two witnesses (11:3) and the victors (12:11).

Given that both of the meanings are supported in the text, we may have created a false dichotomy between them, although the accent in the "testimony of Jesus" passages appears to fall on the latter rather than the former meaning. What Jesus witnessed to in his life and death is precisely what faithful Christians are to witness to in theirs. A true testimony to Jesus means obedience to his commands and faithfulness to his teaching. And, as Jesus openly confessed his allegiance to his Father, so the true Christian openly acknowledges faithfulness to Jesus. Life and word go together; the Christian who does not live like Jesus is a contradiction in terms, as is the idea of a secret Christian. Thus we see in Revelation 17:6 that the saints (not just the best of them) bore testimony to Jesus. In Revelation 12:17 to "obey God's commandments" is the equivalent of holding to "the testimony of Jesus." In Revelation 1:2, 9 and 20:4 the "testimony of Jesus" is a parallel idea to "the word of God." The true Word of God, of course, was incarnate in Jesus (according to Jn 1), came through Jesus and is about Jesus.

That "the testimony of Jesus is the spirit of prophecy," then, means that true prophecy inspired of the Holy Spirit will be in conformity to the life and teaching of Jesus (who was himself in conformity with the rest of the Word of God) and will ultimately point to Jesus. By this standard one may evaluate both the life and the words of a prophet. Revelation itself, then, is on the one hand an attempt to uphold the standards that Jesus taught and lived (such as its call to watching; its rejection of compromise with the world; its demanding that God alone be worshiped; and its rejection of sexual immorality) and on the other hand a call to value the redemption by his blood, live in accordance with his faithfulness unto death, and expect his final victory as King of kings and Lord of lords. While addressed to human beings in seven churches, its ultimate focus is Jesus. It does indeed pass its own test.

In a time when the church is rediscovering the gift of prophecy, then, this verse is very relevant.[2] It is not the messenger who should be honored, but the giver of the message, Jesus himself. He becomes the standard by which all is measured. It is Jesus who clearly distinguishes between John and Jezebel, between the true spirit of prophecy and the spirit of the Antichrist. Thus the true prophet is that prophet who lives like Jesus, teaches in harmony with Jesus and points others to Jesus as their Lord and King.

Notes

[1]Scholars also have believed that some of Paul's sayings and (more controversially) some of Jesus' sayings in the Gospels are the products of Christian prophets, but since none of these are actually called prophecy, even the most sure of them must be classed as disputed in terms of being prophecy. We will therefore keep our focus on what is actually called prophecy.

[2]Note, for example, Wayne Grudem, *The Gift of Prophecy in the New Testament and Today* (Westchester, Ill.: Crossway, 1988); Clifford Hill, *Prophecy Past and Present* (Crowborough, E. Sussex: Highland Books, 1989); and Graham Houston, *Prophecy: A Gift for Today?* (Downers Grove, Ill.: InterVarsity, 1989). Of the three, Hill's is the best, but all of them advocate a role for prophecy (meaning a direct word from God, not simply inspired exegetical preaching) today, and two of them have the imprimatur of no less than F. F. Bruce and I. Howard Marshall, indicating these scholars' positive evaluation of the books' solid exegetical basis.

Bound Him
for a Thousand
Years

He seized the dragon, that ancient serpent,
who is the devil, or Satan, and bound
him for a thousand years.
REVELATION 20:2

We know what it is to put a person in prison for a given term of years, although some unreformed, dangerous offenders we may lock up for indefinite terms, but we normally do not shackle such individuals for the period. These concepts are here in Revelation 20. The setting is the end of the great period of persecution and the judgment of God. The war with the forces of evil has been fought and won by the rider on the white horse who is called "Faithful and True." Then comes the scene of which Revelation 20:2 is a part. What does it mean that the devil is bound for a thousand years? Why put him in prison rather than destroy him? Why put away such a dangerous offender for a mere thousand years? What does this time period have to do with "the millennium," and what does that term signify anyway? This is, perhaps, one of the final puzzles of Revelation for the modern reader.

This verse is another of those places in Revelation in which there appear to be two levels of conflict. In Revelation 12 we saw that there was a conflict in heaven between Michael and the dragon (Satan) and a parallel conflict on earth between the dragon and the saints. Here there is a conflict on earth in the physical realm between the exalted Christ, returning visibly as king, and the pseudo-Christ, "the beast," and his "unholy spirit," the "false prophet" (19:19-20). Both enemies have been summarily dealt with (they are tossed into the lake of fire, or hell) and their army has been destroyed by a word from Christ. All of that happens on a very physical level. But there is still the matter of the devil who inspired and embodied himself in "the beast" (13:1). Now we shift to the spiritual plane (although not to heaven, for the dragon was cast out of heaven in Rev 12) and deal with him.

In this prophecy Satan is taken captive by an angel, bound with a chain for 1,000 years, tossed into the Abyss, which, as we saw in an earlier chapter, is the prison of evil spirits, and locked and sealed in. At the end of this period he is again released, again foments a rebellion among human beings on earth (although now in the tribes outside the Roman Empire), and in the end not only loses his army, but is himself tossed into the lake of fire, where he will remain forever (20:7-10).

"The millennium," then, refers to this 1,000-year Satan-free period during which at least the martyrs are resurrected and reign with Christ on earth (20:4-6). The question that remains is how to interpret this information. There are three fundamentally different positions on the millennium. The first, the postmillennial view, interprets this passage as a look back on history. It sees the millennium as the period at the end of history that ushers in the reign of Christ. At times this is viewed as a spiritual rule of Christ through the triumph of the gospel and at times as a literal period of 1,000 years characterized by the triumph of kingdom values at the end of time. The point is that the physical return of Christ comes *at the end* of the millennium.

The second, the amillennial view, does not really believe in no millennium (which is what "amillennial" should mean etymologically), but in a spiritual millennium. The binding of Satan has been accomplished during the lifetime of Jesus (see Mt 12:29; Lk 10:18; 19:17-18; Jn 12:31; Col 2:15). During the age of the church Christ reigns in heaven and the power of Satan is limited in that he cannot stop the spread of the gospel. The first resurrection is the spiritual resurrection of the person's soul coming to life upon conversion. Therefore the millennial period (the 1,000 years being symbolic of a long time) overlaps the church age, the rebellion in Revelation 20:7-10 being essentially the same as that in Revelation 19:19-21.

The third position, the premillennial view, argues that the text should be taken at face value to indicate an actual period of 1,000 years (or a long time, if the figure 1,000 is symbolic), during which Christ reigns and Satan is unable to deceive the nations. This fits with both the New Testament concept that Satan is alive and active on earth during the present age (see Lk 22:3; Acts 5:3; 2 Cor 4:3-4; 11:14; Eph 2:2; 1 Thess 2:18; 2 Tim 2:26; 1 Pet 5:18) and a common idea found in Jewish apocalyptic. For example, the pseudepigraphical book 2 Enoch mentions the idea that there are seven 1,000-year periods to world history, the last being a 1,000-year Sabbath when God returns (2 Enoch 32:2—33:2). A similar idea is found in a passage in the Talmud (b. Sanhedrin 97b) and in the early Christian Epistle of Barnabas (Barnabas 15). Other Jewish works reveal a belief in a shorter millennium (400 years or even just 40 years) or mention no millennium. In the rest of the New Testament only one other passage (1 Cor 15:23-28) may indicate two stages in the overcoming of evil, but of course the interpretation of this passage is also disputed. At the same time, no New Testament passage excludes this view.

In John's view the millennium consists of several elements. First, Satan is bound so that he cannot deceive the nations (20:3). Second, the martyrs are resurrected and reign with Christ (vv. 4-7). This means that the armies destroyed in Revelation 19:21 are in fact armies, not all the people alive. The population of the earth not destroyed in the final series of judgments remains alive and is ruled by Christ and his martyrs. Third, the end of the period is marked by the release of the devil and his renewed deception of the nations, specifically Gog and Magog, which Ezekiel 38—39 locates in the far north (Asia Minor or beyond) and the Jewish historian Josephus identifies with the Scythians, a tribe outside the Roman Empire (*Antiquities* 1.6.1). All of the identifications appear to indicate that the nations outside of the Empire (now ruled by Christ) gather against the rightful King. Fourth, the rebellion is ended by the destruction of the opposing armies, the consignment of the devil to the lake of fire, the resurrection of all of the dead, and the final judgment (vv. 8-15). This is the end of the history of the earth, for the next chapter takes up the topic of the new heaven and new earth.

One might wonder why there should be a millennium. Several reasons can be given. First, it is a reward for the martyrs (or perhaps the martyrs and those who did not worship the beast, but Rev 13:15 seems to indicate that these would all be martyrs). In their faithfulness they lost their lives. Now they are rewarded with a long life, reigning with Christ. Second, it demonstrates the victory of Christ. That he holds power for 1,000 years will vindicate the rule God has given him and which now is hidden in heaven. His triumph is complete. Third, it vindicates the righteous rule of God, redeeming history. Is it possible that God could not rule this earth any better than human beings (and Satan)? The millennium points to the idea that God can rule righteously and justly from within history. He does not have to simply end history. Presumably this would be when people would experience the just rulership that the world has been rejecting (and yet longing for) since the Fall.

We might further question why the Antichrist and false prophet would be destroyed and Satan preserved? It is clearly not out of any love for or mercy toward Satan! The fact is that when the embodiments of satanic power have been exposed and lost their power, God has no more use for them. Their future on earth has come to an end. On the other hand, God appears to have a use for Satan, but not in the immediate future. He is used for the final probation of human beings after God has demonstrated his just rule. Thus Satan is not kept out of hell for his own sake, but is reserved for

God's own good purposes (although in his own mind he surely rejects this idea). Even to the end God remains in control, including in control of Satan.

As we saw above, the millennium is symbolic for many people. But in calling it symbolic (or in calling it literal, my own preference) we must be careful to preserve the values that John expresses. The reign of Satan is doomed. He will be (or has been) chained. Christ will reign; his victory on the cross will be consummated. His martyrs will be rewarded. And rebellion against God will meet its end. These are the essence of the millennial teaching that must be preserved by any view. The test of a view is whether it best explains the data of Scripture and whether it preserves the values that John is trying to teach.

A New
Heaven and a
New Earth

Then I saw a new heaven and a new earth,
for the first heaven and the first earth had passed away,
and there was no longer any sea.
REVELATION 21:1

As human beings we are all familiar with heaven and earth, for they are part of the world we experience, but what is being said in Revelation 21:1? What does it mean to have a *new* heaven and earth? Why not simply renew or restore the present one? Why would there not be any sea in a new earth? What is the purpose of this change?

In our text we are in the period beyond the final rebellion and the final judgment. Satan is gone forever. Salvation history has totally run its course, for the King of kings has reigned over the world for 1000 years and each person has finally received his or her just reward. Now we are entering the eternal state beyond the struggles of human history.

Within this context there must be a renewal, a new setting for the now purified human race, an earth free from the scars of the rebellion that Satan inspired. This is a need sensed throughout the New Testament. Paul says that there is a new creation in human beings who are in Christ (2 Cor 5:17), which is in tension with the oldness of their own bodies and the rest of creation (Rom 8:19-22). Because of this he can say, "We fix our eyes not on what is seen, but on what is unseen. For what is seen is temporary, but what is unseen is eternal" (2 Cor 4:18). Peter expresses this as "looking forward to a new heaven and a new earth, the home of righteousness" (2 Pet 3:13). Now in Revelation we get a picture of that happening. As God says, "I am making everything new!" (21:5).

There are two opinions about the newness that is being described. Some scholars believe that John is only talking about a renewed heaven and earth. The old will be purified, but not destroyed. In fact, the real issue for John, they argue, is moral purification, not physical renewal, although physical restoration must also be included. This passage, then, describes a return to the goals left unrealized when humanity was driven out of Eden. To document their position, these scholars cite intertestamental literature such as 1 Enoch 45:4-5 and 2 Esdras 7:75 (compare 2 Baruch 32:6; 1 Enoch 72:1; 91:16), all of which speak of a renewal of creation as the expectation of the Jewish groups that the respective writers represented.

While all scholars must agree that the central issue for John is moral purification, the removal of all of the taint of sin and rebellion, some scholars look at such terms as "the first heaven and first earth had passed away" and argue that what we are talking about in our passage is a totally new creation. This appears to fit the language of Peter, who writes, "The heaven will disappear with a roar; the elements will be destroyed by fire, and the earth and everything in it will be laid bare. . . . That day will bring about the destruction of the heavens by fire, and the elements will melt in the heat" (2 Pet 3:10, 12). In other words, according to this view, the heavens and earth are so polluted that what is needed is something like the Genesis flood, a destruction and recreation, but this time the destruction is done by fire, not water. This second position appears to fit the language of Revelation best. Thus while the goal is the moral purification of the world, the moral and the physical are so intertwined (which we are perhaps beginning to understand in our ecological consciousness) that this requires a major physical overhaul, one so extreme that it is called a new creation.

The heavens that are destroyed are not the abode of God (sometimes referred to as the third or seventh heaven) but the observable heavens. Genesis 1:1 describes the creation as "the heavens and the earth." Not just the planet, but all of creation has been polluted by sin. The whole will be remade. In this new creation there will be no sea. Having lived in Vancouver, B.C., I have a love for the sea, the scene of many happy holiday hours, a place of rest, but I must put aside such romantic feelings when I come to read Scripture, for that was not the Jewish view of the sea. In Scripture the sea is normally a negative image. For example, Isaiah 57:20 says, "The wicked are like the tossing sea, which cannot rest, whose waves cast up mire and mud." The sea is also the chaos of water out of which the heaven and earth were originally separated in Genesis 1:2, 6-10. While it is a creation of God (Ps 104:26), the sea is also the home of the sea monster Leviathan, whom God conquers and casts on dry land (Ps 74:13-14). It is no wonder that the pseudepigraphal Jewish work the Testament of Moses 10:6 states that when God comes at the end of the age the sea will retire into the Abyss. In Revelation the sea is the source of the beast and the throne of the great prostitute (13:1; 17:1). Such a symbol of chaos and the powers of evil could not exist in a new heaven and earth.

The new heavens and new earth likewise have a new city, the new Jerusalem. While this is not the place for detailed comment, it is true that here also there is something new. In Scripture the first cities are built by evil people (Gen 4:17; 10:10; 11:1-9). The old Jerusalem was the place in which God chose to put his name, but it was also an unfaithful city, which John could call "Sodom and Egypt" (Rev 11:8). Therefore there is now a need for a fulfillment of what sinful human beings could not produce, the true city with a God-centered community in which peace and justice are actually present.

This whole passage, then, speaks of the fulfillment of the hopes and dreams of humanity in the new creation. Human beings were created to live on earth, so a new earth will be their home. Human beings were created for fellowship with God, so he will dwell in their midst. Human beings were created for community, so a true city will be established. There is certainly a lot of symbolism in what is going on in this passage, yet the symbolism is symbolism of a new reality that straight prosaic description could not capture.

Whether or not the new heaven and earth are a renewal or a new creation, Revelation witnesses to the fact that the universe as we know it is temporal and "will all wear out like a garment" (Heb 1:11-12). Even should we intepret John as saying that the basic structure of the earth remains, he witnesses to a renewal so complete that human culture and creations have been wiped away. History as we know it has come to an end. God is beginning a new chapter in a new history, his eternal history. Yet at the same time human beings are not spirit. They are creatures with bodies, now resurrected and glorified. They do not live on clouds, but in a world and in a city. God provides for them what he designed them for in creation, a home on earth. It is not Eden, but a step beyond Eden, a more perfect development of what might have been, a new earth with a city with God in the midst. It answers an inner longing of the human heart, so it is fitting that John brings the narrative of his book to a close with this description of hope.

CHAPTER 72

If Anyone Takes Words from This Book

*I warn everyone who hears the words of the prophecy
of this book: If anyone adds anything to them, God will add to him the
plagues described in this book. And if anyone takes words
away from this book of prophecy, God will take away
from him his share in the tree of life and in
the holy city, which are described in this book.*
REVELATION 22:18-19

The canon of Scripture is both an emotional issue and a theological problem. It is a problem because the New Testament never speaks of such a canon (which is natural because while it was being written it was only in the process of becoming a canon). It is an emotional issue because, as the only authoritative document of the Christian faith (in Protestant eyes), anything that might add to or detract from Scripture is highly threatening. This emotion and this theology surrounds the end of Revelation. Verses 18-19 come just before the final closing verses of Revelation. The question that they raise is, To what is John referring? Is "this book" a reference to the book of Revelation or to the Bible as a whole? Why did John write these words? What threat to "this book" would he have perceived?

The New Testament was written in a time before readily accessible libraries, communications media and printing presses. Virtually all of the teaching of that period was done orally, for few could read. For this reason John pronounces a blessing on "the one [singular] who reads" the book (out loud to the congregation) and "those [plural] who hear it and take to heart what is written in it" (Rev 1:3). This process of reading such books out loud in a house church (in which the reader might be the only one who could read) would make it very easy to leave out parts of a book being read or to add to it what one wished. It would be difficult for most church members to discover the differences.

John was not the only prophet during the New Testament period to be concerned with proper preservation of his message. Paul was concerned that his message might be falsified by people bringing another gospel (Gal 1:6-9) or a prophecy or a forged letter purporting to be from him (2 Thess 2:2). There was, then, the possibility that, besides the corruption that could be put into the text in reading it, people could deliberately add their own prophetic vision to the text or edit it according to their own perception of what the author should have said.

This type of problem was not unknown in the Old Testament. Deuteronomy 4:2 and 12:32 insists that the Law must be preserved without adding to it or subtracting from it. Later, according to the tradition in the Letter of Aristeas, when the Pentateuch was translated into Greek, those receiving the new translation pronounced a curse upon anyone making any alteration to the text. These verses in Revelation are also a curse, and in placing this curse John is similarly protecting the integrity of his writing and may in fact be thinking of it on a level with Scripture, although a similar curse was also reportedly used by Irenaeus in one of his writings.[1]

John, then, or perhaps Jesus speaking through John (since it is the revelation of Jesus Christ), places a curse to protect the document from well-intentioned or even sinister tampering. The curse itself has two parts. One protects the document from being added to on the threat of the person doing so receiving the plagues written about earlier in the book. The other protects the document from being subtracted from on the threat of the person losing his or her place in heaven, that is, their losing their place in the tree of life (the source of eternal life) and the holy city, the new Jerusalem. The curses are somewhat stylized and strong, as was the custom in the language of the day, so it would not be wise to draw theology from them (for example, as to whether one can or cannot lose one's place in the holy city). But the author intended them as real curses.

The question arises, then, as to whether these curses have to do with anything more than this one book. Do they include the whole New Testament or the whole Bible? Is this a notice closing the canon? We must answer these questions in the negative.

First, we are not certain that Revelation was the last book of the New Testament to be written. Some date Revelation as early as A.D. 68, placing other writings (such as 2 Peter, Jude, or the Gospel and Epistles of John) much later. It would be unwise to base an argument on an uncertain dating.

Second, at the time John wrote the Jews might not have been finished discussing their own canon issues. During the period between A.D. 70 and 90 some discussions about canon took place in the rabbinic center in Jamnia. While there is no evidence that the shape of the canon changed as a result of this discussion, it does show that even the Jews were in something of a state of flux on the matter and could discuss whether certain books (such as Esther) should be included.

Third, John wrote before there was any clear sense of a New Testament canon. There is no evidence that John had ever seen a written Gospel or a collection of Paul's letters. In fact, it would be at least two more centuries before a fixed selection of works would be considered the Christian canon. Some of the works that would be considered seriously and then rejected, such as the Epistle of Barnabas and the *Didache*, had not yet been written.

Finally, while in most modern versions of Scripture Revelation is the last book (even Luther had it last, although he and some of the early English translations put Hebrews, James and the Petrine literature just before it), that was not the case in the earliest period. There was a good deal of shifting in the first three centuries, some people rejecting Revelation, some putting works such as 1 and 2 Clement after it, and some putting it earlier in their list of canonical books. There is no reason to think that this verse would have come almost at the end of the Bible for most Christians until the fourth century.

This does not mean that it is a good thing to add to or subtract from the Scripture. Certainly, even if the proverbial "lost letter of Paul" were found, not to mention some work of a more modern time that people thought might be inspired, it would take a universal consensus of the church that it were inspired to add it to the Scripture, a most unlikely event and thus a miracle in itself.[2] Nor should tampering with the present books themselves be done lightly. We do live in an age when some people wish to rewrite the Bible from their own ideological perspective. The only effect of this process is a distortion of Scripture and the production of a work that no one recognizes as canon. It would be better to write a separate work or a commentary selectively criticizing the existing Scripture, for either approach would be more honest. Even the scriptural authors themselves, when they wanted to reinterpret one another (as Daniel, for example, does to Jeremiah's seventy weeks), did not change the original but wrote their own book.

Therefore John's curse stands as a warning. Its true literal sense applies only to his own book, Revelation, but given that similar concerns were shared by Paul and others it is reasonable to argue that none of the writers of Scripture would have agreed to tampering with their works. Besides, such tampering would defeat the whole purpose of Scripture. The Scripture stands written as a witness to the revelation received in a given place and time. It is to be read, accepted (or, for some, rejected) and interpreted. To rewrite it, however, is to confuse one's own experience of God (or perhaps experience of something other than God) with that of the scriptural authors. It is to take the measuring line of Scripture (which is what "canon" means) and bend it to fit the wall that one is building in the present. In the end one has neither a measuring line nor a straight wall. It may not be the curse of John that one receives, but the resulting confusion will be curse enough and may in fact make one miss having a place in the holy city about which John wrote so glowingly.

Notes

[1]See Eusebius, *Ecclesiastical History* 5.20.2, for a reference to this ending of a lost letter of Irenaeus.

[2]Universal consensus means just that. While we might argue about whether some Christian fringe groups (such as certain Christian groups in Africa or the remnants of ancient heretical groups) should be included in such a consensus, it must at least include the basic Protestant (that is, most Protestant denominations), Roman Catholic and Orthodox branches. Who could conceive of these groups agreeing on anything, let alone that a given book was inspired by God?

Index to Scripture and Ancient Writings

Index of Modern Authors